Parachuting into
Poland, 1944

Parachuting into Poland, 1944

Memoir of a Secret Mission with Józef Retinger

MAREK CELT

Edited and annotated by Wojciech Frazik
Translated by Jan Chciuk-Celt

McFarland & Company, Inc., Publishers
Jefferson, North Carolina, and London

LIBRARY OF CONGRESS CATALOGUING-IN-PUBLICATION DATA

Celt, Marek.
    Parachuting into Poland, 1944 : memoir of a secret mission with Józef Retinger / Marek Celt ; edited and annotated by Wojciech Frazik ; translated by Jan Chciuk-Celt.
    p.   cm.
    Includes bibliographical references and index.

    ISBN 978-0-7864-7460-8
    softcover : acid free paper ∞

    1. Celt, Marek. 2. Retinger, J.H. (Joseph Hieronim), 1888–1960. 3. World War, 1939–1945 — Underground movements — Poland. 4. World War, 1939–1945 — Personal narratives, Polish. 5. Diplomatic couriers — Poland — Biography. 6. Poland — History — Occupation, 1939–1945. I. Frazik, Wojciech, editor. II. Chciuk-Celt, Jan, 1955– translator. III. Title.
    D802.P6C41413 2013
    940.53'4380922 — dc23   2013013224

BRITISH LIBRARY CATALOGUING DATA ARE AVAILABLE

© 2013 Ewa Chciuk-Celt. All rights reserved

No part of this book may be reproduced or transmitted in any form or by any means, electronic or mechanical, including photocopying or recording, or by any information storage and retrieval system, without permission in writing from the publisher.

On the cover: Military canopy parachutes and wheat field (iStockhoto/Thinkstock); night sky (Zoonar/ThinkStock)

Manufactured in the United States of America

McFarland & Company, Inc., Publishers
  Box 611, Jefferson, North Carolina 28640
  www.mcfarlandpub.com

Acknowledgments

Without the dedicated cooperation of Polish historian Dr. Wojciech Frazik, this book would still be an unfinished manuscript in my late father's desk, but he agreed to edit what my father had left behind into a finished book, which was published in Poland by LTW in 2006. Furthermore, Dr. Frazik's annotations added an invaluable measure of historical depth. I wish to express my heartfelt gratitude to him for getting involved.

Once I had the translation complete — with enormous support from my family — it was Angie Jabine who very generously shared her editorial advice with me, and she, too, is owed a debt of gratitude.

I'd like to acknowledge the invaluable assistance of Karolina Sikora of the MHPRL (Museum of the History of the Polish People's Movement) in Warsaw, where she curated an exhibit dedicated to the memory of Tadeusz Chciuk-Celt, and of Marek Jastrzębski at LTW, the original Polish publisher. "Dziękuję!" Also, I'm grateful to the Rev. Dr. Elizabeth DH Carmichael of St. John's College, Oxford, for her gracious cooperation regarding the excerpt from *By Parachute to Warsaw*, and to Luke Celt, my brother, for his help with indexing.

—*Jan Chciuk-Celt*

Table of Contents

Acknowledgments v
Introduction by Jan Chciuk-Celt 1

ONE. Prologue 27
TWO. Prehistory 31
THREE. With Captain Paisley in Bari 49
FOUR. 4.4.44 69
FIVE. Salamander, the Conspirator 89
SIX. The Tragedy of the Jews 114
SEVEN. Patient Józef Brzoza 117
EIGHT. The Third Bridge 140
NINE. The End of the Song 161

Appendix 1. Salamander's Report 179
Appendix 2. Source Documents 182
Chapter Notes 201
Index 209

Introduction
by Jan Chciuk-Celt

This book is the fourth and final volume of my late father's memoirs concerning his activities during the Second World War, written in Polish under the pen name Marek Celt. It deals with his second parachute mission into occupied Poland, Operation Salamander, which dropped him and Dr. Józef Retinger near Warsaw on April 4, 1944, and the subsequent events, culminating in the mission to pick them both up again on July 26, 1944, which was called Operation Wildhorn III. The book was almost, but not quite, finished when my father died in 2001, and his manuscript was edited into its final form by the eminent Polish historian, Dr. Wojciech Frazik. The original Polish edition (*Z Retingerem do Warszawy i z powrotem — Raport z Podziemia 1944*) has done quite well in Poland. I got involved by translating the book into English, principally because I felt that it told a thrilling story, taken right from the pages of history — a story that *deserved* a wider reading audience, i.e., the English-speaking world. Beyond that, this book constitutes a significant addition to the rather meager body of available written material about Dr. Retinger, and I felt that it was important that it should be translated. I was also able to include some source material that has never been published before, namely, a few frames of the microfilmed information my father brought back from Poland to the authorities in London. I've tried to keep my translation as straightforward as possible, adhering closely to exactly what was written, and taking only minimal liberties with some sentences.

At the time of this mission, my father was a 27-year-old Polish junior officer (Second Lieutenant), doing commando assignments which involved parachuting by night into German-occupied Poland. The men who went on these missions were an elite group of special forces called the *Cichociemni*, literally "the Silent Dark Ones." I call them Silent Shadows in this book. They've become something of a heroic legend in Polish war lore, with their adventures adapted into made-for-TV movies, miniseries, documentaries and the like. These parachute missions were vital to the Polish Government-in-Exile, and the daring men who went on them were a little larger than life in the eyes of the Polish people. Dozens of these Silent Shadow missions were flown, out of England at first and eventually out of southern Italy. The planes, training and equipment were provided by the British S.O.E., or Special Operations Executive, while the Polish side provided well-trained and highly motivated special forces, and coordinated events on the ground. The risk factor was extremely high; several planes were shot down on the way to Poland, and the *Cichociemni* lost a lot of fine men in action on the ground. My father was in fact the only man to survive two of these Silent Shadow parachute missions, complete his assignment and return to base.

What Was Operation Salamander?

This operation was unique in the annals of the *Cichociemni* missions in several ways. To begin with, the entire human payload of Operation Salamander consisted of two men, both of them on a strictly civilian political mission, where more typically a team of about six mostly military men, dressed as ordinary civilians, would be dropped into occupied Poland. (The mission did also deliver eighteen containers of supplies and military materiel.) Even though my father held the rank of Second Lieutenant, he was sent on this mission in mufti as an emissary of the Polish Interior Ministry. The man he was accompanying was a 56-year-old political advisor named Dr. Józef H. Retinger, who had never in his life strapped on a parachute before — not even in training.

The operational mission was purely political and intelligence-related — aside from the pre-arranged air drop of equipment and supplies, receipt of which was handled very surely and swiftly by the forces on the ground. Acting as a personal emissary of the Polish Prime Minister, Stanisław Mikołajczyk, my father was assigned the urgent task of explaining to the key political figures in Poland that the Allies, following through on the promises they had made to Soviet leader Joseph Stalin at the Teheran Conference, were now fully backing the Soviet Union and its Red Army in their fight against the Germans, and that consequently Poland would soon have to accept Russian soldiers on Polish soil as they pushed the Germans back — detestable as the prospect might seem. It is worth mentioning that Stalin, who was already preparing a Communist cadre for the takeover of power in Poland, had broken off diplomatic relations with the Polish Government-in-Exile several months earlier, under the absurd pretext that the Poles were cooperating with Hitler. My father and

Dr. Retinger were now going to have to explain to the Polish underground leaders that resisting the Russians would be futile, a waste of time and blood, and an irritant to our only allies, the Americans and British. Exhausted though they were, many leaders in Poland wished to fight the Soviet Red Army at any cost, even though they were completely unprepared to take them on. Driven by patriotism, they simply wanted no part of what they saw as caving in to the Russians, or indeed a treasonous betrayal of Poland. The Government-in-Exile, located in London, had to explain that from their point of view, working with our allies in the midst of a much larger war, we simply had no choice but to accept the inevitable. The patience of the British was already wearing thin as they waited for the Polish side to get with the program. Foreign Office Undersecretary of State Sir Anthony Cadogan had already expressed his frustration to Retinger personally, telling him, "The Poles are incorrigible idiots, and Poland will drown."[1] We Poles simply had to come to terms with our role as expendable pawns in a larger game, and the government in London had some explaining to do to the people in Poland. Toward this end, my father was intensively briefed for several weeks on all the personalities he'd be meeting with, the various political groupings and their viewpoints, and the geopolitical background against which all of this was playing out. He was specifically trained to be a "human gramophone," memorizing large amounts of information and classified intelligence that he was to "replay" verbatim when he got to Poland, then switching to "record" mode and committing to memory the details of certain conversations he was to take part in, which were held at the highest levels of the Polish underground. He wasn't supposed to keep anything at all in writing, in case he got caught by the Germans, but he did in fact keep a tiny coded notebook in one of his socks. Upon his return to London, these conversations he had "recorded" were then transcribed as faithfully as possible and included in his report to Prime Minister Mikołajczyk, who had personally sent him on Operation Salamander.

In addition to his mission as an emissary of the Polish Prime Minister, my father was given charge of the lone other passenger on this flight, who was none other than the mysterious and enigmatic political advisor, Dr. Józef Retinger. Although this distinguished gentleman was 56 years old, awkward and frail physically, and a novice parachutist, he was nonetheless willing to risk his life for a chance to talk to the key political figures in Poland, to try to salvage what could be salvaged of the Polish nation in the face of what seemed an inevitable Soviet takeover. Even though Retinger was viewed with suspicion in some circles of the Polish Government-in-Exile, and many people simply assumed that he was a British agent (or was that a Russian agent? Vatican?), there is archival evidence to support the claim that the whole mission was Retinger's own idea, undertaken on his own initiative, and that he'd had to talk both the British and Polish Prime Ministers into giving him the green light for this highly risky and dangerous project.[2] He was given the code name "Salamander" by the British S.O.E., and the mission to parachute him into German-occupied Poland with my father was named Operation Salamander.

One thing Operation Salamander was *not* connected to was the Warsaw Uprising, which commenced on August 1, 1944, just days after my father's return to London, and lasted 63 days before the Germans crushed it and then blew up the city, house by house. The Uprising turned out to be a tragic and very costly failure, and there has been speculation that Celt and Retinger were sent to dissuade the Polish Home Army, or AK (for *Armia Krajowa*), from undertaking this desperate enterprise, but that was simply not part of the mission. They may have discussed it with people, but they were there on other business. The AK went ahead with its doomed uprising, as chronicled in depth by British historian Norman Davies in his book, *Rising '44: The Battle for Warsaw* (Penguin, 2005).

Who Was Józef H. Retinger?

The man whose care and safety had been entrusted to my father was a Polish political advisor who had been particularly close to the previous Prime Minister, General Władysław Sikorski. Code-named "Salamander" and carrying identification as "Captain Edward Paisley," Józef Hieronim Retinger (1888–1960) had already spent a lifetime behind the scenes of political power. To say that he was an interesting fellow would surely be a monstrous understatement. He was truly charismatic, a magnetic personality who made friends with ease and inspired loyalty in the people who knew him. At the same time, there were suspicious people in the innermost circles of power in the Polish Government-in-Exile who deeply mistrusted him, questioned his motivation, and accused him of all sorts of treachery or deviousness. His life story, already filled with adventures, accomplishments, highs and lows, was about to take a completely new turn as he set off on this self-motivated do-or-die mission. The future of Poland was at stake.

A brief biography would be in order here.[3] Józef Hieronim Retinger (often written Joseph Hieronimus Retinger) was born in Kraków on April 17, 1888, the youngest of four children, at a time when there was no Poland on the European map. The Germans (Prussians), Russians, and Austrians had neatly divided up the country almost a century earlier. The southern part of Poland, including Kraków, was a province of the Austro-Hungarian Empire known as Galicia, so technically and officially he was born an Austrian subject.

Like so many Poles who had endured seemingly endless decades of partition and occupation, Retinger was fervently patriotic and wished more than anything to see Poland become a free and independent nation again. As a young man, he once told a friend, "I wish Poland would soon be free again so I would not have to be a damn patriot!"[4] But a patriot he was, and in 1944 he was willing to risk his life to save his country in Operation Salamander.

His father was Józef Stanisław Retinger, a brilliant lawyer who served as private legal counsel and advisor to the eminent Polish nobleman Count Władysław Zamoyski. His mother was Maria Krystyna Czyrmiańska, whose father was the Dean of the ancient and renowned Jagiellonian University in Kraków. His siblings included University of Chicago Chemistry Professor Julius M. Retinger and society doyenne Maria Dobrowolska. The Retingers were a well-to-do and highly respected Polish family.

The senior Retinger had represented Count Zamoyski as lead counsel on the winning side of a lawsuit in 1889 against Kingdom and Crown (i.e., the Austro-Hungarian Empire) in the matter of the ownership of certain particularly beautiful lands near the winter resort of Zakopane, including the spectacular Lake Morskie Oko. The lands stayed in Polish hands, and Count Zamoyski later bequeathed them to the Polish nation as national parks, which they remain to this day. It was a major triumph for the fiercely patriotic counsel, who had changed the spelling of the family name, originally "Röttinger," to its more "Polonized" form, Retinger. The name in its original spelling indicates that the family would have come from the German town of Röttingen at some point, but by the 1880s they were Polish through and through.

The elder Józef Retinger died suddenly in 1897 while the younger Józef Retinger was still a boy, and Count Zamoyski took little "Józio" under his wing. The boy was contemplating the priesthood as a teenager, and even entered the Novitiate of the Jesuits in Rome, but withdrew after a few months upon concluding that the requirement of celibacy was going to be too much of an obstacle. Thereupon Count Zamoyski sent him to study at the Sorbonne, covering all his expenses. Young Joseph Retinger (his preferred spelling of his given name when not in Poland), aged 18, arrived in Paris in 1906. Being the protégé of the magnificent Count, he was granted entrée into Parisian society and set about befriending an impressive array of people, including the young composer Maurice Ravel and the young painter Pierre Bonnard, before they both became world famous, and the dapper Marquis "Boni" de Castellane. Retinger's personal friends included numerous other highly creative types, including the dazzling pianist Ricardo Vinez, composers Eric Satie and Francis Poulenc, writers François Mauriac and André Gide, and many more. His active social life and the many hours he spent at the Café Vachette didn't take anything away from his work ethic, though, and he got his PhD in literature in 1908 at the age of twenty, establishing a record as the Sorbonne's youngest PhD ever.

Retinger continued his studies at the University of Munich, reading Comparative Psychology (*Völkerpsychologie*). In Munich, as in Paris, he met and befriended a lot of bright people, including Hans von Weber, publisher of the legendary *Hyperion* artistic monthly, who taught him a thing or two about the world of publishing. Retinger traveled a lot between Paris, Munich and Kraków between 1908 and 1912. During this time, he started publishing a literary and artistic monthly of his own in his native Kraków. Many writers gave him manuscripts for publication, among them Arnold Bennett, Franz Bley and André Gide, who let him serialize his book *La Porte Etroite* before it was even published in France. Despite its heavy-hitting talent roster, though, Retinger's monthly *Miesięcznik Literacki i Artystyczny* didn't last very long. It folded after a one-year run, January to December, 1911. In the midst of all this activity and travel, he married Otolia Zubrzycka (1889–1984), a lovely Polish girl from a good family — her father was the head of the Chemistry Department at the Jagiellonian University, and her mother had an estate of her own. The word is that Otolia, whom everyone called Tola, was a prize catch who turned away all other suitors in favor of the small and ungainly Józef Retinger.

Retinger's political activity first began in the years before World War I. He was asked by a group of Polish politicians from Galicia to open a bureau in London, in order to advocate for Polish matters in Great Britain. In modern parlance we'd say he was doing public relations for Poland. His "bureau" was a one-room office in Granville House on Arundel Street, and he set about making contacts among people who might one day be influential, doing what he could to promote the idea that Poland, which was split up between three partitioning powers and did not exist on the map, was in fact a nation. One example of a small but symbolic triumph involved the Third All-British Jamboree of the Boy Scouts, held in Birmingham, England, in 1913. Retinger talked to Andrzej Małkowski, known as the father of Polish Scouting, and got him to go along with a plan to set up an area for Boy Scouts from "Poland" at the jamboree, even though the scouts were technically from Austria, Germany or Russia. They flew the Polish flag. This little P.R. stunt must have irritated the three partitioning powers, who had no interest in acknowledging any kind of Polish sovereignty, but it was allowed to blow over. He had made his point. Slowly and gradually, the cause of Polish nationhood, which had been more or less a non-subject for decades, began to get mentioned in the press. "Retinger did not belong to any political organization or group, but he consistently upheld the idea of Polish sovereignty vis-à-vis all three partitioning powers," writes Zdzisław Najder.[5]

While in England, Retinger and his wife, Tola, met and befriended the Polish writer Joseph Conrad (Józef Konrad Korzeniowski), who gained international renown as the author of the English classics *The Heart of Darkness* and *Lord Jim*, among others. They met in 1912 through a mutual friend, Arnold Bennett, whom Retinger had known during his Sorbonne days and who had written for his literary monthly. The Conrads (Joseph and Jessie) and the Retingers spent a good deal of time together, later memorialized in Retinger's book *Conrad and His Contemporaries*.[6] They were in fact vacationing together in southern Poland during the summer of 1914 when World War I broke out, and they had to scramble to get the Conrads out of there on a train. It took a while. Joseph and Jessie Conrad finally got to Vienna on October 10, 1914, on a night train filled with wounded soldiers.

Józef Retinger in Paris, 1908. He had just received his PhD from the Sorbonne at age 20, setting the record for youngest-ever PhD at that University (Chciuk-Celt Family Archives).

As the Great War went on and the death toll mounted to horrific levels, Retinger tried to use his influential contacts and personal charisma to bring about an end to the slaughter by persuading Austria to withdraw from its alliance with Germany and sue for a separate peace. Boni de Castellane tried to help; there were meetings with Asquith,[7] Clemenceau,[8] Northcliffe[9] and Berthelot,[10] but in the end his plan didn't work out, the two Kaisers didn't go for it, and by his meddling Retinger had managed to seriously offend some important people. He further offended the powers that be when he got involved in arguments over the legal status of the Polish Army of the West under General Haller — he was extremely concerned that Polish soldiers might be classified as traitors and face summary execution. Again, he was accused of meddling and over-reaching, and was declared *persona non grata* by Austria. The Germans reportedly had a price on his head, he was suddenly unwelcome in Britain, and he was expelled from France — penniless! Furthermore, his marriage to Tola, who had given birth to their daughter Wanda in Lausanne in June of 1917, was falling apart. Joseph Conrad tried to help by wiring him some money and writing letters on his behalf, but basically Retinger was on his own, down and out with no place to go.

He wound up in Mexico, where he spent quite a lot of time in the 1920s. Once again, his amazing ability to make friends came into play, and he got to know many of the key players, trade unionists, politicians, and so on. Plutarco Elias Calles, who went on to become the President of Mexico, was his personal friend, as was the union leader and future politician Luis Negrete Morones. One notable area of Retinger's activity in Mexico involved advising the Mexican government to nationalize the country's significant petroleum reserves and the industry that went with it. This set up a major source of national revenue for Mexico, but it seriously irritated some powerful Americans, since the companies poised to make fountains of money from the Mexican oilfields were all American. Consequently, Retinger had enemies in Washington, even though he also had friends in high places, including Supreme Court Justice Felix Frankfurter. The one side had him in jail the moment he set foot on American soil; the other side intervened to get him out. He describes it all with a good deal of humor in his book, *Memoirs of an Eminence Grise*. In the midst of this renewed series of travels and adventures, in 1926 he married Stella Morel, the daughter of British Labour Unionist E.D. Morel. They had two girls: Maria was born in 1927, and Stasia in 1930. Stella died in 1933, and Józef eked out a fairly meager existence for the remainder of the 1930s by writing articles, books and essays — but he kept up his contacts.

Things took a very nasty turn for Poland in September of 1939, when the country was invaded and crushed by the Germans from the West and the Soviets from the East. After Warsaw surrendered, there was a scramble to put together a Government-in-Exile, and this entity eventually became the official face of the Polish government, headquartered in France at first, and then in London after France fell to the Germans. When General Władysław Sikorski became the Prime Minister of the Polish Government-in-Exile, his close friend and political advisor Józef Retinger was at his side. Sikorski owed Retinger a debt of gratitude, as the latter had personally borrowed Winston Churchill's airplane to fetch the General out of France when things were collapsing there in 1940, in an amazing bit of derring-do that must have greatly impressed Sikorski. After that, the General came to rely on his friend and advisor, who also served as a key link to the British government, where he clearly had excellent connections at the top level and no trouble with the language. Retinger was able to see to it that the Polish government's relationship with its principal ally was kept on an even keel, and the General appreciated it. When General Sikorski went to visit the Polish military contingent in the besieged city of Tobruk, he took Retinger with him — the only civilian in the group. Sikorski was killed in a plane crash in Gibraltar in 1943, leaving his close friend Retinger devastated, but when a new government was formed around Prime Minister Stanisław Mikołajczyk, Retinger continued to play an important advisory role. Having been told point-blank by British Foreign Secretary Anthony Eden that the Allies were not going to fight a war against the Soviets over Poland or its borders, he knew that some concessions would have to be made, and he was acutely aware of the urgency of the situation. The Russians were coming and no one was going to help the Polish side, which simply had to accept the facts and try to enter into negotiations with the Soviet Union, or else get steamrolled completely. Retinger was, by his own account, acting entirely on his own initiative in the early days of 1944 when he undertook a mission to parachute into Poland, and that mission is the subject of this, my father's last book.

After World War II was finally over and Poland had been reduced to a smoking heap of rubble by the Germans, only to be promptly handed over to the Soviets, Retinger managed to use his contacts in England once again, persuading the demobilizing British Army to give a substantial amount of valuable surplus military materiel to Poland, where equipment of all kinds was so sorely needed. They shipped blankets, field kitchens, tents, many thousands of pairs of shoes and boots, and even a few Bailey bridges to Poland.[11] My father, whom he'd gotten to know well during their time together on Operation Salamander, served as his secretary during this time.

When the Communists grabbed the reins of power in Poland and started cracking down hard, Retinger very wisely got out of there while he could, returning to London, where he lived out most of the remainder of his life. In the late 1940s and into the 1950s, he made it his personal mission to bring about a united, peaceful Europe. Retinger was one of the initiators of the European League for Economic Cooperation, a precursor to what would eventually become the European Economic Community and finally today's European Union, of which Poland is a proud member. Nowadays, therefore, when we drive across the former East Germany and enter Poland without any hassles at the border crossing, we have Józef H. Retinger to thank for getting the ball rolling. He is one of the founding fathers of the European Movement that made these changes possible.

Retinger's final achievement was also his most controversial — and he'd had his hand in plenty of controversies before. It is the one thing he is associated with nowadays in some circles — his claim to fame, as it were. What he did was this: building on his excellent contacts and peerless personal connections, in 1954 he arranged, with the help of Prince Bernhard of the Netherlands and some other highly influential people, to convene a unique conference at the Bilderberg Hotel in Oosterbeek, Holland, bringing together into one room all of the most important players and decision-makers in the entire international scene for a conference dedicated to completely unfettered, off-the-record dialogue among all of the people present. At that time — the early 1950s — there was an atmosphere of considerable mutual distrust between the Europeans and the United States, even though we were ostensibly cooperating beautifully, what with the Marshall Plan and NATO. Retinger thought that the best way to cut through the red tape was by not having any red tape to begin with, and that the best way to get things done was by gathering together all the people who could actually get things done, and letting them talk freely and openly.

This was more or less the technique Retinger had employed while in Warsaw in 1944 on Operation Salamander, when he called a meeting of all the top Underground people in a café in the middle of the day — much to my father's dismay, as it presented him with a security nightmare and the Germans, should they get wind of it, with an easy major target. The Germans never came, though. The meeting was called specifically so that all of the key players could speak their piece and be heard out, and was kept so successfully hush-hush that none of the attendees, nor any of their staff, breathed a word. He pulled it off: it was a very useful meeting. It could be said that this afternoon get-together in a café in wartime Warsaw served as a model for that first meeting at the Bilderberg Hotel in Oosterbeek.

The meeting at the Bilderberg was a success as well. The template seemed to work: invite the key players to attend personally; keep publicity to a minimum and the press (or the Germans) at a distance; meet to talk freely and openly; address the most pressing issues of the day; and finally, take no formal action and issue no policies or communiqués. The group started meeting on a regular annual basis, and although the list of attendees varied from year to year, Dr. J.H. Retinger acted as Secretary of the Bilderberg Conferences — as they came to be known, regardless of where the meetings were taking place — until his death in 1960.

In the years since then, the Bilderberg Meetings have come to represent for some people the presence of a conspiratorial cabal which seeks to rule the world. The name of the Illuminati is often invoked in reference to these ongoing annual meetings of "everyone who really counts" on the global scene, held under tightest security under absolute exclusion of the press, and the name of Joseph Retinger is often held up as that of the architect of this supposedly dark and evil conspiracy. Thus he remains a controversial figure more than fifty years after his death, reviled in some circles and greatly admired in others. With this book about the time he spent with Dr. Retinger on Operation Salamander, my father has attempted to add to the rather meager written account of this extraordinary human being by drawing an accurate picture of the man exactly as he saw him.

Who Was Marek Celt?

The author of this book about Operation Salamander and Operation Wildhorn III used the *nom de plume* Marek Celt, but his real name was Tadeusz Chciuk-Celt — my father. He was one of the elite Silent Shadow commandos, and Operation Salamander was his second parachute mission into German-occupied Poland. His code names were Celt and Sulima.

When he was born Tadeusz Chciuk in Drohobycz on October 17, 1916, he, too, was technically an Austrian subject, as the Austro-Hungarian Empire still ruled Galicia, but by the time he was in preschool the map had changed, and as a result of the various post–World War I treaties and the Polish-Russian War of 1920, Drohobycz was in the new nation of Poland, back on the map after a 125-year absence. Tadeusz, nicknamed "Dzidek," was the fourth of five children born to Michał and Maria Chciuk. His father was a civil

Tadeusz Chciuk's high school graduation picture, taken by Studio Tycjan in Drohobycz, 1936 (Chciuk-Celt Family Archives).

engineer involved with river regulation, and his mother was in charge of the family home. The Chciuks were a prosperous middle-class family until the Great Depression brought much leaner times in the 1930s. Young Dzidek was active in the Polish Boy Scouts, liked playing ice hockey, and did well in school. After graduating from Jagiełło High School in Drohobycz, he went on to study law at the University of Lwów, while simultaneously getting his intermediate music degree at the Conservatory there. He was an able performer of Chopin's piano pieces. The ink on his master's degree in law was barely dry when the Germans and Soviets invaded Poland in September 1939.

In the early months of the war, he was a "White Courier," specializing in leading small groups of people across what was then the Hungarian border to relative safety, as there was no war being fought on Hungarian soil in those days. While the principal assignment of these couriers was to ensure the steady flow of information between the resistance organizations in Soviet-occupied Poland and the Budapest field office of the exiled Polish authorities, they also provided a guided cross-border transfer for numbers of young men eager to join the Polish army units then being formed in France, as well as for people fleeing from the nightmare of the ongoing mass deportations to Siberia. They were called White Couriers because they were dressed in white to avoid detection in the snow.[12] One of these groups, led by his comrade-in-arms Władysław Ossowski, led my mother — then a teenage high school student named Ewa Lovell — to safety, allowing her to spend the war

Tadeusz Chciuk at the chessboard, in his Polish Boy Scout uniform, 1938 (Chciuk-Celt Family Archives).

years relatively unscathed at the Polish school in Balatonboglár. It wasn't until much later, in November of 1944, that she was injured when the Germans dynamited a Budapest bridge she happened to be crossing in a streetcar.

My father managed to join the Polish Army units in France in the spring of 1940. As the European situation deteriorated that summer and the Germans seized control, he made his way to Great Britain, where the Polish units were forming up anew. His three brothers were all involved in the war effort, too, with Władek (Pilot Officer Władysław Chciuk, 1915–2006, awarded the *Virtuti Militari* medal) distinguishing himself as a particularly fearless and aggressive fighter pilot. Their eldest sister Stasia, along with her two young daughters, was hauled off by the Soviets on a brutal forced march to Kazakhstan, where one of her little girls, Basia, died.[13]

Second Lieutenant Tadeusz Chciuk in Lintrose, Scotland, 1941 (Chciuk-Celt Family Archives and MHPRL Warsaw).

Stasia and her surviving daughter, Krystyna, were eventually able to make their way, through many trials and tribulations, to London, where they were reunited with Stasia's husband, Leopold Sklenarz, in 1943. She is listed on my father's mission papers for Operation Salamander as the person to notify in case of death, with a London address. My father, Tadeusz Chciuk, was initially stationed with Polish units in Biggar and Lintrose, Scotland, and went through Officers' Training School. After a brief stint as a motorcycle courier (he recounted to me that he enjoyed riding the big British Nortons) he was enrolled in a parachute training course, in preparation for deployment on Silent Shadow missions into Poland. The paratrooper commando candidates were trained at a facility in Ringway, near Manchester, where they practiced by jumping off moving trucks or being dropped from a tall crane that looked like a jungle gym.

His first such parachute mission, Operation Jacket, which took place in late December of 1941, involved a deadly firefight with German forces right off the bat. That shootout was described in his book *Koncert,* which could be translated as *Concerto for Four Colts*.¹⁴ He had been sent with a small team on Operation Jacket as a courier of the Polish Government-in-Exile, which was then led by General Sikorski. This was one of the earliest such missions into German-occupied Poland, and the pilot mistakenly dropped them a few hundred meters into actual German territory, so that the very first thing the men had to do was to cross the well-guarded border back into occupied Poland. Four of them, including my father, were apprehended by the German *Grenzschutz* (Border Patrol) and taken to a small outpost, where the Poles had to shoot their way out. That was the "concerto." In a separate nearby incident, the two other members of the Operation Jacket team engaged a group of about twenty-five German soldiers and were both killed in the ensuing firefight. My father and the rest of the Jacket team survived and made their getaway, with hundreds of German soldiers looking for them and "Wanted — Bandits" posters all over the place.

Second Lieutenant Tadeusz Chciuk in Scotland, 1941, shortly before Operation Jacket, his first parachute mission into German-occupied Poland (Chciuk-Celt Family Archives and MHPRL Warsaw).

The way the political setup functioned at this time was that the Polish Prime Minister and his cabinet were in London and served as the officially recognized face of the Polish government, while the man in charge of representing this government in Poland itself was called the Chief Delegate. His was a very dangerous job indeed, with the term of office usually shortened by death at the hands of the Gestapo or the Russians. The Polish side lost several Chief Delegates that way. Naturally, with the seat of government separated from the

Introduction

nation's capital by 900 miles and the Third Reich, communications were a major challenge. The Silent Shadow couriers, by parachuting into Poland and reporting personally to the leadership, served as an indispensable communications link between the Government in London and the Delegature in Warsaw.

In addition to delivering news, intelligence information and instructions from London — as well as gold and cash — my father's mission on Operation Jacket had been to meet with the key figures in the Underground, make a thorough assessment of the situation in occupied Poland, return to London "by whatever means possible" (a wonderful military term) and submit a report to the Prime Minister. This he did. The report itself — what's left of it — is stored at a Polish military-historical archive in London. His hair-raising adventures in the Polish Underground, personal eyewitness account of the Warsaw Ghetto, arduous journey across half of occupied Europe in a variety of disguises, capture and incarceration in a Spanish prison, followed by a stint in a concentration camp, and return to base are all described in his book *Raport*

Second Lieutenant Tadeusz Chciuk being awarded the Virtuti Militari, Poland's highest military decoration, in London, 1943. Left to right: General Kazimierz Sosnkowski, Tadeusz Chciuk, Franciszek Moskal (Chciuk-Celt Family Archives and MHPRL Warsaw).

z Podziemia 1942, or *Report from the Polish Underground, 1942*.[15] (That book has yet to be translated.) It was an amazing mission to have accomplished, and he was awarded Poland's highest military decoration, the *Virtuti Militari*, in recognition of his courage and gallantry in action under extremely trying circumstances.

In the months between the completion of Operation Jacket and the inception of Operation Salamander, my father had been put to work at a secret underground radio station called Radio Świt (which means "dawn"), which was supposed to give the impression that it was a clandestine broadcast being beamed from within underground Poland, when in fact it was actually being transmitted to Poland from the U.K.

On this, his second parachute mission, my father was being sent to Poland as the personal emissary of the new Prime Minister, Stanisław Mikołajczyk. His predecessor, General Władysław Sikorski, had perished in a bizarre — not to say suspicious — plane crash at Gibraltar several months before,[16] and now it was up to Mikołajczyk to pick up where Sikorski had left off. The new Prime Minister also asked my father to safeguard the life and well-being of Dr. Józef Retinger while in Poland. Following that, my father's assignment was to get Retinger onto one of the planes flying the daring new Wildhorn missions (which involved actually landing a plane on Polish soil "right under the Germans' noses" to deliver men and supplies, picking up a handful of passengers and communications, and returning to base) and see to Retinger's safe return to London. Despite numerous roadblocks, sabotage and at least one attempt on Retinger's life, he did manage to accomplish his mission: he talked to the people he was sent to talk to, and he got the old man on a plane, even if he had to carry him in his arms. He returned to his superiors in London and filed his report. A copy of this report is now held in the archives of the Hoover Institution in Stanford, California, and its contents serve as the original source material for this book.[17]

Tadeusz Chciuk returned to Poland in December of 1945 and married his fiancée, Ewa Lovell, right away, at St. Anne's Church in Kraków. Theirs was indeed a very long engagement — over six years — during which time they were each notified by the International Committee of the Red Cross that the other had died. Very much alive and together again at last, the young couple tried to settle in Kraków, but they were both arrested, imprisoned and interrogated by the Secret Police. My father was suspected by the Communists of being a British agent. His pregnant wife wasn't suspected of anything, but was held as a way of putting pressure on him. He was taken to a small interrogation room exactly seventeen times per day and asked the same questions every time. My parents were released after about six weeks of captivity, allegedly after Dr. Retinger intervened personally with Soviet Foreign Minister Vyacheslav Molotov. They lived in Kraków for two more years — under surveillance — with their baby daughter (my eldest sister, Aleksandra), until it became clear that they were about to be re-arrested, whereupon they hastily fled the country in late September 1948. Many of their friends and acquaintances spent the next eight years in prison. After crossing the border into Slovakia, making their way to Vienna on a night train, and continuing to Innsbruck, where they stayed for a couple of weeks, my parents and their young daughter got to Paris around November 20, 1948, and that's where they stayed for about three years, living in authentic poverty before my father was recruited to the Polish editorial team of a new American-funded radio station, Radio Free Europe. He was to spend the next forty years working for

Wedding photograph of Ewa Lovell and Tadeusz Chciuk, Kraków, December 19, 1945. They were engaged in 1939 and spent most of the next six years not knowing if the other was dead or alive. They did have two weeks together in the summer of 1942, while the author was trying to return to England after Operation Jacket. While they were apart, each was separately notified by the International Committee of the Red Cross that the other had died (Chciuk-Celt Family Archives).

R.F.E. in Munich, Germany, where I was born. It wasn't until he retired that he began writing his World War II memoirs, of which this is the fourth and final volume.

My Personal Perspective

This is my father's story, his own eyewitness account of what happened on Operation Salamander and his attempt to portray the supposedly mysterious and enigmatic Dr. Retinger exactly as he saw him. I undertook the translation project because I simply felt it needed to be done. I'm personally involved in it, though, beyond just the translation. This fearless commando, this decorated national hero laid to rest with fullest honors at the Polish National Cemetery in Powązki, who has a school and a Boy Scout troop named after him, was just Dad to me. His comrades-in-arms referred to him as a "young god" in a surviving report, but I didn't know anything about that.[18] Even though he practically never talked about his wartime adventures when I was growing up, and most certainly didn't glorify them, I feel that I can relate to my father and to whatever it is that motivated him and Dr. Retinger to go on this extremely dangerous mission: good old-fashioned patriotism, doing anything you can to save your country, even if it means dying in the process. I can picture us on the same side, so to speak: the Polish side, whose one preeminent goal has always simply been a free and independent Poland.

I grew up stateless, living in Munich, during those decades when Poland was neither free nor independent as the Cold War went on and on, and it seemed our dream of freedom and independence would remain elusive for the foreseeable future. We'd sing the Polish national anthem, which is called "Poland Hasn't Died Yet as Long as We're Alive," and finish every Sunday's Mass with a fervently sung entreaty to God to someday let us return to a free fatherland. Even though we were incredibly proud when our family, after being stateless refugees for two decades, became American citizens in 1968, and I live in America with my American wife and children, I grew up in a Polish family, speaking Polish at home. When I get wrapped up in my father's account of what happened to Poland during and after World War II, I do take it personally. This is what was done to *us*, this is what happened to *us*.

When the whole Communist show collapsed around 1989–91 and free elections were held at last, we all shared in the triumphant feeling that my mother and father had successfully outlived the decades-long Soviet domination of our homeland. He and Dr. Retinger had parachuted into Nazi-occupied Poland to try to help save the nation from going under, in the face of a forcible takeover by the Soviets. It took about forty-five years, but we finally

Ewa and Tadeusz Chciuk-Celt in Planegg, Germany, some 45 years after they were married in Poland in 1945. They stayed together till death did them part. Photograph by Jan Chciuk-Celt (Chciuk-Celt Family Archives).

got the free elections in 1991 that we'd been promised in 1945. Today we have a free and independent Poland, fully integrated into the European Community. Dr. Retinger's dream of a free Poland taking its rightful, regular place in a peaceful Europe is now a reality.

My father, Tadeusz Chciuk-Celt, was finally able to return in 1991 to visit the country he had fled with his wife and toddler daughter, taking only the things they could carry, in 1948. In all those intervening years he would have been arrested at once as an enemy of the state if he had tried to enter Poland, but in 1991, as a new Poland was born, he returned to a splendid welcome. When word came that his old friend Władysław Ossowski had survived his decades in the Soviet Gulags and was returning from faraway Krasnoyarsk to Poland to be reunited with him, their meeting at the airport in Wrocław after fifty-one years apart was carried live on national TV. I was there to witness their reunion — a moving event. Even the news cameraman next to me had tears running down his cheeks. I had the privilege of driving these two old friends around Poland as they gave interviews to the media in city after city. Even though their life stories since they'd last seen each other in 1940 had taken such drastically different paths, with one man digging ditches with a hand pick in the frozen Siberian ground and the other broadcasting into Poland over Radio Free Europe under a pseudonym ("Michał Lasota") while living in exile in Munich, they both had the same happy ending: "It's good to be back."

Political and Historical Context

The purpose of Operation Salamander was purely political: to bring the key players in Poland up to date on the major changes in Poland's international situation as a result of the Teheran Conference of late 1943, at which U.S. President Franklin D. Roosevelt and British Prime Minister Winston Churchill had essentially turned Poland and the rest of Eastern Europe over to Soviet dictator Josef Stalin, declaring those areas to be within the Soviet "Sphere of Influence."

It may sound hard to believe today, but the flow of news was so restricted under German occupation that many people in Poland hadn't even heard about what had happened at the Teheran Conference, months after the fact. Those who'd heard of the conference were largely unaware of its implications, which were truly devastating from the Polish point of view. We were busy fighting the Germans, with increasing success at that, and didn't have much free time to ponder our perilous predicament vis-à-vis the "Sphere" we'd just been assigned to without even being consulted. Mikołajczyk, the Prime Minister, was in a tight spot. Since he was in contact with Churchill and his Foreign Secretary, Anthony Eden, he was painfully aware of the fact that the Allies now fully supported the Soviet Union and were not going to fight them over Poland's borders. Anthony Eden had told him so in person. Stalin was getting everything he wanted from a compliant Roosevelt and an indifferent Churchill, and Mikołajczyk was powerless to do anything to prevent the Allies from sacrificing Poland altogether in the name of their broader geostrategic goals. Poland really had no cards left to play. If we resisted and protested, we'd just be seen as making trouble, and we couldn't run the risk of annoying our only real allies. The political and military leaders of the Polish Underground would now have to be talked into negotiating with the Russians, not fighting them, if there was to be any chance of saving the nation, already so badly damaged and exhausted by four and a half years of war, from being completely taken over by the Soviet Union.

The problem with this was that the Poles in general detested and deeply mistrusted the Russians, who had invaded Poland to begin with on September 17, 1939, barely two weeks after the German invasion that sparked World War II. The Soviet forces behaved very brutally, killing a lot of people on the spot and hauling many thousands of others off to forced labor in the Gulag prison camps of Siberia and Kazakhstan. My father's close friend and comrade-in-arms from the "White Courier" days, Władysław Ossowski, had disappeared in 1940, nabbed by the dreaded Soviet Secret Police, the NKVD; he was presumed dead, but was in fact serving a life sentence at hard labor in Siberia. There were many thousands of Polish prisoners in those Gulag camps. Furthermore, everyone in Poland knew that it was the Soviets who had rounded up and executed the entire officers' corps of the Polish Army, as well as mass numbers of Polish POWs, intellectuals and political prisoners — some 22,000 men in all — in an infamous place called Katyń and a series of other sites, in 1940. The NKVD were an instrument of really brutal terror during those first two years of the war. The Soviet occupiers were bad news, bringing death, devastation and deportation. In view of all this, it seems understandable that the Polish political and military leadership would balk at the idea of doing an abrupt about-face and "making nice" with the Russians; it was seen as treasonous. Although the Communist cause did have some believers, the overwhelming majority of Polish people reviled the Soviet Union and its brutally oppressive system.

Seeing that the British and Americans now fervently embraced the Soviet Union as an ally, and that this ally was expected to re-invade Poland with their full blessing this time, Prime Minister Mikołajczyk was acutely aware of the fact that he was probably going to have to make some territorial concessions to the Russians if there was to be any chance of Poland surviving as an independent country. Armed, fed and supplied by the Allies, the Red Army had the upper hand, and the first thing they wanted back was the territory that Poland had reclaimed in 1920. By early 1944, they were already taking over in some of the eastern Polish areas, such as Wołyń with considerable harshness. President Roosevelt had made it clear that he had no problem with Poland going Communist under Soviet control — but our Prime Minister certainly did! So he sent my father to talk to the various players in the Polish Underground, and with him went Dr. Retinger.

There were going to be several very bitter pills for people to swallow, and it was going to require some desperate salesmanship to persuade the political and military leaders to accept the facts. Retinger was a distinguished political figure with real connections, and although he had made some enemies, he definitely had a lot of clout.

The first and most bitter pill of all was the very idea that we should agree to give up a large part of our pre-war territory to the Soviet Union, and move Poland's eastern border back to the so-called Curzon Line, which had been drawn on the map by an English Lord with that name. Those lands east of the Curzon Line were won back from the nascent Soviet Union in 1920, when Poland actually repelled a Russian invasion and trounced the Bolsheviks in a military conflict, forcing them into a hasty retreat. As a new nation, reborn after 120 years of non-existence, the Poles were attached to all of their territory. If Poland's border were to be taken back to the Curzon Line, the area we might have to give up to the Russians would include a major city, Lwów, and a very productive oil field. My father happened to be from this part of Poland, so this had to be personally agonizing for him. Vilnius, too, was a Polish city at that time, and we were unwilling to simply give it away.

A second bitter pill was the idea that we were going to have Russian troops in Poland—again. This time, they were pushing back the Germans, so they were supposed to be our allies now. "Not bloody likely" is what most Poles thought of that. It looked for all the world as though the Russians were going to try to take over our country again. We were far too worn out, having been in the war since Day 1, to give them much of a fight, but we still didn't see them as liberators.

Even the acceptance of the Communists as a legitimate political party was a hurdle. The horrors of Soviet rule in the 1930s in the nearby Ukraine were an object lesson in the reality of applied Stalinism, and a great majority of Poles emphatically wanted no part of it. There was a Communist Party in wartime Poland, but it certainly didn't have enough support to win any elections. A lot of people thought the Communists should be shut out of the government entirely, but now we were being pressured by the Americans and British to give them a seat at the table.

Józef Retinger in a British officer's uniform, as "Captain Edward Paisley," shortly before Operation Salamander, 1944 (courtesy MHPRL Warsaw).

The British had come up with the nickname "Stem" for Mikołajczyk, as in "St. M." (his initials), since they were known to have a real struggle with the pronunciation of foreign surnames. They also called him Prime Minister Mick. My father got used to calling Prime Minister Mikołajczyk "Stem," and used that name for him in this memoir almost exclusively, with only the occasional reminder that "Stem" was in fact Stanisław Mikołajczyk, the Prime Minister.

Certain other people's code names and pseudonyms are vital to this story as well. Foremost among these is Józef Hieronim Retinger, who had been given the code name "Salamander" by the British, carried ID papers saying he was a British officer named Captain Edward Paisley, and used other pseudonyms while in Poland, such as Mr. Józef Brzoza, which would be like calling himself Mr. Joseph Birchtree in English. In this book, my father refers to Dr. Retinger most often by his initials, JHR, but also as Salamander and sometimes by his proper surname.

My father had code names, too. His proper given name was Tadeusz Chciuk, and his rank was Second Lieutenant. His code name was "Celt," made up by combining his initials with those of his fiancée, Ewa Lovell. After the war, he had his last name officially changed to Chciuk-Celt, and that's my last name as well. In the secret dispatches from London, however, he is code-named Sulima. And while in Poland, he carried fake identification papers under the name Marek Jurkiewicz.

Important people in Poland were often referred to by their code names. The Chief Delegate, the government's top man on the ground, was a man named Jan Stanisław Jankowski at the time of this mission, but he was known by his code name, Sobol, which means sable (the animal). The women agents were known by their code names too, with the notable exception in this book of my father's Cousin Hanka. Practically the entire military chain of command operated on code names. You got used to it. No one used their real name.

It's clear now, going on seventy years later, that Operation Salamander was up against some very serious resistance from within the Polish Government, even though it was ordered by the Prime Minister himself, in full consultation with our allies. Some people in the top-level leadership of the Home Army, or AK, were dead-set against the whole idea, and took all sorts of steps to delay and finally sabotage the mission. The notion of giving up half of Poland's territory to the Soviet Union without a fight was just unthinkable; they didn't trust Retinger, suspected him of being an agent, and didn't want him to fulfill his mission in Poland; they most certainly didn't want him to return to London.

Even though Józef Retinger remains a controversial figure to this day, most famously because he convened the original Bilderberg Conference in

1954, plenty of people were talking about him behind his back in the 1940s, and had been doing so since World War I. He was 56 years old at the time of this mission, and willing to risk his life in order to try to save Poland, but he was suspected in various quarters of being a British agent, a Soviet agent, a high-ranking Mason, a Jesuit, a Jew, a Knight of Malta, a Vatican agent, an American agent, a homosexual and the Devil's Cousin. (When told of these rumors, he was known to smile and say, "...and that's not the half of it.") He'd already had a colorful and adventurous life marked by numerous distinctions and marred by several periods of being homeless and broke.

During World War II, most of the buzz and gossip about Retinger was centered around his role as principal political advisor and close friend of General Władysław Sikorski. Although General Sikorski was undoubtedly seen as a hero and leader by millions of Poles, he did face some internecine opposition. Evidently some factions left over from the ultra-right wing Polish government of the 1930s, who were now in the opposition, didn't think General Sikorski was sufficiently vigorous in his defense of Polish interests and Poland's independence. They viewed his closest advisor with a great deal of suspicion. Even so, Retinger was valuable to the General because he was in personal contact with British Prime Minister Winston Churchill and Foreign Minister Anthony Eden, so he could get things done. He really was amazingly well-connected. Who else could talk Winston Churchill into lending him his plane? His activity may have been behind the scenes for the most part, but he was an influential advisor and a faithful friend to the General.

With Mikołajczyk as Prime Minister after Sikorski's shocking and suspicious death in Gibraltar, the internecine tensions within the Polish Government-in-Exile only intensified. Mikołajczyk's situation was completely different from Sikorski's. Where General Sikorski had had unified command as military Commander-in-Chief and Prime Minister, Mikołajczyk had to cede command of the military to General Kazimierz Sosnkowski. They didn't always see eye to eye, to put it mildly, and consequently Mikołajczyk's authority was weakened. Aside from the one unifying theme for all Poles at that time — to resolutely fight the Germans using all available means — there was a lack of harmony in the Government. When the British S.O.E. gave Operation Salamander the green light, some people in Mikołajczyk's own inner circle saw it as a sinister undertaking which was to be thwarted at all costs. The whispered innuendos laid at Retinger's feet as quasi-criminal charges (enumerated above) added up to such a ludicrous litany that it may have sounded funny, but the fact is that he was widely suspected of being an agent with a sinister secret agenda. But just whose agent, and what agenda? Some said he was in the service of the Soviet Union, since his aim was to persuade people that it would be counterproductive to try to fight the Russians, and that therefore he was implementing the Soviet agenda. But he was clearly working closely with the British, so maybe that was it? Rumor-mongering, guessing games and innuendo kept Retinger's reputation under constant attack. He knew so many important people personally that it was hard to tell if anyone owned him. He himself insisted that he was strictly acting on his own.

In any event, certain rogue elements within the Home Army (AK) appear to have taken the lead in sabotaging this mission. A scenario emerges in which we have a Prime Minister who personally orders this daring and vital mission, in full consultation with our allies, only to be blocked behind his back by members of his own armed forces! These opponents finally ordered Retinger killed, detailing the AK's Liquidation Squad, Unit 993W, to do the job. He was kept off the plane that had come to pick him up (Operation Wildhorn II) and was crucially delayed by almost two months in his eventual return to London. The paralysis which so nearly cost him his life was not caused by a fall into an icy stream (as Retinger himself believed at the time), but by a poisoning. The military nurse/assassin from Unit 993W who administered the poison, Izabela Horodecka, recounted it all in detail for Polish TV years later. She clearly and emphatically stated that the order to kill Retinger came from the AK top brass in London. There is a surviving document — a telegram from Col. Franciszek Demel of the General Staff in London to Col. Iranek-Osmecki, head of AK Intelligence in Warsaw — stating that Retinger's mission was to be thwarted "at all costs."[19]

In spite of these obstacles, the mission was accomplished, inasmuch as the two men met with the key players in Poland and attempted to present to them the appalling new reality facing Poland. Ultimately, though, Operation Salamander could also be called a failure, in that they didn't convince people to accept the position of the Government-in-Exile that the Soviet Union was to be treated as an ally. It was not so much a military problem as a political one. The Polish forces were willing to accept the Soviet army as an ally in the fight against the Germans, but the problem was the matter of what price Poland was to pay Stalin in order to get him to consider the Poles as allies. That price was nothing less than Poland's independence, and the Polish politicians knew it, even as they persisted in deluding themselves that the Americans and British were going to come to Poland's rescue. Stalin himself had set up political conditions that made it impossible for the Polish side to treat the Soviet Union and its army as an ally. The Polish government did indeed wish to come to some kind of understanding with the Soviets — they were simply unwilling to give him an unconditional surrender. They never did reach that political understanding, and the rest, as they say, is history.

Dr. Retinger was left poisoned and helplessly paralyzed, so that my father had to carry him in his arms like a child, but he got back to London and recuperated at the Dorchester Hotel. He briefed Churchill and Eden on the situation in Poland, even as Warsaw was going up in flames during its doomed Uprising, while the Red Army — the ally of our allies — stood by and watched from across the Vistula River and did absolutely nothing to help.

This, then, is the true account of Operation Salamander, a kind of "Mission Impossible" in which Dr. Józef Retinger and 2nd Lt. Tadeusz Chciuk parachuted into Poland to try to save the nation.

ONE

Prologue

(Planegg, Germany, 2000)

My life is already behind me now.

My thoughts at this point are all about reaching the end, without anything grating on my conscience or any important matters left unattended.

Thinking about all this, I keep coming back to 1944. Something inside me — could it be "History" with a capital H? — keeps calling out: "Tell 'em about what you saw back then, what you heard and experienced, because you can't take it with you to the other shore." Might this story be of some use to those people who remain, or to those yet to come? I've been asked so many times to write a follow-up to my *Report from the Polish Underground 1942* — serious people have urged me to do this, indeed they've demanded it.

All right, then: this is the way it was. In the course of well over a half-century, I've spoken about those days many times with Polish people of different generations: with those who took part in the fight for freedom against Hitler's Germans and against the Soviets; with younger people who couldn't fight because they were just too young back then; and with totally young people who were years away from even being born yet — and just about every time, just about everybody urged me to give this account of what happened in the Polish Underground prior to the Warsaw Uprising of 1944, and the people and events of that time. This would be the story of Poland fighting, the way I saw it in 1944, which was from up close, not only in Poland but also in London. The issue then, perhaps more than ever, was whether our country was "to be or not to be." The Teheran Conference had left Poland crushed, given away by the Allies to the grace and mercy (or rather the wrath) of Joseph Stalin. After 1943, a year of awful setbacks — the outright lies of the Soviets regarding the Katyń massacre, swallowed without any resistance by the Allies; the death of General Sikorski; the Teheran Conference, with the hypocrisy of the West giving away half of Europe to the yoke of Commu-

Dr. Józef Retinger standing amid the ruins of Warsaw. Photograph by Tadeusz Chciuk-Celt (Chciuk-Celt Family Archives).

nism — after all that came 1944: the complete breach of faith by our erstwhile friends; the Polish nation suffering beyond its limits; our fight for the very life of our nation. How best, now, to understand those times of our struggle against the heavy hand of the Soviets, with the Allies completely indifferent? The things I saw then, the things I lived through, the events in which I often played a part — I really ought to describe all that.

I have reflected often, and for years, about my mission and duty as an emissary. I'll admit that for a long time I didn't answer the call. I put my pen aside. I had serious health problems, after all.

Finally, I gathered my strength and collected my thoughts. I got to work on a book about "The Underground Before the Uprising" — that was the title I wanted to give the book. I thought at first that the nucleus of the book should be the report I submitted after returning from Poland to London in the summer of 1944 at the behest of the Prime Minister of the Polish Government, Stanisław Mikołajczyk, who had sent me to contact the Polish Underground that same spring as his personal emissary.

I wrote my account of the Underground before the Uprising, just as the Uprising was in progress. I didn't want to do it, asking counselor Siudak,[1] minister Banaczyk,[2] and finally even Prime Minister Mikołajczyk himself if there was any point in writing my report, since the situation on the ground had completely changed as a result of the Uprising. But they all firmly gave me the same answer: "Write the report, write about everything you saw; your report will surely be useful, if not now then some other time." I couldn't refuse.

So I wrote, while back there our nation's capital was being reduced to a pile of rubble, while magnificent people were dying. They were the soldiers of the Underground, not even underground anymore but fighting openly, fighting for our freedom. Many a tear fell onto my manuscript. Often I would interrupt my work to listen to the latest radio reports from Warsaw. Often I'd find it hard to get back to work, crushed by the news of new losses and lost battles in the Uprising. I heard about the deaths of a lot of friends, colleagues, scouts — people with whom I had only recently shared the underground life. It wasn't easy.

But upon further reflection, I've decided not to publish my report of fifty years ago. That isn't reading material for today's average Pole, especially for the young people, the new generations of Poles. That's a matter for historians to deal with; they can take the account of a young man (at the time) who was enormously burdened by the tragedy of the Uprising, feeling hopeless and embittered, and therefore not always writing about what he saw and heard with a cool detachment — and arrive at the truth of those times.

Over half a century has passed since those days. My report is in the archives; it's material that historians can research. Will they find my observations useful, will they reach for them some day? I don't know, that's not for me to say. But I do know that for today's reader, those observations couldn't be enough.

That's why I've decided to tell the story anew, reaching occasionally for my notes from years ago.

During that expedition in 1944, my companion was Józef Hieronim Retinger (hereinafter referred to as JHR), and this story will mostly be about him, about the man himself, about his many enormous merits and his few faults or quirks, and also about his — our — adventures in Poland. I would like my book to play a part in setting straight the many opinions and rumors circulating about JHR, disseminated in various books (not just books about the war) as well as articles in the press and people's personal recollections. These opinions, which are primarily hurtful put-downs of the man, are based not on facts but rather on gossip and outright fabrications. I decided to give an account of the things I personally saw and the things I heard knowledgeable people say about JHR, and to share what kind of assessment of the man I was able to make.

Fate commanded me, or rather allowed me, to experience many magnificent moments with JHR. I thank God that there were times when I was able to help this extraordinary person and that he helped me so very much — more than I admitted, even to myself — during his lifetime. It seems to me that from the time I met JHR and entered into his environment, took an interest in his interests, and — as much as possible — immersed myself in his philosophy of life, I became a different person, fuller, more rounded than I had been before. I'm not the only one for whom this holds true. He was one of the most interesting people I ever met, and amongst those most interesting people, he was the closest friend.

So let's make this testimonial about JHR the final mission of the emissary named "Celt."

Two

Prehistory

The whole thing began in a purely military manner, just the same as in Hemar's well-known poem:

> They called on a paratrooper,
> A farm boy right out of Kossak's painting—
> "Hello!" they said, "at ease!
> Listen up. The matter is this ..."[1]

"I've taken you away from your work at Radio Station Świt, and maybe even for good." That's how I was greeted by "Stem" when I appeared, straight from the train station, at the Presidium of the Council of Ministers. "I have a different assignment for you; I have a proposition."

"Yes, Sir, Mr. Prime Minister."

His words shot out as if fired from a rifle. "Would you agree to another flight mission to Poland?"

I was stunned. I was actually not fully prepared for such an eventuality, what with just having returned to base a couple of months previously from my parachute mission to Poland as a courier. Coming in on the train, I was wondering what it was they might want from me in London: maybe something connected to Radio Station Świt; maybe an evaluation of some event that had taken place in the Underground, or an explanation of some complicated telegram; maybe they wanted to send me around Great Britain on a lecture tour, or maybe they wanted to ship me off to some outpost? And now, just like a punch in the head: a flight mission to Poland!

Shivers ran up and down my spine; I started feeling hot and cold. I wavered, wondering stupidly if perhaps I wasn't dreaming; then there was an unclear feeling of joy, followed by a very clear feeling of pure fear. All of these feelings must have been visible on my face, which I could feel going pale. "Stem" was looking at me with a combination of great interest and something like sympathy. He looked at me and didn't say anything. After a moment, all

> **MINISTERSTWO SPRAW WEWNĘTRZNYCH**
>
> L.dz.K.5954/43
>
> Londyn, dnia 20th Oct.1943.
>
> TO WHOM IT MAY CONCERN
> ---------------------
>
> The Polish Prime Minister's Office states herewith, that Mr. Tadeusz T. CHCIUK is an employee of the Polish Ministry of the Interior, Social Department.
>
> DIRECTOR
> /Paweł Siudak/.

Affidavit from the Polish Interior Ministry in London, dated October 20, 1943, stating that Mr. Tadeusz T. Chciuk is an employee of its Social Department. It was in this capacity that he was sent on Operation Salamander (Chciuk-Celt Family Archives and MHPRL).

the while looking me dead in the eye, he reached deftly with his left hand for a match and struck it against the matchbox, then brought the flame close to his lips, into which his right hand had put a cigarette. If a third party had observed us from the side, I think they might have sensed some similarity to a hypnotist's seance, but we both knew that this was simply a brief exchange of meaningful looks between two people who knew and understood each other well. The smile which slowly spread across his face was surely nothing other than a reflection of the joy that had triumphed in me, and that allowed me to voice doubts of a strictly technical nature.

"I'll fly," I said at last, "but I'd like to know what kind of assignment I'm going on, and whether I'll have enough time to prepare properly, because last time ..."

"Yes, I remember, I read your report. This time we won't make the same mistakes, we won't rush anything."

"Meaning ...?"

"You'll have plenty of time to study your assignment — about a month, that ought to be enough. I just received a telegram from Italy. As you surely know, that's where we've moved our departure point base; it'll be closer to

Poland from there than from England. However, the weather conditions there are very unfavorable and the whole thing is going to take some time. Not only has no one taken off to Poland from there this season — meaning since November — but for the next four or five weeks, it's doubtful whether there will be any expeditions from that base."

"In other words, I'll have a month to prepare, a few days to get to Italy, and in early March we'll fly over and parachute in?"

"If everything goes well, then yes. Except that once you get to Italy, you won't be waiting in any queues. Your mission will be treated as special and immediate. And in that 'special immediacy' lies the answer to your question about the nature of your assignment. Of course, we'll discuss the details later, in detail."

"Is it something that important, Mr. Prime Minister?"

"Something very, very important."

"Stem" got up from behind his desk, walked around it and took hold of me by the shoulders. He was smiling, but also looked quite moved. Only now did I begin to realize how very important it was to him that I not turn him down.

"I knew you'd agree to it, Tadeusz, I knew it, but even so I must say you've taken a tremendous weight off my shoulders. I had no one else to turn to, but I have to do this. It's been really hard for me lately, you know, this business of being Prime Minister."

"Ever since Teheran?"

"Yes. In Teheran, the Big Three pushed us onto a steep, slippery slope."

"And my mission is related to this?"

"Yes, it is. And that's why I have to send someone strong on this dangerous escapade. A tremendous amount depends on it. I know I'm repeating myself, but this has been weighing me down. Someone has to fly to Poland and tell them where matters stand. And the matter is pressing; your departure has to happen quickly. That's why I decided to ask you, even though you've only recently returned from your last mission in country, a mission during which you certainly couldn't complain about a lack of dangerous travels, in Poland as well as on your long way back. At least you won't have to go through that long and arduous training in that — what do you guys call it? — jungle gym of a paratrooper's school, with all those Silent Shadow cowboy exercises. You'll be able to devote your entire time to preparing for your assignment. You'll need to memorize a considerable amount of material, you'll have to read up on all the subjects you'll be briefing people on, and prepare for your conversations with important people from the government and the various political parties — and with me. That's one thing. Secondly: especially in view of the fact that you've just recently returned from there, it'll be easier for you to move around, with the underground network still fresh in your memory. And finally: you've been sitting for several months now at Radio Station Świt, so you're more familiar with the political situation than some complete greenhorn. Your question, when you mentioned Teheran, is proof of that. In a word, I didn't have any other choice but to ask you. To ask ... and to apologize."

He embraced me once again, and after a moment he said, "I'm very grateful to you, and I thank you."

I was quite moved myself, maybe even more so than "Stem," but I tried not to show it on my face. I tried to sound as natural as possible when I said, "Well, as we say in the Army: For the glory of the Fatherland!" And then I added, "and if all goes well, I'll be the first man to complete two of these Silent Shadow missions."

Mikołajczyk smiled.

"And when am I to get to work on this, Mr. Prime Minister?"

"At once. You have a hard month of solid studying ahead of you — just like preparing for a difficult exam. We'll begin the preparatory conversations this evening at home, at my place. Now please go see Paweł,[2] so that he can start taking care of all the technical matters for you, because you're not going to have time for that. And please have him arrange for an apartment for you, something close to my place. In any event, you'll also have a little corner you can sleep in at my place, in case our talks should drag on late into the night."

And that's the way the whole thing started. That same night, we were up talking until dawn — or rather, "Stem" did most of the talking, while I listened, interrupting him from time to time with a worried question, for they were some very sad things he was telling me about, and taking notes about certain details. We were distracted a little by the Luftwaffe, which just happened to be getting busy bombing London's West End more intensively than they had been in the previous months. Hyde Park, which was only one city block away from his apartment, was being hit with numerous incendiary bombs, and began to bear an uncanny resemblance to a Polish cemetery on Hallowe'en, glowing, sparkling and smoking, full of eerie living shadows being cast by the trees. An ammunition cache belonging to the Home Guard, right next to the Serpentine, took a direct hit from a German bomb and belched fire all night long, with explosion after explosion as the cases of rifle shells caught fire. Several times, when there were particularly loud detonations, we'd have to interrupt our conversation. At one point even "Stem" began to wonder if we mightn't be safer in the basement. A hotel on the Bayswater Road, not far from us, burned so brightly that it lit our room all night, with the blackout curtains drawn.

My preparation resumed the next day at noon, with another long talk with "Stem," and then another, and then several more. When did this man have time for sleep, and how much sleep could he possibly be getting? Our conferences would surely have gone on without stopping at all, if it weren't for the fact that my eyelids would start getting heavy, at which point he'd call a break. Even so, this went on for nearly a month, with hardly a pause — maybe just enough to give my heavy eyelids a little rest, or to allow him to deal with those pressing needs of the Presidium which couldn't be put off. My talks were with Mikołajczyk himself, as well as with government ministers, the heads of various political parties, and advisors to whom I'd been directed. I was turned into a gramophone record, onto which all kinds of information was recorded, in order that I should replay it with maximum fidelity to the right people in the right places in Poland.

As far as the Polish situation in London was concerned — the Polish Government-in-Exile — it sometimes happened that I got conflicting information, since I was getting it from various political parties, unions and other groups. More than once I'd hear complaints from the right about the left, and from the left about the right, on the same day; the opposition would complain about the government even as the government complained about the opposition. I'm sure I could have made a fine mess of it in Poland if I replayed the concert I was getting from the right to an auditorium full of the left, or vice versa!

Surely, however, the substance of my mission couldn't be an update on our internal squabbles and conflicts in exile. I was to brief the Chief Delegate in Poland, and the National Unity Council, on everything that was known about the Teheran Conference, and about the positions that the United States and Britain were taking concerning our eastern lands. These were currently being invaded by the Soviet Army and their secret police, the NKVD, who had announced that they were occupying the western Ukraine, western Byelorussia and Lithuania, and commencing immediately with running things their way: mass arrests, deportations, bullets to the back of the head ...

It was just at this time that Prime Minister Churchill first unveiled, clearly and in public, his relationship to Poland — far removed from his previously declared friendly position. He called into question our ownership of the eastern territories, and referred in the plainest terms to the Curzon Line as our eastern border.[3] The BBC Polish Service never said a word about this in their broadcasts; they hushed it up, since after all, the Polish people might still be of some use in this war.[4] Our own Radio Station Świt couldn't have said anything about it even if we'd wanted to, since we were supposedly an underground station and as such couldn't possibly have had access to this kind of information. Anyway, there's not much to say about it, since I know from the post-mortem what Radio Świt could and couldn't do. Our English "protectors" had the final word on what went out on the air, and they could at any time politely and graciously block any programming content that ran counter to the wishes of His Majesty's Government. Our programming wasn't broadcast "live," but was recorded onto acetates and then broadcast at a later time. In other words, we were unable to keep the nation informed about what was going on at this most distressing time, just when they really needed to know what was going on in order to take an active part in the policies of the National Unity Council and the Government Delegature in Poland. Mikołajczyk rightly feared that if we couldn't persuade the Allies in time to accept our point of view (which they could have accepted), if we were unable to come, with their help, to some sort of understanding with the Soviets, with whom it was known we no longer had any diplomatic relations ever since the murders of Katyń had been brought to light, then decisions about us would soon be made entirely without any input from us.

The matter was indeed urgent. We needed to inform the Chief Delegate and the National Unity Council as soon as possible and in the greatest possible detail, but there was no way to do this using coded radio broadcasts, for technical reasons as well as our need to preserve the strictest secrecy. This is exactly why "Stem" decided to send his personal emissary, well acquainted with the problem, into Poland. The choice fell on me, and this is why I had to familiarize myself with the problem in depth.

My evenings, and often my nights, were devoted to reading the reports coming in from the government, analyzing transcripts of important conversations beginning at the highest level and ending at the lowest, studying the debates concerning our situation in the House of Commons, and reading newspaper articles from around the world. These things were all prepared for me on a daily basis by Mikołajczyk's secretary, Mrs. Lieberman. In my conversations with "Stem," and with ministers, diplomats and trade unionists, I was able to clarify any grey areas, asking for vital explanations in a few key matters. We'd reach back sometimes into the distant past, then again we'd project into the foreseeable future, studying the developing situation and trying to arrive at some conclusions as to what lay ahead for Poland. Unfortunately, it became increasingly clear in these conversations that a dark tableau was taking shape: the fate of Europe, divided into "spheres of influence," and the fate of our country, given away by Great Britain and the United States to the mercy of the Soviets.

From the reports of these conversations, I remember very clearly the following statement by Churchill, who, upon his return from Teheran and following a bout with an illness, spoke with Mikołajczyk about the Teheran Conference and the conclusions that were to be drawn from it by the Polish government: "We decided in Teheran that the seat of the Polish nation will be between the Bug and Oder Rivers." There followed pressure on Mikołajczyk to agree as soon as possible to the Curzon Line as our eastern border. Mikołajczyk replied that "a nation doesn't have wheels" and couldn't just be rolled from east to west, asserting that Lwów and Vilnius were cities dear to every Polish person and were at the very heart of Polishness, and that the Poles should be moved less to the west and lose less of the east. He showed Churchill a map prepared and documented by Minister Seyda, arguing against the Curzon Line. Churchill didn't even want to look at the map, and replied sharply that Vilnius had been taken away from the Lithuanians in defiance of the will and the admonitions of the British government. I don't rightly recall that any single conversation ended with a definitive conclusion. In these conversations the British mostly lectured the Poles and instructed them on how they were to act with respect to the Russians. Mikołajczyk basically went along with their advice, with the exception of two points: 1) He believed that he could work out a deal with Stalin concerning Lwów and Vilnius — later, he didn't believe in Vilnius anymore but counted only on Lwów; 2) He didn't want to abandon the platform of the Polish Constitution of 1935, arguing that the moment he dropped it, he and his entire government would lose their legal standing (which was, in his opinion, one of his government's biggest trump cards against the Union of Polish Patriots)[5] at which point the Russians wouldn't even want to negotiate at all with the Polish Government in London.

Going along with the advice of Anthony Eden, the British Foreign Minister, Mikołajczyk led the entire so-called public negotiations with the Soviet government.[6] He did this, as he told me, purposely; and even took it to the degree that before any declarations were made, he would take the text, which had already been approved by the government, and check it with Eden and make important changes in accordance with Eden's wishes. He did this in order to get the British more involved in Polish matters and obligated to help. He put it this way: "Our failure (if I run every text past Eden for his approval) will ultimately also be Eden's failure."

I couldn't escape the painful thought that I was preparing to give the Chief Delegate the hardest day of his life: I would unveil to him the tragic situation of the Polish nation in all its danger — a situation in which there were so very few ways out, and each of them so dangerous — and that I'd be calling on him and all his ministers and the National Unity Council, in other words the whole Underground Nation, to take part in choosing one of these ways out and to take upon themselves part of the responsibility, for the sake of the nation and history. For without this, the nation might collapse or even — God forbid — disintegrate. So there was really no other way. "Stem" was giving them the straight story over there in the Underground. He didn't keep anything secret, he didn't gloss over any details, he outlined clearly a dangerous reality.

It seemed that now, for the first time since the war had started and the roles were divided between the Government-in-Exile and the underground in country, the government in London and the Polish nation were truly to become one body, reaching decisions together about the most essential political matters. But — I thought to myself — why so late? And I didn't keep this thought to myself, either: I expressed it in my talks with the Prime Minister. I declared that the authorities in Poland might very well have an issue with this government on this point: why is it that only now, literally at the last moment, you are showing us our cards, however awfully weak they may be — and then telling us to take responsibility for the game?

"Stem" looked me in the eye and said, "I've only been Prime Minister for half a year."

We were both silent for a pretty long while, after which "Stem" added:

"I've always been in favor of keeping the country fully informed, of having the Chief Delegate be the Vice-Prime Minister and all his deputies be ministers, so that they could have more of a say in the government's policies. But it hasn't been easy to maintain contact with the country; it wasn't easy for General Sikorski, and now it isn't easy for me, and not just on account of the distance and the known technical challenges. It's also because the people in Poland, cut off from the rest of the world, are often guided by their fervent wishes; they idealize the western allies, they magnify the meaning of statements and phrases like "the inspiration of nations" and the resolutions contained in the Atlantic Charter, and they don't want to believe that reality can be different, completely different. In the Underground, people say prayers at Mass for the ailing Churchill, while he ... and even so, it isn't easy, taking their cherished illusions away from them. It's an enormously painful thing to do. And as to taking responsibility for a game played with weak cards, well, I'm going to have to take it myself, regardless of whether anyone else supports me or not. Because what's at stake here, weak cards or not, is the future of our nation. You yourself, Tadeusz, brought Witos's words back from Poland: What is the most important thing? To save the nation! To strengthen the nation so that it may live through this dreadful time, for if not, if the nation is ruined and bled to death in today's hopeless battle, then there won't be anything left to work and fight with in the future. It's about the future of our nation."

A little while later, he added, "Saving the nation! That's something best done with all of our united effort. Tell them that in Warsaw. And tell them that if we can't save everything, we'll have to save as much as we possibly can, even if it means taking a great loss. The nation is more important than the state. Even a nation without a state, or with a weak, carved-up territory, still has a future, and the more we can preserve of our strengths, the better. A state without a strong, healthy nation might have no future at all."

Again, after a while, he said, "I don't know, maybe a simple analogy to a farm might be in order. If a farm is threatened with total ruin, the loss of its land and buildings, and the farmer has to make a choice between packing his bags and leaving, or giving up part of his land to save the rest — is he going to take long to make up his mind? He's tied to that land. Without it he's lost! A city dweller might possibly let everything go and set out into the wide world, but a farmer? And isn't our entire nation in that farmer's predicament right now? Are we all going to emigrate? Scatter to the winds? You know we'd be lost. If there's no other way out, wouldn't it be better to save part of the farm? Then, later, we could try to get back what was lost, and if that didn't work out, then at least we'd stay on the part we still have. Stay on the land! And the faster we try to save part of what could be lost completely, the more we might save. And the more we save, the quicker we might get back what was lost, in time. Isn't that right?"

I asked, "Maybe we could manage to save Lwów, Vilnius, the oil fields? Because you know ..."

"I don't know, it's hard to answer that question. Maybe. There have been various statements from the Anglo-Saxon side, not binding at this time, that there might even be some significant changes made to the Curzon Line, to our advantage. We're going to fight for that, if there's absolutely nothing that can be done in the matter of ... the whole farm."

Yes, an awful burden rested on the shoulders of this "farmer." Every day, in my conversations with him and with other representatives of Polish London, I became more and more aware of this. What a steep slope we'd been pushed onto at Teheran!

Toward the end of my preparatory studies for this mission, another problem absorbed my attention. A completely different problem, yet maybe somehow connected to our general Teheranian quandary. In one of my last talks with "Stem," I was suddenly informed that I was to have one more rather specific duty on my Silent Shadow mission, in addition to all the things that had already been spelled out for me in the course of the previous month. An integral part of my assignment was to "protect" a certain "Mr. Salamander," also known as Dr. Joseph Hieronimus Retinger. (I'll refer to him as JHR).

"What's that?" I asked "Stem," not quite believing my ears.

"Yes. Retinger's been waiting for quite some time for a flight to Poland."

"Impossible! He's an older gentleman, and besides, he's ... Retinger."

The Prime Minister replied, "He's an older gentleman, yes, and on top of that he's physically weak and not that coordinated. But he's bold and decisive. You shouldn't have too much trouble with him. It's true that he's never done a parachute jump, but he claims to have familiarized himself with it in theory and that that's enough for him. It's even possible — and now get ready to hear another bit of news — that you guys won't even have to jump, because there's some hope that finally, *finally,* we'll be able to pull off one of those 'Air Bridge' operations we keep saying we're going to do, you know. In that case you two would go as the first ones."

Well, how about that! So many surprises in one day. Retinger! An air bridge operation! Why, I'd heard this and that, about Retinger and about an air bridge. Well, bridge, schmidge — I didn't really believe that that would ever work out, landing an Allied plane on the ground in occupied Poland, right under the noses of the Germans, bringing into the country a lot of our emissaries, mail, money, arms *en masse,* and then taking back from the country a lot of emissaries and a large volume of mail. But maybe ... maybe we'd live to see such a bridge and take a stroll across it. But one way or the other, the two of us were headed to Poland, this older gentleman and I, his guardian. But why with him? And why was he flying to Poland? There had been so much written about him in the émigré press, and there was even more that was whispered about him back in the army and here in London ...

I finally asked the question that had been on my mind from the moment Retinger's name was mentioned. Mikołajczyk had clearly been expecting it.

"Is it you who's sending him?"

"Yes. But I didn't ask him to do it; after all, who would ever come up with such an idea! He came to me himself with it, persuaded me, made his points, until — well, I reached the conclusion, we both concluded, why not? I agreed to it. I assume that either Eden is sending Retinger or, far more probably, Retinger managed to convince Eden that his trip to Poland was necessary.[7] Indeed, let him go — his trip might help us a lot, and I don't see how it could hurt. After the death of General Sikorski, Retinger couldn't seem to find a place for himself anywhere. He went to Scotland and was supposed to be writing memoirs about Sikorski, but they say he spent his nights weeping, and nothing ever came of the memoirs. And then he shows up here one day at the Presidium and comes to me with this proposal of his, which was as surprising to me then as it is to you now. He has a lot of important English friends; they trust him, they'll believe without reservation whatever he tells them about the state of the Underground in Poland. Let's let them know as much as possible about our underground state. Let them hear all about it, and not just from the lips of young couriers and emissaries whom no one knows, or from copies of our dispatches. I know that they often suspect us of exaggerating our reports on the resistance, the Home Army, the underground government, our secret intelligence, about the bigger picture of what's going on in the life of the underground. Well, they'll believe Retinger."

"He cried after the General died?"

"Yes. That's what I was told, and there's really nothing strange about it. I had moist eyes myself at that time, and he was truly close to the General, maybe the closest of anyone outside his immediate family. And I mean not just politically, but personally. This was an authentic friendship that was mutual, although the General didn't particularly show it and even joked about it from time to time. Retinger was devoted to the General. Then again, to tell the truth, without Retinger's initiative it's doubtful whether we'd all be here in Great Britain, our army in Scotland, the government in London. I don't know if we'd have had the ability to carry on the fight. For it was he, an advisor in our embassy at the time, who talked Churchill into bringing Sikorski over from France when everything was falling apart over there; he went to get the General himself, brought him over to talk to Churchill, he was helpful — he helped. That was a dangerous, treacherous expedition, and yet so crucial to us all. Only a person completely lacking in objectivity could fail to recognize that."

"I was completely unaware of that. Well, how about that! I didn't read a word about it anywhere — in fact I read something totally different."

"Exactly: something different. People who are pigheaded and completely lacking in objectivity write bad things about him. The former right-wing regime held it against him that he traveled abroad and spoke the truth about their *coup d'état* and the subsequent succession of governments. He organized international protests — they'll never forgive him for that. Take "Cat" Mackiewicz, for example.[8] You know how those guys — especially Cat — can whack about with a pen, with no sense of restraint. They insinuate, and then other people just spread it around, that Retinger is an English agent, or a Soviet agent, or God knows what other kind; he was supposed to be an Arab agent, a Mexican one ... the one you hear most often is that he's an English agent. I keep asking for proof of that, and never get any. And I know well that an accusation of being an agent, coming from the lips of some of our so-called politicians, is the charge that's leveled against pretty much any opponent that they can't get to any other way. So I'm not too surprised to see Retinger on that list of English, even Soviet supposed agents; who knows if I won't end up on one of those lists myself someday, I think to myself, for not toeing their line? They fight against Retinger more sharply than the others, because he's a versatile man, full of ideas; there's a lot that he can do, a lot he knows how to do, especially here in England, where he's had many friends for years. They fought against Sikorski with everything they had, so they really blasted anyone who supported him — Professor Kot, too, for example."[9]

"But as far as I know, Professor Kot doesn't like Retinger that much, either."

"Tadeusz! I don't like Retinger that much myself. As far as the professor goes, even though I value him greatly, I don't always agree with him. Kot doesn't like Retinger, Retinger doesn't like Kot, but politics isn't a matter of likes and dislikes. People's opinions of Professor Kot aren't always brilliant, either, by the way, but I never heard a word from the professor about Retinger being an agent."

"Well, Mr. Prime Minister, why is it that you don't like Retinger that much?"

"It's because he's incorrigible, because he always knows better (although he is sometimes right), because he goes his own way. He doesn't belong to any party, but he wants to make politics for all the parties. He's a kind of political egocentric, but he's ... useful. Very."

"Can you guarantee that he's not an English agent, Mr. Prime Minister?"

"I can not, and I don't want to knock myself out worrying about it. But I'll tell you that even if he were an English agent, which I don't believe he is, I wouldn't hold him back. Let him go ahead and fly to Poland, let him come back and tell them everything he saw and heard! He'll tell them the truth and that won't hurt us. Let's have our ally know what the other allies are thinking and how they're fighting. Besides, that's exactly why I'm sending you, so that you can inform the Chief Delegate about how I feel about Retinger, and to tell him not to give Retinger any information that they wouldn't want the English to know about. And the things that Retinger is going to tell people in Poland will be the unvarnished truth as well, and that will also be to our benefit. He's fully aware that we can't exactly count on any help coming from Great Britain and the United States in our tragic struggle with Stalin. He agonizes over it. As for Churchill, he's been saying for ages that that man will be our undoing someday, but no one ever believed him. He thinks we need to inform the people in Poland in total detail and in the plainest terms of our dangerous current reality — that if they continue on their present senseless course of a blindly anti-Russian and anti-communist policy, they'll bring it about themselves that Russia and only Russia will be making all the arrangements for the Polish state, and only the Communists will have anything to say in it. If Retinger should manage to convince the Underground that they really must seek some sort of realistic way of ironing things out with the Soviets, that will help me a lot. I want you, too, to tell them the same thing clearly, and the sooner, the better. But since people in Poland might not want to believe this alleged agent, I want you to tell them that he can be trusted, that I trust him. Tell them about this conversation we're having right now, and the thing I want to repeat in conclusion: that Retinger has Poland at heart just the same as we all do."

"I'll tell them that. A moment ago, I was asking myself why you were sending me, since Retinger's already going to fly to Poland. Now I understand. The people in the Underground are to find out about the total threat facing us, from two sources. And besides, you want me to let them know that this "Salamander" source isn't a poisoned one. Right?"

"Right."

"Well, then I just have one more question, Mr. Prime Minister. You said that Retinger's already been waiting for quite some time for a flight to Poland."

"Yes. He's waiting in Bari, in Italy. Code name Salamander. The whole thing is being kept in strictest secrecy; very few people know about this. The Poles in London think Retinger's in Scotland writing his memoirs of the General."

"And you waited until now before you decided to give him a "guardian?"

"No. He already had one of our couriers keeping him company in Bari, ready for a mission to Poland. You know him, code name Cable."[10]

"Ah, yes, Cable. So how come there's been this sudden change from Cable to Celt?"

"I'm not exactly sure. There must have been some sort of conflict between the two of them over there, because I suddenly got a telegram from Salamander, asking me to call off Cable and send someone else. And since so much happens to have changed in our political arena, with all these new developments — which is what prompted me to ask you to take on this mission and inform the Chief Delegate of the latest events — I decided to combine the beautiful and the practical, and saddle you with the additional burden of taking care of this older gentleman during your jump (or possibly landing) and then also on the spot, in country. You two ought to get along all right."

* * *

Not long after this conversation with "Stem" about Retinger, during my flight from England to Bari via Gibraltar, Algier, and Tunis, I had time to think, going over the more important items over and over in my mind. With my head battered by the ceaseless roar of the engines, all kinds of thoughts whirled around my brain: news reports of every variety, entire pages of reports and accounts, the worried voices of the people I'd been talking to. At times, in a kind of half-dream, I'd see the faces of my sister and her husband, who had put such a sincere, though fruitless, effort into getting me to drop this project, which they thought would break my neck.[11] But aside from that, one thought kept stubbornly lurking around my brain: how's it going to be with this Salamander, how is it that he's "theoretically prepared" for a parachute jump, how will I be able to help him, how is this escapade of his supposed to work out? This was all enormously unsettling, this Salamander aka Captain Paisley — for he was to meet "Marek Sulima," in other words me, wearing the uniform of a British Captain and using that name, in the royal city of Bari.

Of course, I thought to myself, it's a good thing that Retinger is flying to Poland. I figured that they should have sent in a serious mission long before, be it Polish or even Allied. And behind that would follow a larger, broader stream of help from the West to our Underground. Maybe Retinger would fill in the gaps in their information, if only partially, and give them a solid account. Well, the situation had changed ever since the Teheran Conference, with brutal pressure coming from the Soviets now, and with the Allies' complete submission to Stalin. What mattered above all now was the relationship between our Underground and the Soviets, the need to arrive at some kind of acceptable compromise, some kind of dialogue (if it's possible to have a dialogue with a gangster), and not squander our energy organizing this or that further fight with the Germans.

But was he even going to get to Poland? — and these were the thoughts that were prevalent for the time being — and why should I, of all people, be a nanny to a parachute jumper who has only "familiarized himself in theory" with parachuting? I cursed myself for having agreed to it. A conflict with Cable? What kind of conflict? Why doesn't Cable go ahead and take care of him? — that's the way I'd put it when I saw him. I had my own mission to see to in the Underground! On top of all the things with which "Stem" had burdened my heart, several new points of business had taken shape during my month of study and preparation: among others, making arrangements with the Delegature for a northern access route to Sweden; problems with the underground outpost in Hungary, and a conflict between its chief and the Delegature; matters pertaining to the Boy Scouts, which I'd specifically been asked to look into by the Supreme Scouting Council in London (Olga Małkowska, Kazimierz Sabbat) ... and now this guy Retinger! At the beginning, when "Stem" called me in for that meeting, there hadn't been any mention of any Salamander, any parachuting ignoramus whom I was going to have to teach the trade. How the hell can anyone familiarize himself with parachuting in theory? Out of what book? From some fairy tales, maybe?

And the air bridge? Go on with that bridge! Who was going to believe that? So much had been said about it, there had been so many plans, preparations, deliberations during parachute training, that the only result was this: when somebody's hair had a bit too much of a tendency to stand straight up on the back of his neck before a practice jump, the owner of that hair would hear taunts from his buddies, like "you must want to get out of a plane the normal way, on a nice roll-up staircase! Just wait, you'll get to go on the air bridge!" This pretty much amounts to the guy getting cut from the team, because if he folds in training he isn't going anywhere, because there's never going to be any bridge.

Besides — on the subject of folding — I didn't feel at ease personally with this whole business of a bridge. When "Stem" first mentioned it, I remember the first thought that crossed my mind when he said, "You two will be the first to go." Aha! In other words we were going to pioneer this thing — sure! — we'd be laying the groundwork for others. The whole thing didn't look good to me at all. I'd already been a guinea pig once before, as a member of the six-man team executing Operation Jacket, jumping in 1941 without a landing team to receive us, a shot in the dark — "and if it works out, then maybe others can follow in your footsteps if need be." The tragic outcome of that little show is still traumatically etched on my mind to this day. And now there's to be the first air bridge attempt ever made, and I'm supposed to be its passenger?

* * *

Well, enough already with this kind of thinking, I have to go for it, especially since the action is already in progress: I'm in an airplane flying from England to Italy, and then I may fly after all with Salamander to Poland, as Silent Shadow parachutists or even as passengers on the air bridge.

* * *

I left London on the 27th of February 1944. In the company of Lieutenant Tadeusz Starzynski, an army courier, I was taken by car to one of the more remote British airfields. We couldn't avoid an accident on the road — luckily without anybody getting hurt. I felt like the accident was a sign of good luck, a kind of guarantee that everything was going to work out and we'd get through the mission in one piece. I'd had a similar automotive mishap right before my previous parachute mission from England to Poland on the 27th of December 1941.

An airplane was already waiting for us at the airfield. We got in, along with several other passengers, and after an hour we found ourselves at ... another British airfield in southeastern England, Port Reath, where we were instructed to wait for three days.

Dirty bedsheets, cold as hell, no news from London, boring company (with the exception of Lieutenant Tadeusz Starzynski), a piano hopelessly out of tune, stupid American movies at the field cinema — these are the things that we endured for those three days. On top of that, we were in a daily, constant, fruitless state of readiness.

Finally, though, we escaped from there in our Dakota and got to Gibraltar.[12] It was like waking up in another world. Oranges and bananas, a warm breeze, and the realization that we were quickly approaching our new wartime adventure — all these things cheered us up considerably.

We soon left for Algiers. Once airborne, I said a short prayer for the soul of the late General from my bird's-eye vantage point. However, after twenty minutes we landed again, in ... Gibraltar. Luckily, my companion had noticed that the cap had fallen off of the external fuel tank on the right wing of the Dakota, and a steady white stream of fuel was pouring out, leaving a white, misty trail that could catch the slightest spark from the engine and blow up the plane, or else in the very best case scenario we'd quickly run low on fuel and have to attempt an emergency crash landing or a water landing.[13]

Our return to base unleashed a real storm. God only knows how many reprimands, tickets, days in the brig, curses raining down on the officers' heads, and demerits came out of that mishap. They were even cursing the poor Polish crewman who'd had to see to it that the fuel tank was properly capped and closed.

The result of this little accident was that we departed an hour and a half later than planned. We reached Algiers at 1500 hrs., in bad weather and with no flights leaving for Italy. I had never imagined that Africa — we were practically on the edge of the Sahara — could be so cold and wet. We were taken from the Maison Blanche airfield to the city, where we were quartered in some dreadful sleeping-cars. Everything was overcrowded and dirty. Pesky little Arab children begged shamelessly for money, or offered us the love of their sisters, even more shamelessly. In spite of the fact that we were totally exhausted, I prevailed upon Tadeusz to go out to the opera with me.

It's kind of curious to see *Rigoletto* in Algiers a couple of days after being in London and a few days before being in Warsaw. Every once in a while, one or the other of us would sigh. I'm not sure exactly what was on my mind —

Two. Prehistory

my girl Ewa, my Mom for sure — but I know exactly what was on Tadeusz's mind: his wife and children. He'd told me so much about them.

En route to Poland in wartime and with lousy weather, Algiers is only good for a day. The offices of the Allies were a mess, you didn't know whom to ask for directions — stick with the Americans and English, or maybe turn to the French — so it was with considerable relief that we flew out of there on the morning of Friday, March 3, 1944, with snow-capped mountains on the horizon. This was not the way I'd pictured Africa.

While switching planes from one Dakota to another, it turned out we were "only" missing two major containers of military hardware. Tadeusz had a fit, but neither shouting nor filling out forms brought any results. The equipment had been left behind in the U.K.[14] Too bad — we would have to go on without those containers.

We landed after a flight that was so short that I had to wonder if it could really be Bari. I hadn't thought it was that close. It turned out we were only in Tunis. We got out of the plane for a cup of tea, with our departure scheduled in one hour. It's easy to say "one hour," but we had forgotten that there are Americans in this world. One of them latched onto us, said he was from

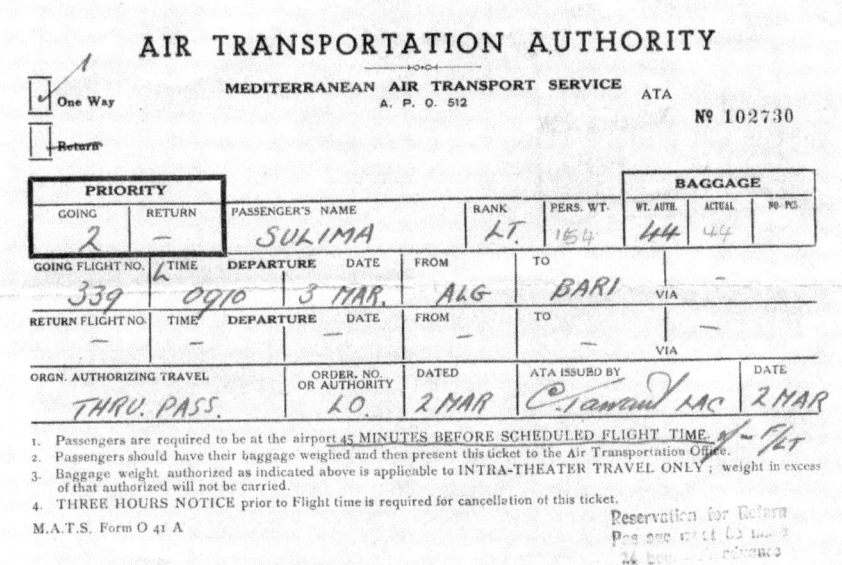

One-way Air Transportation Authority ticket for "Lt. Sulima" from Algiers to Bari, departing March 3, 1944. The stamp in the lower right-hand corner reads: "Reservation for Return Passage must be made 24 hours in advance." (MHPRL Warsaw).

Security and told us he wouldn't let us out of Tunis because we didn't have the right papers. He didn't even know who we were. He had a point with the papers — we actually didn't have the ones he needed to see. But what was it all about? It was because I, traveling as a chronic civilian, didn't have an English Officer's Identity Card, and Tadeusz had surrendered his in England on the express orders of his hosts. Our interaction with the obstinate American was long and stormy. We took turns, alternating between trying to tell him who we were, and getting offended. Finally, he gave up and told us angrily, "All right, you can go, but the responsibility is yours." That was the end of that. The clever American must have thought they'd catch us in Bari, anyway.

Meanwhile in Bari, it was raining when we got there, and that must have been the reason why no one checked us out, not even a dog. We could have done anything we wanted with that fine airplane, or gone out on the town. No one was interested in us on the Polish side of the airbase, either. I began to regret getting involved in this whole project. How nice it would have been to be sitting somewhere in England just then, listening to the sound of my block flute playing the call signal for Radio Świt, and getting on the microphone to light into the Germans or the Bolshevik so-called patriots from Radio Kosciuszko![15] Meanwhile, here we were....

I can attest to the fact that traveling in the world of the dollar and the pound sterling must have been fairly enervating for any Axis spies. Conversely, I can attest that for Polish paratroopers, traveling was significantly more difficult still. Had it not been for a certain telephone number that I'd gotten from Major Hazell of the Special Operations Executive at Port Reath right before we took off, Tadeusz and I would both have been stuck in the mud at the end of a rainy runway in Bari.

As I took Tadeusz to the address I'd been given after calling the aforementioned phone number, I felt pleased that if it hadn't been for my taking action as a civilian, then he, a representative of the Ministry of Defense, would surely be tearing out whatever hair he had left while waiting for orders from above.

That same evening, Tadeusz was shipped off by the British to the Polish airbase at Brindisi, whilst I, on the recommendation of the Prime Minister, found myself face to face with the wrinkled countenance of Captain Paisley, aka Salamander, or properly Dr. Retinger.

Three

With Captain Paisley in Bari

Just as planned, in the first days of March, 1944, I finally stood in the presence of "Salamander." I have never regretted it since. My very first conversation with this exceptional person made me aware of what an interesting and unique acquaintance I was making. Even though I thought I knew quite a bit about him from all the things I'd read and heard, the man I was getting a good look at wasn't anything like the image I'd built up in my mind. Listening to what he said, and looking at his wise, sparkling eyes, I realized at once that my preconceived notions of the man as General Sikorski's evil spirit, as an Eminence Grise or even a meddling political busybody, were disappearing by degrees. In fact, my initial antipathy toward this parachuting know-nothing began to melt away, while at the same time I took a kind of satisfaction in knowing that, for good measure, JHR was going to be something like my subordinate.

I suppose it would be a considerable exaggeration to claim that JHR's face was one that was any great pleasure to behold, especially when his eyes were closed or when he looked serious. However, one forgot about this at once as soon as JHR opened his eyelids and looked at his listener with those uncommonly bright eyes. If, moreover, he should add a smile, a person might feel that their aesthetic concerns had been laid to rest. It's a similar feeling to the one you might get after a hard rain abruptly stops and the sun comes out from behind the clouds.

If one's gaze, normally riveted to JHR's face, might sometimes allow itself to wander a little, then it would probably be in order to look at his hands. Just as his eyes were enormously lively, quick, penetrating and yet not particularly beautiful, his hands, though not always moving, were magnificent, you might say thoroughbred. They were very shapely and smooth, with long, slender fingers ending in almost feminine fingernails. JHR was proud of his hands, and it was evident that he liked it when people admired them.

This was indicated by the way he held a cigarette or shook hands with someone. I remember how, after we'd known one another well for several months and he was giving me a hard time about something, half in jest and half seriously, I got a good laugh out of the fact that I'd never yet gushed openly about his hands.

Thinking now about that time in Bari, I imagine I must have been a fairly unusual and maybe even burdensome acquaintance for him. There was a certain specific way in which I was different from the people who usually surrounded him. Everyone, as I've said, would pay attention first and foremost to his eyes and often his hands, simply not daring to turn their gaze onto any other parts of JHR's body. But I was just the opposite! Owing to my duties as the commander of our upcoming parachute mission, I had to have a good look at his whole body, to evaluate his legs and shoulders so that I could form some sort of opinion as to his physical strength and coordination. Only then could I arrive at any conclusions about his stamina, and set up a corresponding game plan.

The results of this research did not give me any great joy. If I had to describe his physical characteristics in one word, then I suppose the best word would be: awkward. It wasn't with any feeling of anger, but rather a secret sense of alarm, that I thought about the responsibility which awaited me. I couldn't imagine that JHR could run twenty steps, or jump up even once, or land gracefully on the ground. From that time on, I started imagining various scenarios in which JHR played the lead role, and not a happy role at that. For example, I pictured with my mind's eye how he'd be lying on the ground with a broken leg from the jump, or else he'd be trying to run from the Germans but couldn't, or else he'd be dragged along the ground by the wind and be unable to turn over onto his back, unable to feel the central release with his hands; he wouldn't know how to rotate the shield, he wouldn't know that you have to pound the release with your hand to get free of the parachute harness, which, if it feels like dancing along with the wind, is welcome to do so, but kindly without the parachutist still attached. Every time I'd imagine this kind of thing, or turn my attention to the dangers awaiting even an old hand at this silken line of work, I'd start to look at JHR with a hopeless look, wringing my hands in despair so you could hear my knuckles cracking. And this was supposed to be a parachutist whose very first mission was to be a combat mission into enemy territory! And I'm responsible for him ... it gave me the shivers. I'd pray in my soul, too, looking at JHR, that that damn air bridge might finally work out. It was no longer a matter of my being less than thrilled about my role as a guinea pig; first and foremost it was about JHR not having to jump, with me watching him and being responsible. But unfortunately, he had to do it, I had to do it, we had to do it!

The issue with Cable, who had been playing the part of Salamander's nanny up to now, came to light after a few days. It turns out Salamander gave him a sharp talking-to about the eighth commandment. I was amazed to find out that Cable had claimed, no less, that it was he who had been in Poland and not I, that it was he who had played the *Concerto for Four Colts* and not I, and so on. And Cable had informed me personally that none of us knew anything about him, that his real name wasn't Wiktor Karamać at all, and that he was plotting against the whole of exiled Poland. After officially and ceremoniously confirming once more the entirety of what he'd told Salamander, Cable went to the base in Brindisi, after signing a sworn statement that he would never speak to anyone on the subject of Salamander until we had met with the Chief Delegate. We stayed in Bari.

Long, hard days of waiting for our flight now commenced. Interesting conversations with Salamander, boring games of dominoes with him, playing solitaire, every possible concert and opera, the Garrison Cinema, sleeping, eating, sleeping — these were the things that made up my days and led me, not infrequently, to feelings of blackest despair. I'd open my eyes at eleven in the morning, which was when Salamander would usually enter my room and graciously inform me that I could go on sleeping because our little operation was off, as the British had just informed him from headquarters by phone. We could do whatever we pleased until the following morning, with the only condition being that we should be sober and well-rested in case the message should come in that the operation is on. These were times of dreadful idleness, gaining weight and waiting for fate to smile upon us and give us good weather. Boring as hell.

JHR's departure to Poland was to take place in total secrecy. Of course, it was hard to hide him from the officers at the Polish base in Brindisi, so at the very least, an effort had to be made to conceal the identity of the secret emissary. That's the very reason we were quartered in Brindisi rather than Bari, where we would have been together with the other army personnel and civilian couriers and emissaries awaiting their flight missions to Poland. Nonetheless, I had to report to the base every four days to meet with Lieutenant Jurek Zubrzycki (by a twist of fate, he happened to be JHR's brother-in-law)[1] and receive updated particulars for our mission: the location of the spot where the AK would be waiting for us, nearby contact addresses, and so on. This was because the landing site couldn't be kept at one spot for too long, for understandable security reasons. Sometimes I'd return from Bari with the unpleasant news that if the operation were to be on in the next few days, we'd have to jump somewhere in the Świętokrzyskie Mountains, or in the Lublin area, or even in the foothills of the Tatras. In such an event, the trip to Warsaw would be long and dangerous, and our mission would be further delayed. On the other hand, sometimes Lieutenant Zubrzycki would smile at me and show a landing spot on the map that was so close to Warsaw that we could be on Marszałkowska Street literally a couple of hours after the jump.

Lieutenant Zubrzycki was always discreet, and it was only when we were saying our good-byes, as I got into the jeep after an ample dinner and got ready to return to Bari, that he would say, "and please give my regards to your companion!" The other officers wouldn't give me a moment's peace, constantly asking, "Who is he?"—"What's he here for?"—"Is he army or civilian?"— "Curious thing that you guys have to be first in line to fly even though you've only just got here from England, when we've been hanging out here since November," and so on. Sometimes Salamander's relative would ask me with a kind smile (for he was a kind person generally) if I knew what Dr. Retinger was up to in London; sometimes another officer would secretly inform me that Section VI knew who Salamander was anyway.[2] But I didn't let myself be provoked, and kept my tongue behind my teeth, so to speak. And would you believe it—JHR clearly held that against me! He would have preferred that his fate be openly known and that the BBC should broadcast it to the world in at least as many languages as he knew himself. When I'd tell him about Jurek's smile, and about the pestering questions from the other buddies, he'd moan and complain that God had punished him by sending him such a non-talker for a companion. His sole hope was that Jurek would figure it out and at some point, after overcoming "those reservations of his," he'd say a peep about Salamander. Indeed, one of JHR's flaws was that he fully believed in the principle of self-promotion as the engine of success in politics. If he could have, he would have announced to the whole world that he was flying to Poland.

Of all the things that gave us a little variety in our lives, some of the worst were the car accidents that would be set up by stubborn Italian fascist saboteurs, who would make refined booby-traps out of roadside rocks and trees. There was one close call that would have left little more of us than a stain on the road. A certain tree trunk found itself about four inches from my head. But, as I've said, I see car accidents as a sign of good luck for the upcoming flight, so I wasn't too concerned about it.

From time to time I'd do a little target practice on the beach with my pistol; from time to time I'd study my notes from London and my maps of Poland, and that was about it.

Three. With Captain Paisley in Bari

* * *

Actually, though, there was more to it than that, because that's only the way it was at the very beginning of our wait. After that, there were more and more of those interesting conversations with Salamander, and they started getting more and more interesting. The days on end of boredom became a thing of the past.

My companion practically never left the house. He did a lot of reading, and listened to the radio often. If there was anyone there to listen to or talk to, he would listen and talk. Sometimes Major Richard Hewitt of the SOE would visit him, and they'd get into rabid discussions about English literature, and only marginally get into strategic military deliberations, as if the events unfolding around them were of no concern to them at all. Salamander's English was excellent, spoken with a strange, Eastern accent but delivered like machine-gun fire. They'd get into conversations in Spanish at the same tempo, since the Englishman had spent quite a bit of time on the Iberian Peninsula during the Spanish Civil War and was equally enamored of Spanish literature. We were also visited daily by "Captain Paisley's" orderly, who would come for culinary requests and bring in all kinds of delicacies for JHR, who loved to eat well — God only knows where he got them from, but he would have fish, turkey, seafood and other wonders, fixed by our Slovenian hostess. The orderly came from Malta, so Salamander spoke Italian with him. He'd listen to various radio stations — French, English. At first, he mostly read books in German, because we had "inherited" our apartment in Bari from the Gestapo station chief, who had an ample library containing more than just *Mein Kampf.* But after that, the British supplied him with at least a dozen books in English, including Plato's *Dialogues,* which he read with delight — devoured them, as he said. I was amazed and enchanted by this polyglot nature of his, and by the enormously wide range of his interests.

But JHR impressed me most with the things he said in Polish and about Polish matters. I knew that our upcoming escapade together was constantly on his mind, and yet he never started a conversation on that subject. He'd ask about the working conditions in the Underground, about occupied Warsaw and Kraków, about the people I knew in the Underground, about the Boy Scouts; but as far as the flight to Poland, his parachute, the jump, the spot on which we were to land (or not) — he never once asked about any of that. And whenever I would try to broach the subject, or make a sarcastic remark about his "theoretical preparation" as a parachutist, he'd cut in with a smile, saying, "well, it's possible that you'll have quite a problem with me, but that's your problem. It's not my business." And then he'd change the subject; and the fact that he did so jokingly, intelligently, that he was able to interest me or amuse me with whatever new subject he raised, made it hard for me to pin him against the wall of the Silent Shadows and say he didn't measure up.

For example, I found it enormously entertaining to hear about his two collections, as he called them. "There are those who collect postage stamps, or coins, or paintings," he would say, "but I collect ... people and world records."

"Like what? What people?"

"Well ... people. I just find people interesting. Not all people, just ... interesting people are interesting. And anyone who's really fascinating, not stupid, but with character, I want to have as a friend right away, or at least get to know him very well."

He told me stories about a few of the exhibits in his collection, about Joseph Conrad, about General Sikorski, about Ravel, Stempowski, Hemar, Paul Henri Spaak[3] and Zygmunt Żuławski. About the first of these he had written a book, *Conrad and His Contemporaries,* among which contemporaries he also counted several of the other exhibits in his collection. About the second, he said he had tried to write something, but that nothing had quite worked out yet.

He also collected people from the distant past, mainly Poles, and specifically those who had somehow contributed to the progress of civilization. About these he had written another book, *Polish People in the World's Civilizations.* He promised to someday give me copies of both books, "if we succeed in the thing that must succeed."[4]

When we talked about the Boy Scouts, he said he knew Andrzej Małkowski and "did public relations for him." Where? When? At the Third All-British Scouting Jamboree in Birmingham in 1913. There was no Poland on the map then, and yet Polish scouts from all three partitions (German, Austrian, Russian) were there. The red-and-white Polish flag flew over their camp, and over the entrance was a sign that read "Poland." The protests of the three partitioning powers went unheeded by the British. Those scouts represented Poland, which ... didn't exist. Andrzej Małkowski played first violin among the Poles there, and submitted a report to General Baden-Powell,[5] played host to him, kept him informed, while young JHR assisted him and wrote articles for the English press, which up until recently hadn't even recognized Poland. Now, thanks to the Polish Bureau that JHR had established, the English press was increasingly paying attention to our country.

When JHR found out about my music studies in Lwów, he started telling me stories right away about his acquaintances among the French composers. His collection included Erik Satie, and Francis Poulenc was there, but first and foremost came Maurice Ravel.

He cracked me up with one particular story concerning Ravel. One time he was at the *Bolero* composer's home, in the company of several of the French genius's friends. Ravel sat down at the piano and treated his guests to his latest composition, after which he asked the assembled company for their impressions and evaluations. Musicologists and admirers started talking up a blue streak, praising the new work to the heavens out of authentic or feigned conviction. At that point Maurice turned to JHR, who had somehow been silent up till then —

"Et toi, Retingé, qu'est-ce que tu penses?" ("And you, Retinger, what do you think?")

"Me? If I were in a hurry to catch a train, I wouldn't stay to hear it all the way through." This produced an explosion of laughter, with Ravel laughing loudest.

I heard more stories of this kind directly from the lips of JHR. He loved cynical remarks made at the most unexpected time, in idealistic or romantic conversations. Those who knew him, knew he was kidding. Those who didn't know him, hated him in a huff. As for me, I was getting to like my future subordinate paratrooper more and more.

"Well, what about those world records? How many of them have you collected, Doctor?" I asked, with a strong undertone of irony in my voice. "In which sporting discipline exactly do you excel?"

"You rather like making fun of me, Marek," he said (for that was the name by which JHR addressed me then), "but you seem to forget that there are records in other areas besides sports. I stay well away from sports; there are others who can jump, run, shoot and so on. I'm all about *ex-cep-tional* matters. My records aren't athletic but rather ... war records."

"Aha. So, what records, then?"

"Well, one was a sort of introductory record, not connected to this war. I was the youngest PhD —*Docteur es Lettres*—at the Sorbonne."

"Really?"

"Yes. But those are *tempi passati*.[6] The serious records of our time are different, they're not academic, not cultural."

"Like what?"

"Number 1. I am the only civilian who was in Tobruk during the siege."

That stunned me. "Well! How about that!"

"Oh yes. No one else accomplished that. Therefore, it's a world record, is it not? General Sikorski was visiting the Carpathian Brigade at Tobruk, and I was with him — just as I went practically everywhere with the General from June 1940 onward — I rode with him, flew with him, in this particular case sailed with him — and I was the only civilian in his retinue. I'll tell you, the

Carpathians looked at me with *ad-mi-ration*—both at my suit and at my hat. You can't argue with that—no other civilian got to the city in those days, surrounded as it was by Rommel's Desert Rats, hence: a world record!"

"All right, what about number 2?"

"I'm not a hundred percent sure about it being a world record, because maybe somewhere out there some American or Japanese has ambushed it, but certainly a European record, and a Polish record by all means. But as long as I don't find out that someone's beaten me in this competition, I consider myself the world record holder."

"Well, what's this all about?"

"I have logged the highest number of flight hours in this war. For I not only flew everywhere that General Sikorski flew, but beyond that I flew separately, independently, for example, I flew to Moscow ahead of Professor Kot, and then as a kind of Polish chargé d'affaires, I flew around Russia."

"You're right. I'm sure that not many people have traveled by air as much as you have during this war. The *Luftwaffe* doesn't exactly encourage these kinds of escapades, so the only people who fly are the ones who really have to."

"Exactly."

"And you always accompanied General Sikorski?"

JHR grew thoughtful, looked out the window for a long time, finally turned his gaze in my direction and said sadly, "with the exception of that last trip to the Middle East, to visit the 2nd Corps."

A silence fell on us, each of us lost in his own thoughts, but surely thinking about the same thing: about General Sikorski and that fateful day in Gibraltar.

After a while, Salamander said softly, "That was the most tragic day for Poland in recent years. For myself as well."

"For all of us, Doctor."

He also told me about how he'd been thrown out of several countries for political reasons. Here I gave him a macabre reassurance, that he wouldn't be able to add being thrown out of Poland by the Germans to this record, since in the event that they should catch him, they'd probably hold him captive until the end; and if they should throw him out, they'd only be throwing out the remains of the youngest-ever PhD from the Sorbonne; but when JHR went on about his records, he didn't usually mention any breaks in the action.

Now he was promising himself one more record, this one a title as well: World's Oldest Combat Paratrooper. He admonished me on this point, saying that even though I might take his other records lightly or indeed question them, I wasn't going to be able to do that with this parachute jump. So once, when he'd been cheating a bit too much at dominoes, I picked up a copy of the *Stars and Stripes* and got busy reading it,[7] and then after a moment I began reading aloud with an innocent voice about some heroic airborne action by the Americans and British on the Dalmatian coast. Into the middle of this article I inserted an entirely invented bit about a sixty-five-year-old Colonel who was parachuting in along with his unit. JHR immediately uttered a foul oath, then gave me a look and scattered all the cards in the game of solitaire he was playing — which in this case wasn't going too well for him, even in spite of his fudging. With a croaking voice, he said, "will you show me that paper?" and this time the deception that was revealed was mine.

"Aha, you wanted to relieve me of my record! No, my dear Marek, that's not going to work. I'm the oldest combat paratrooper in the world, and right here, here on my chest, is where you'll see that gleaming eagle, or hawk, or other falcon with golden talons and a golden beak,[8] and that isn't something you'll take away from me."

Well, there was little I could do other than mutter something like "don't shout hurrah until you've jumped out of the plane and your parachute has opened," under my breath — after which I started spinning gruesome yarns about how some guys beat their head to a pulp against the plane's door frame when they jump; and if not, then they get their feet tangled in the lines and land on their backs, after which they don't get up, because it's very hard to get up with a broken back; and if not, then they die a very unpleasant death of natural causes. JHR, who pretended that he hadn't heard a single word, suddenly interrupted his game of solitaire and asked,

"What does that mean again, a very unpleasant death of natural causes?"

"A death of natural causes is when your parachute doesn't open at all. And it's really unpleasant as well, since a person doesn't get to experience the thrill of parachuting. And to make things worse, at the end it's hard to give a person a decent funeral, I mean, how do you bury a splattered stain? I guess you'd sprinkle some snow on it or cover it with a little sod..."

This kind of stuff was just child's play to JHR, but one time I did get him pretty worked up. I had just come back from the base, and told him that the other guys were asking lots of questions about my secret "James." JHR listened with some satisfaction, whereupon I told him that the scuttlebutt around the base was that the secret man was Professor Kot.

"Sure, oh yeah, Kot, and how! Please! I ask you, just why isn't Kot going on this mission, if he's so bold?"

"Well, Sir, surely you wouldn't deny that Professor Kot is a bold man! Even his die-hard political opponents and personal enemies acknowledge his daring."

This was like adding oil to a fire. From the things that JHR then said, I concluded that he had more than one beef with Professor Kot. They had had, each in his own way, a considerable influence on General Sikorski, and it must have been this rivalry that divided them more than anything else. So when JHR found out that people were thinking he was Kot, he wanted to do something to bring the truth to light, at any price. But what could he do, if the British didn't want his identity revealed?

JHR spoke with me often about English matters. Since at that time — in Bari — I was only faintly familiar with the key English figures, I don't remember very much of these conversations. I was struck by the fact that he had such a wide range of acquaintances amongst English politicians — he knew the most distinguished Conservatives as well as Labourites and Liberals. He told me a lot about his cooperation with General Sikorski from 1939 until the time of the General's death. When Sikorski formed a government in France, Retinger came to see him from London, where he was reportedly living in difficult material circumstances and had secured a position as advisor at the embassy in London. And then he himself went to Churchill and initiated the idea of bringing in General Sikorski from France to discuss the whole matter of evacuating the Polish Army and civilians to England. Churchill gave him the use of his airplane, and the entire action was a success. It seemed unusual to me that Churchill would have discussed these matters with JHR, an advisor at the embassy, and not with the Ambassador personally. Later on, after the government was installed in London, JHR's position grew immeasurably. The General took care of everything through him, beginning with contacts with the British and ending with renting office space and apartments. JHR told me that General Sikorski had this method whereby, just before he was to meet a new Englishman, he'd ask JHR what he thought of the man and how best to proceed with him. JHR kept a diary of his meetings for him, as well as a little book describing people's characteristics; he organized luncheons and meetings, international press conferences — he was everything in the office of the Presidium of the Council of Ministers. He recounted these days as among the happiest in his life — since General Sikorski's cooperation with the British, through him, was a smashing success.

Our conversations became more and more candid, even sincere. He would listen raptly to my stories about being with the White Couriers — about Tońko and little Władzio, Rudek and Szczepan, about the Boy Scouts and the tough jobs they had to do, about life under Soviet occupation. He asked me in great detail about the "Concerto for Four Colts," and about my impressions, my work, my contacts with the Underground in 1942, about my yearlong return trip to London. I told him about Hungary, about my Ewa —

my God, where might she be? Things were going badly there just then, the Germans had entered Hungary and installed their fascist footmen as a government — the fate of the Poles living there seemed worse than uncertain. JHR listened sympathetically and tried to cheer me up as best he could.

When I told him about my greatest dream upon returning from Poland on my first mission — of handing over my courier report to General Sikorski personally, and of telling him how much he personally embodied the hopes of the Polish people, what he meant to those unhappy people I'd met everywhere — and then how that dream was shattered by Sikorski's plane crashing at Gibraltar ... JHR's lively, dark eyes grew moist, he wiped his pince-nez and was silent for a long time. And then he in turn started talking about how those Poles who had been saved in Russia from the most miserable Hell on Earth would bless the General's name for rescuing them — their blessings flowed upon the General from a thousand lips.

And that's the way our conversations would intertwine pleasant matters with tragic ones, personal concerns with general observations. JHR had an opinion concerning the plane crash at Gibraltar which I found it hard to share. He thought it had been an accident, not sabotage. He responded to my doubts by saying that of course the General's death had been convenient for certain people and power bases: for the Soviets above all, the Germans, but also for the British and even for certain Poles; but that he had no data to support the idea that it was anyone's dirty work, rather than a simple twist of fate.

There in Bari, I would often go to concerts, to the opera, to the movies, as I've said. At first I went out compulsively, but gradually, as I developed a taste for conversations with JHR, I went out less often. It was in Bari that I first heard a live performance of Gershwin's *Rhapsody in Blue,* Franck's *Symphonic Variations,* and the *Bolero* written by Salamander's pal. I renewed my fervent love of Beethoven's Seventh Symphony. I went out to see *Rigoletto* for the umpteenth time at the opera, having already seen it that season in London and Algiers. This version distinguished itself by the fact that the Duke of Mantua was ... struck dumb. The principal tenor had taken ill, and his part was played — but not sung — by a stand-in from the choir, and the effect was such that in those places where there was supposed to be an aria sung by the Duke, all you heard was the orchestra. This worked out particularly badly in the third act at *La donn' e mobile,* and at the famous quartet in the cave by the River Mincio.

Even so, during these cultural activities my thoughts would often wander over to my "record-holder." I was drawn to him, to his stories, to our conversations. There was one question that was on my mind most often: what about all the stubborn rumors that JHR was an agent? Was he an agent of some foreign intelligence service? And if so, then which one? Or which ones? I'd heard and read so much about this, even if it all seemed like it didn't amount to anything, but he never reacted to the things people were saying about him. Why was that? Didn't he have an answer to these accusations? Was he afraid of an open discussion on this subject? I resolved to wait for an opportune moment, when he was in a pleasant mood, and ask him about it. Delicately? Outright? Well, we'd have to see.

An extraordinary opportunity presented itself. One morning, we got the news that the operation was off. Dominoes with JHR. Conversation. A stroll to the center of town for the afternoon concert. On this particular day, the concert had been cancelled. Heading back home, I stopped in at a small nearby church to say a little prayer for our upcoming jump ... or would it be that bridge?

In the middle of the dimly lit nave, one solitary person was kneeling. I only saw him from behind and didn't take a closer look; I just noticed someone's back, someone's dark head out of the corner of my eye. I knelt in the shadows. We were praying, each in his own way having a conversation with God. But when he stood up from the pew and turned around, the light caught his pince-nez, and I recognized JHR. And I saw that those prayers of ours were for one and the same thing. I observed him, unobtrusively. He didn't notice me. After a moment, he walked right by me, dipped his fingers in the holy water, crossed himself and left.

Well now, how about that! When I'd heard about people calling him an atheist, a Jew, a Mason — and now here's this prayer!

That evening we got into a cheerful conversation — that is, he did most of the talking, and I listened. I decided to go ahead and spit out the question that had been bugging me.

"I saw you in church today, Doctor."

He looked at me attentively, took a drag off his cigarette and asked, "What about it?"

"I didn't know you were a practicing Catholic, Sir."

"Well, maybe not all that practicing. But long ago, in the misty, distant past, I was going to be a priest, a Jesuit even. However, nothing came of that. The thing was, I liked the fair sex..."

"In other words, you were in church now on the principle that when you're in a tight spot, you turn to God?"—I fired back.

He cracked up laughing.

"Yeah, I guess so," he said cheerfully, "and I'll bet you follow the same principle. It isn't a very devoutly Catholic approach to God, but hey, everyone believes as best they can. To me, for example, Pascal's argument is very appealing. Do you know his saying about God? The one from his *Pensées*?"

"I suppose I do. I might not have it exactly right, but I think you mean that wager of his, about the unnecessary risk. If there's no God, then a person who believes that God nonetheless exists risks nothing but could gain everything. But if God does exist, then the person who doesn't believe in Him loses everything."

"Yes, something like that. Reason orders us to choose faith in God, not atheism. It's logical! And I like logic. Anyway, Blaise Pascal, now that was somebody. SOMEBODY. He's one of my role models, although I get the shivers at the very mention of the word 'ascetic' and have to reach for the whisky."

"Do you have more role models?"

"I do, I do. For example, William of Orange — *Guillaume le Taciturne*, in other words he didn't say much. I really like his position on determination, his attitude toward that which constitutes the duty of a person who's fighting for higher values, his faithfulness to his principles. You know French, so listen: *Point n'est besoin d'espérer pour entreprendre, ni de réussir pour perseverer.* Do you understand?"

"Well, more or less. 'You don't need hope at all to undertake some activity, nor do you need success in order to keep going.'"

"Something like, he didn't need hope in order to fight for his country and his ideals; and he didn't need to succeed in order to persevere in that fight. He was losing, but he didn't lose."

After hearing these words from JHR, I thought to myself that since he gets into these deliberations about God, determination, perseverance, being true to one's principles, maybe this would be the time...? I gathered the courage to say:

"Are you an agent of the Intelligence Service, Sir?" I blurted out the words, at once a little frightened and disgusted by my own question.

Calmly and seriously, he looked me in the eye. After a moment, the wrinkles in his face dissolved in a smile.

"I knew you'd ask me that question sooner or later. It's not the first time I've heard it, but I pretend not to hear it and don't answer. I'll answer you, because we could get the news tomorrow that we're flying, and the day after tomorrow I might be gone, whereas you might get through our little Silent Shadow adventure in one piece, as you've already done before. You have several lives, like some kind of cat, and I even think that I may survive with you. But, to answer your question ... well then, yes" — he said it so quietly, softly — "I am indeed an agent, but not British, nor Soviet, nor Mexican, as some people have tried to insinuate. I am, if I may put it this way, a Polish agent;

I freely devote myself to the service of Poland, my country for several generations. And that's it! I'm a free agent. A *franc tireur*.⁹ I don't take orders from anyone, just my own conscience. And I don't have to have hope that what I'm doing will succeed, in order to get to work on it; nor do I need to succeed in order to keep at it and not yield."

I said nothing, but got a warm feeling around my heart. I guess it was that atmosphere of waiting for the next major turning point in my life that made me so disposed to a little pathos. And that afternoon prayer in the church, when each of us was asking for God's help in his cause, and the cause was one and the same.

JHR added:

"Actually it's been my dream for years to also be a European agent.¹⁰ A United Europe — do you understand? In a united Europe, it would be easier for Poland, being between Russia and Germany. So these two dreams of mine complement each other: a free Poland and a united Europe. Don't you think?"

"Yes. Definitely. I'm glad you told me that, Sir. But why don't you ever say it *coram publico* ("in public")? People tell so many stories and write all this stuff about you, they wear out their tongues and their pens, and you say nothing?"

"Responding to slander, correcting gossip — that would be beneath my dignity," he said calmly. But then he smiled a little impishly and added, "and anyway, what harm does it do me if they say unheard-of things about me? Let them say whatever they want. It's better than no one saying anything."

"Hmm. There's a Latin saying, *calumniare audacter, semper aliquid haeret.*" ("Go ahead and slander, some of it's sure to stick.")

"But there's another saying, a Polish one: the truth, like olive oil, always rises to the surface."

I would like — with all my heart — that the truth about JHR be that olive oil, that it might rise to the surface, and that of all of the views of his slanderers and unwitting gossipers, none of them might stick.

I went through many difficult and trying times with him. We had our brushes with death. I observed him in dramatic circumstances. I saw his patriotism, determination and perseverance in the things he considered to be true and worthy of effort and battle. I'm sure many people knew him better than I, but I daresay none of them could see the man from my point of view, my insight into him, my opportunity to see him without blinders. I saw him as he was — and at the time he couldn't be any other way. I knew what he really thought, for he couldn't have thought any other way just then. I witnessed the way he did things, about which I will still have much to tell in the pages of this book. I know that he always had the greater good of Poland at heart, that he was her free agent, her *franc tireur*.

* * *

The month of March dragged on.

Three times, we were led on. We'd be told the operation is a "go," they'd send a car and we'd pack in all of our secret bundles and be off to Brindisi. Once there, we would prepare meticulously for our flight: putting on all the pieces of our Polish civilian outfits, checking the contents of each pocket, getting into the coveralls, putting on the money belts and checking our firearms. (Salamander didn't do that, for he was afraid that his pistol might fall on his foot, and besides, I took his weapon and belts and everything heavy and added them to my load.) After that we'd get into the parachute harnesses. He was issued a parachute meant for a very large man, which he wasn't, but that — and being freed up from having to haul any heavy equipment — made for an extra margin of safety for our "theoretically prepared" parachutist. Well, after this cruel torture and all kinds of sweat, we'd find out at the last minute that "owing to weather conditions," etc., etc. — and it was back to Bari with us. The British were sorry, we were angry, and that's the way it would go.

Once, on the way back from one of these escapades to Brindisi, when we were dressed in civilian clothes and only had German identification papers on us (that is, *Kennkarte, Arbeitskarte, Ausweis* and such), we were stopped by the British Military Police, who wanted to know who we were, where we were coming from and where we were going. Luckily, our driver somehow talked his way out of actually having to produce any documents. We laughed about it for a long while — that situation could really have been hilarious.

In the end, all of those evil spirits that had stood in the way of our flight — raining at the base, foggy at the base, a storm in the flight path, raining in Poland, foggy in Poland, lack of radio communications *et cetera omnia* — brought us into a kind of state of numbness, of not taking reality seriously, of getting wrapped up in the anticipation of danger. Every morning, the danger would cease hanging over our heads for twenty-four hours, only to regularly revive like one of the heads of Hydra, to thwart any kind of normal life, normal thoughts, normal longings. JHR would read Plato for days on end, loudly swearing about two or three times per page of text — not swearing at the text, of course, but at his own accompanying thoughts. It would even happen that he would sit for several minutes in a row, with me or someone else in the room, and be silent. Anyone who knew JHR will know what kind of depression he had been pushed into! I even suspected that he was writing his will.

Gradually, I stopped believing that our flight was going to work out — and what about Salamander, who had now been waiting for eleven whole weeks? I even started to doubt that I was in Italy, that I was supposed to fly to Poland, that I was alive at all, etc., etc. — and dreamt only of sleep and peace and quiet. Besides, I was getting pretty tense, thinking about this companion of mine, whom I was supposed to not only lead but also take care of. He was actually not very graceful (to put it delicately), not particularly strong and definitely not young — well, and he'd never jumped before. What if he should break his legs, what if something should happen to him, what if I'd have to carry him for miles?

Since we couldn't wait for the weather over the Tatra Mountains, Poland and the flight path, we would work every day on our own new operational plans. For example, the dark drop (in the dark, no landing spot), a trip to see Tito (i.e., Yugoslavia),[11] or Hungary — and then onward from there on foot, by train or whatever. Of course, someone would have to be bribed. What people won't do for money! But the English called our plans unreasonable. Of course, we were turned off of Hungary not only by their opinion, but also because Hitler had decided just then to occupy the Magyar Empire. I really held this against him, because I knew that my Ewa was in Hungary. My God, what was happening with her? What about the Poles over there? What about Station W?[12] Lech?[13] Béla?[14]

We kept waiting. Multi-course dinners, games of dominoes and car accidents all totally lost their appeal. My conversations with JHR continued to be gripping, but subconsciously I was concerned with the problem of my emissary mission. The lack of new information from the Foreign Ministry was giving me fits. Every passing day meant I was less up-to-date. The whole purpose of my mission depended on my quick arrival in Poland from London. Our mission! "Stem" had emphasized that.

Even my magnificent sleeping bag lost its appeal. It's true that I continued sleeping eleven hours a day, but I was already sick of it. I was tired, and more and more ... sleepy. JHR's spirits were far lower than mine. At times he would sadly discuss our "devaluation" as emissaries, and he spoke of time working against us.

During our stay in Bari, Major Wilkinson of the SOE,[15] who knew JHR well, returned from Yugoslavia. They had a long talk in private about Yugoslavia and Wilkinson's impressions. Afterwards, JHR told me that on the basis of that conversation, he could see that his departure to Poland was unusually important, and he regretted very much that the weather conditions kept getting in the way. He concluded that what was happening in Yugoslavia was a living blueprint for what was shortly going to happen in Poland, and that this was the final bell for bringing about, at any price, an understanding between the underground movement directed from London and the underground movement directed from Moscow. At that point, since Polish society overwhelmingly supported the Delegature of the London Government-in-Exile and the Home Army (AK), and not the National Council and the People's Army, it would be possible to hang on to the most important political positions and outvote the Communists. If some attempt to come to an understanding between the two sides wasn't made at once, then it would soon be too late and the Communists would outnumber everyone else, the way they had just done in Yugoslavia. Besides, this kind of action would put a stop to the fragmentation of the Underground, which looked bad from an outside point of view, and it would serve to bring Polish matters to the attention of the Americans, as well as increasing the engagement of the British in our cause. And finally, this step would immeasurably strengthen the prestige of the Government-in-Exile in London, which would direct the entire underground movement, including the Communists. Then, with more help from the British, they could more easily reach some sort of understanding with the Soviet government in the matter of establishing diplomatic relations, and move to liquidate the Union of Polish Patriots, a dangerous organization over which the government would assume control. The National Council and the People's Army would be similarly taken over.

Everything that JHR said seemed to me to be too hurried, too revolutionary—and when I told him that he was likely to encounter a solid wall of opposition in Poland to the idea of signing off on the Curzon Line, getting the People's Party involved, and so on, he replied that the thing had to be done in a quick and revolutionary way. He said Mikołajczyk was moving too slowly even though he did indeed possess a kind of civil courage, but only to a degree of ninety-five percent; and that he was always afraid they'd call him a traitor and a sell-out; and in any event Eden had told him (JHR) upon his departure: "Tell the Poles that we will not go to war over the eastern border of Poland, and that if they don't want to lose everything and make any further help from us impossible, they should come to an agreement with Russia as quickly as possible."

There was only one good side to this torturous wait, and that was that perhaps in the meantime they would finally set up that air bridge. We couldn't get rid of that stubborn hope. But you'd have to be kidding! If maybe one of us were the old man in a certain children's song, then maybe they would build us this bridge in the air; but the way things were looking, it seemed far more likely that a different song from childhood days might be more apt: the one about the ring that ends with "we all fall down."

When we were told in late March that the air bridge project had definitely been postponed by a whole month, and the weather had calmed down to the extent that the first parachute mission would probably happen in a few days, I thought JHR was going to have a fit. His indignation, his nervous pacing from corner to corner with a double helping of curses and expletives, led me to suspect that perhaps his boldness and courage, which I'd heard people talk about so many times, might be rather Einsteinian, so to speak. I thought to myself that the old man had lost his nerve, and that was that. As long as there was any hope of an air bridge, he played the hero. Now, I figured he would probably quit. Even though I liked him and admired his lightning intelligence, his versatility, detailed knowledge of human nature, and command of six languages (and he had plenty to say in each of them), I looked at him at that time with a certain disdain.

JHR was so acutely intelligent that it seemed at times as though he could read people's minds, and that's how it was this time as well. He was walking around the table, swearing under his breath and following each swear-word with an almond, fig or date, of which there were whole heaps on the counter. Suddenly he looked at me and stopped in front of the sofa I was sitting on.

"You think I'm scared, right?"

How was I supposed to reply? You don't say things like that to people. So I sat still and didn't look him in the eye.

"But I'm just furious!" he finished with a passion.

After a brief silence, I replied, "There's no other way out for you, Sir, than to either jump or call it off."

"But no, you are fundamentally wrong, *fun-da-men-tally*. I have no other way out than to jump. And that's why I'm furious."

I looked at him with a wondering, questioning gaze.

He continued, "Because for me, a jump pretty much equals a broken leg, and then what? I'll have to hold meetings in my damn bed!"

I was surprised by his tone and bewildered by his strange reasoning, in which his personal safety seemed not to play the slightest part. That wasn't the old man's fear speaking — quite the opposite. Unable to make sense of my feelings just yet, I sat there silently, waiting for him to swallow that fig and continue speaking.

"I'm not saying anything about your speeches assuring me some measure of safety and delivering me from the landing spot to Warsaw. I'm not concerned about that, it's your business. But I'm directly confronted with one thing, and that is that I'll have to call off at least half of my important meetings. Real friends will come to me, but I'll have to go visit the questionable ones myself. I'm talking in political terms, of course. That's why I was counting on that bridge. I wanted to have my whole legs and be able to move around Warsaw, and not be lying there in one of your so-called safe houses, waiting for someone to take pity on me and come for a talk. I wanted to have my whole legs..."

"Precisely!" — I interrupted — "Your whole legs!"

"Well, because — what?"

"You were counting on that bridge, Sir, and you didn't want to go through regular parachute training. You familiarized yourself with it *in theory*," I barked sarcastically, because that matter had been bugging me from the very start.

JHR stopped in front of me again, and looked into my eyes very seriously. Calmly, he started to explain.

"I guess you still don't understand me. Of course I was counting on that bridge, and why is that? I just explained it to you a minute ago. I didn't go to parachute training, not because I was afraid, but because, as I've said, I anticipate breaking a leg on my first jump. So I prefer to break my damn leg and fulfill my mission as an emissary, even if it means doing it from my bed and only half way, rather than breaking it at that Ringway place of yours during a practice jump and winding up in an English hospital whose doctors would naturally unravel any dreams of mine about going to Poland. It's because I have weak and rather brittle bones, Marek. And then there's my age ... I'm coming up on sixty."

Something grabbed me by the Adam's apple and held on tight. I was moved, the way I used to be moved as a kid when my brothers and sister and I would get swept away reading Sienkiewicz's *Trilogy*. A fleeting memory ran through my thoughts, of how as kids we'd once gotten into a discussion of the individual characters in Sienkiewicz. Skrzetuski? A hero, yes, but practically a saint already. Kmicic? A hero as well, but a little too much of a bully. Wołodyjowski? A hero, and what a one! The most authentic, throughout all three volumes of the *Trilogy*, without exception. Zagłoba? A hero — fiddlesticks, a coward! — not at all, he was very brave, he cut Burlaj to pieces — because he had no other choice, chump! — Stasia, tell us, is Zagłoba a hero or a coward? — and Stasia would decide the matter on the authority of her being a student at the academy in Lwów. "Zagłoba was first and foremost a wise man. He didn't want to risk his hide if he didn't have to. But if it came to it, he was ready for anything," she declared.

Yes, I thought to myself now, there is certainly a strong touch of Zagłoba in JHR. There are differences, sure: he's slim, has no moustache, he's no good with a sword and it's hard to imagine him on horseback. But the similarities were far greater: he talks a lot, just like the other man, he loves to embellish, definitely toots his own horn, doesn't let good vodka go to waste, and — just as Stasia had said — he doesn't like to risk his hide unnecessarily: he'd prefer to fly in via the air bridge. But since the air bridge probably wasn't going to work out, and he had to go to Poland — he was ready to jump, too.

After that conversation, I looked upon JHR with totally friendly eyes. The old man had captured my heart.

In an altogether different matter: the approaching parachute mission was stoking my growing fears about those "weak and brittle" bones of JHR's. When I thought about my first flight to Poland, with Effendi, Buka and company, and considered that similar adventures might be our lot this time, I shuddered to think that I was going to be alone with JHR, whom I was supposed to take care of, and who might break a leg when he landed, or slam into a tree the way Marian had done on my first mission; or some other kind of accident could happen. What would I do with him then? I mean — I wouldn't make it!

Four

4.4.44

At last our little Italian comedy came to an end. Departure! The third of April. We were excited and happy — I more so, JHR less so. For me, besides the fact that I was flying to Poland, there was a further reason to smile, which he didn't have, to wit, I got to see Salamander's hilarious mask, with eye slits and a mouth hole cut out of the canvas, and his glasses glinting underneath. The British had fiercely insisted on keeping JHR incognito to the very end. I just about burst out laughing when, just before we got in the car to head for the airport, already dressed in our parachute gear, an English sergeant stuck this monstrous mask on JHR's head and told us both that it was not to be removed until the plane had taken off. And if by chance we were unable to fulfill the mission and had to return to base, that mask was to be on JHR's head before the airplane door was opened at the airport. I kidded him without letting up, calling him Professor, pointing out people at the airport — here's his relative, Jurek, here's another officer who knows him — and wondering how it could be possible that they think he's Professor Kot. Salamander was fuming, but I was having a ball. I smiled at the pilots around us, who made no secret of their delight with the black mask. There were Poles among them. Suddenly, Salamander grabbed me by the arm and said breathlessly, "Shield me, Marek! I see that rascal Chłapowski over there.[1] He might recognize me by my moves."

I shielded the Black Mask.

Finally we loaded our things into the Halifax.[2] We'd be flying with the same kind as that other time in 1941. God willing, there would be no losses this time.

Maybe it would work out! Our landing spot wasn't too far from Warsaw, near Minsk Mazowiecki. Code word "Clock." The code name for our mission was "Salamander," after the pseudonym of my charge. He could soon add a new record to his collection: world's oldest combat paratrooper. I smiled at

> **Signal from LONDON** MOST SECRET. 19.March.44.
>
> A. PAISLEY considers infiltration via Hungary most dangerous and unwise.
>
> B. Understand weather improving.
>
> C. Suggest PAISLEY SULIMA take first opportunity drop anywhere in Poland moon or non-moon.
>
> D. Otherwise propose suggest to Polish Prime Minister PAISLEY should return to U.K.

Signal from London, dated March 19, 1944 and stamped "Most Secret," referring to Retinger ("Paisley") and Chciuk ("Sulima") and their planned mssion to parachute into Poland (courtesy MHPRL Warsaw).

the thought, and at a second, parallel thought, and a third. For I was going to set a record as well — not a world record, to be sure, but a Polish one. The thought crossed my mind more than once: I'm going to be the first guy to go on two Silent Shadow missions. And besides — this is that third thought — just like in the days of being a White Courier, I was going to be a "one" who had a "plus one." That first time, it was a strapping lad from Lwów, the unforgettable Tońko, and this time it was to be a man from Kraków, JHR, whom I was sure I'd never forget, either. I had good luck with my "subordinates."

1920 hrs. — takeoff — and we're on our way!

It was still fully light out. The sun had only just gone down behind the roofs and chimneys of the city from whose port Cicero once bade farewell to Italy. The giant Halifax lifted off, stowed both wheels and, falling into the measured rhythm of its four throaty, roaring engines, began moving majestically into the darkness of the Adriatic. Other than the flight crew, there were only the two of us on board: JHR, my subordinate, and I, his commander. I was the commander of a weird parachute mission: in my charge were one older gentleman and eighteen containers of arms, ammunition, radio equip-

> **MOST SECRET.**   23.March.44.
>
> <u>Operation SALAMANDER</u>
>
> 1. Details of a reception committee in the Red Group suitable for this operation have not yet been received. The Blue group finishes today, and re-commences on 27th.
>
> 2. Committees in the Red group are only available near KRAKOW and LUBLIN. It is estimated that the operator will take at least a week to reach his destination from these areas. In my view he is unlikely to succeed in reaching it as the committees are situated far from regular communications and journeys of at least 100 miles on foot would be necessary.
>
> 3. In these circumstances it is suggested that the speediest way for him to carry out his assigned task would be to wait until 27th March when the Blue group committee will again be available.
>
> 4. Sulima should therefore report here for re-briefing at 1800 hours on 26th March.
>
> 5. It is regretted that the inadequacy of line communications between this Unit and your H.Q. have made earlier notification impossible.

Communication from the Special Operations Executive in London to the Polish base in Brindisi, dated March 23, 1944, and stamped "Most Secret," with operational details of Operation Salamander. Retinger is referred to as "the operator" and Chciuk is "Sulima." (courtesy MHPRL Warsaw).

ment and other marvels for the AK and the Delegature. Being in charge of the containers was easy: they sat quietly in the bomb bays; at the touch of a button by the navigator, they would willingly and nimbly leave the airplane, their parachutes opening automatically; they'd land surely and without injury, and then they'd obediently let themselves be led off by the underground soldiers to a concealed depot. If there were ever to be any trouble with them, then it would have been this one thing: that after the containers landed, they might disappear from view in the thick grass or forest and lie in wait there, causing the landing detail plenty of headaches trying to find them. With the older civilian gentleman, however, the situation presented itself rather more unfavorably. On board the airplane, even though he sat there like a lamb, he might be more trouble than the containers; he could be dashed to pieces upon landing; he might not hear or understand an order, and so on. Above all, he could stall right before the jump — not jump at all, or jump with a delay of several seconds, which would lead to the two of us being so far apart on the ground that it would be difficult to gather our things together — especially if JHR should really break his brittle leg and lose consciousness, for example, and with it his voice as well.

 I had time to think about all of this and mull it over, sitting on the aluminum floor of the Halifax and gazing at JHR's dark figure, his back leaning against the opposite wall. The result of my ruminations was that I moved over to him and announced that he would jump first and I second, which was the opposite of the way it had been agreed to before. This way, I eliminated the danger of having too long a lag between the first and second jumps; and, well, I could be sure that he was even going to jump at all. For if he should get terrified at the last moment, with the hatch already open — which has been known to happen to certain overly sensitive people, let's just say — then I'd push him out into the abyss myself, I swear to God. And then I'd dive in right after him, focusing all of my attention in his direction while in the air, so that I might have a clear mental picture of where he landed.

 Thoughts like these, alternating with prayers, went around in my head as I stood by the Halifax's little window. Meanwhile, the flight to Poland went on, and it was ... magnificent. Twilight came while we were still over the Adriatic. The shoreline and the Balkan Mountains were already bathed in deep shadows. As we entered Hungarian skies, the moon was rising, bathing everything below in a silvery glow as it floated delicately in the air, broken up by the four mighty propellers. If it hadn't been for that unbearable feeling of danger gnawing at one's insides like an indigestible meal, stuck at the very center of one's thoughts, like some jagged reef against which those thoughts would be smashed as soon as they were born — then we could have more fully appreciated the fairy-tale quality of this trip. I, especially, had reasons for having a heart filled with emotions, because I was looking from high above at the ribbon of the Danube, shaped like my girl Ewa's beloved Orion, winding beneath us and falling, way down yonder to the right, into the black stain that was Budapest, where at that very moment the person dearest to me was nestled in sleep. And I was with my Ewa with every thought. I prayed. "Lord,

Four. 4.4.44

protect us," just like way back when. "Redeem us in any misfortune..." Redeem my Ewa — us.

A marvelous night. The plane sped along evenly. There was no wind, no clouds. It was indescribably beautiful. I thanked God for that flight.

A little farther to the north, another little ribbon caught my eye, glued as I was to the pane of that small window. It was narrow, *way* narrow compared to the Danube, but somehow alive, changing from silvery in the pale moonlight to a matte grey in the shadow of the little clouds. I gazed at this marvel for a long time, unable to connect it to anything from the real world. Finally I took off my parachute, moved over to the cockpit and asked the pilot.

"Germans," Lieutenant Szrajer answered calmly, "they're pounding toward Budapest.[3] That's a huge motorized column, maybe even armored."

Oh yeah, I remembered. The *Magyarorszag* (Hungarian Empire) had actually been under German occupation for a couple of weeks now. The Germans were no longer guests now, courteous allies, the way I remembered them from my previous time in Hungary. They were occupiers now, pouring a steel stream of armed forces into the subjugated country. Looking at the enemy column snaking along, I started thinking about Hungary's sad fate, and above all about the sad fate of the Polish refugees, several thousand of whom continued even then to benefit from the hospitality of our Magyar brethren.

"If it weren't for you gentlemen," Lt. Szrajer interrupted my train of thought — "and if it weren't for this mission we have to accomplish, we'd tear up that column sure as two and two's four. It's a real pleasure to think about how much confusion we could create, and how many Krauts we could wipe out. Opportunities like this don't come along often. They don't have any protection, they're moving with complete confidence. Look, Sir, they even have some lights on. Too bad..."

He sighed deeply, after which he reluctantly took his gaze away from the ground and shook his head sadly. But after a moment he was looking down there again and hollered right in my ear,

"Tough luck, this time we'll have to get by with just a look, because if we started any trouble, some Focke-Wulfs would surely latch onto us, and then there's no telling what would happen.[4] But if we should get a similar freebie on the return flight, we'll try to take some sort of action." He smiled broadly and winked a couple of times. "We'll only be responsible for our own skin then, and not for that bigwig you're with, eh? Because he is a bigwig, right? All that mystery about the gentleman, masks and what not."

"Uh-hmm," I replied, pretending not to understand what he was getting at. I'd been sounded out like this before.

"What's the guy doing?" Lt. Szrajer asked after a while, evidently unable to wait for my comments any longer.

"He's sitting."

"He seems kind of calm for a bigwig."

"Yes — on the plane."

"Why don't you bring him up here, Sir? We'll be over the Tatra Mountains in a minute, it'll be something to see."

I went back to JHR to propose that he check out this spectacular view, but he didn't want to. When he heard that we were about to fly right over Lake Morskie Oko, his eyes evidently began to perspire — he was clearly moved. I wondered aloud why he wouldn't want to take a look at these treasures of the Tatra Mountains — this was the only opportunity. He just cleared his throat and turned his head away. He must not have wanted me to see the tears in his eyes, but still he didn't move. It wasn't until after the jump, when we rendezvoused at the landing spot, that I understood that motionlessness of his. So I didn't keep trying to talk him into it, and hurried back to the cockpit, not wanting to lose a single second of this view of the Tatras. And how very right I was....

The farther north we flew, the more beautiful the world below us seemed to get. The wings of our airplane were bathed in the milky silver moonlight, and the landscape slipping past us below, although it still created the impression that it was some magic fairy-tale land, was as bright and clear as the palm of my hand. Presently we floated over the territory of Slovakia; to the left, we passed by the heavy mountain range of the Central Tatras, crossed diagonally over the valley of the White Wag and then ... we tore into an utterly real Land of Fairy Tales and Spells.

For that one view of the Tatras, for that majesty of mountaintops seen from above, it would have been worth risking a hundred times more, I thought to myself, none too intelligently. Here and there in the clear moonlight, bright spots of snow sparkled just like jewels; they contrasted in a magnificent way with the darker blue shadows of the mountaintops, the glitter of the cliff faces, the dark blue of the forest depths and the black of the crevasses. And all of this was in a state of constant motion, as if in a mad escape. The Tatras raced away to the rear below us, dusky, blurred together so I couldn't tell them apart. Farther up, near the horizon, they ran more slowly until they crouched and hid behind the backs of their larger companions of the *avant-garde* so that only their tips were showing.

The sight of this procession of the Tatras moving below us was so lovely that it took my breath away. I completely forgot about any danger. The mood of this scene, the feeling that our existence was unreal, was only made stronger

Four. 4.4.44

yet by the ceremonial parade of the stars above us and the mighty music of the motors' orchestra, an uninterrupted chain of *crescendo* and ***diminuendo***, and that feeling flowing from my subconscious, reminding me that every link in this chain, every measure of this music, every flashing revolution of the propellers announced that we were getting closer to our own country. I felt happy, but my whole body trembled at the thought that this feeling couldn't last, that the four motors were single-mindedly pushing northward, racking up more mileage in the silvery-blue air. I felt sorry the mountains were slipping by, but also grateful, for I knew that this view of the Tatras from the sky was just the prelude to an even greater happiness. In just a moment, we were going to be within the borders of the Republic. Not many people get to experience feelings like these, framed by views like these.

"Mount Gerlach on the left!" the navigator hollered right in my ear.

I began to awaken from my ecstasy. My eyes searched mechanically for that regal peak, but I couldn't make it out. My wide-eyed gaze was still drinking in the entirety of the Tatras; I didn't have any free space inside me, not even a fraction of a second to spare for details.

"Zakopane on the left!"

"Where?" — I finally snapped out of it completely, because this meant we were already over Poland and that soon ... I took a more clear-headed look down below. The scenery somehow darkened and got murkier; the silver fairy tale ran away from under our wings. A few lights far below us indicated Poland's winter capital.

I stood with my face glued to the curved glass of the turret. I was looking at Polish land in the darkness below, the way you look at the embers of a dying campfire or at the cascading water of a waterfall: with an absent, absorbed gaze that reads from our souls rather than from the world around us. The mad movement below us gave way to some kind of darkened film running in slow motion. The plane flew on as calmly as before, the stars hung above us as steadily as before, but the complete change of scenery below us, the lack of snow and mountains and the disappearing light of the suddenly dejected moon, made me feel clearly that a new stage was beginning: I'd begun living in Poland, breathing Polish air. Just the jump now, and I'd feel the hard ground under my feet — the ground I literally flew to on wings, racing the wind — the ground I would greet by unfurling the great silken flower of my parachute.

"We're close to the Pieniny Mountains, but I can't see anything," the skipper's voice reached my ears. "You'd better get back and put your parachute back on. The dispatcher's already warming up the intercom, and he's right, because you guys don't have much more waiting to do."

I sat back down, across from JHR, who wiped his glasses and spoke in my ear: "That was Lake Morskie Oko, won by my father in a lawsuit against Hungary. Now we're coming up on Czorsztyn, my part of the country. What a strange coincidence. Flying to Poland this way ... after all these years."

The dispatcher, or bouncer, got after us to sit down, speaking Polish with a weird accent. Another hour, maybe less, and we'd be over the landing spot. I resolved to have a chat with Salamander about that court case in the matter of Lake Morskie Oko — later, on the ground, if the jump worked out and anyone had anything to talk about.

At last we were sitting ready to jump. In front of me was Salamander's dark, crooked shadow, and above him there was a little white spot. That was the moonlight, peeking in through a little hole in the plane's roof, poking around its dark interior and landing on the aluminum wall. For a long time, I sat without moving and without feeling, gazing vacantly at the little white spot, which barely budged. Maybe I was dreaming with my eyes open; maybe I was saying some kind of pagan prayer without being conscious of talking to God. The black, wordless roar filled the scene.

Suddenly the little white spot went crazy. It did an awful pirouette and then hid somewhere in the tail of the Halifax. Almost immediately it returned over JHR's head, then with a quick, fluid motion it went to the right toward the floor, brushed against my legs and landed like a butterfly on my shoulder; then, as if running away from something, it swam toward the face of my companion. After a moment it reeled to the right and left, darted to the side and disappeared. For several seconds I followed it with my eyes, the way you'd follow a sun spot that your classmate was making with his mirror during lessons. After the spot disappeared for good, I suddenly came to the realization that there must be a deeper explanation for this wild behavior of the hitherto motionless spot. I also became aware that from the moment the little spot went nuts, the floor of the airplane and the wall behind my back had started acting strangely as well: first I'd get the feeling they weren't there next to me, because I felt so light in those places where I was touching the aluminum; then I felt the brutal pressure of the metal crunching my back and tailbone. Finally, I figured it all out and tore myself off the floor with a sudden move. A brief conversation with the sergeant/bouncer confirmed my suspicions and filled me with a cruel fear.

"Hans, that son of a bitch, he's on our tail," he roared in my ear. The bouncer hadn't been to Poland in a long time. He was a Pole from Brazil.[5] But he could cuss in Polish all right.

I looked over uneasily at the outline of JHR's shape. It would be better if he didn't find out about this. He'd get mad, and then there could be trouble later.

Pointing out the seated old man to the bouncer, I said, "Don't tell that guy."

"You got it," he said with a knowing twinkle in his eye and tilted his head. He turned away with his back to me, heading into the interior of the plane, but I stopped him impatiently and wanted to know the details of whatever kind of danger we were in. The plane's sudden moves made us tumble around on the floor while trying to talk; finally we were sitting almost helplessly by the wall.

"It's better like this," the sergeant said, "because if he starts firing at us, you'll get hit sooner if you're standing than if you're sitting."

"And maybe he's already firing?" I moved uneasily and looked around. It started seeming to my agitated ears that the roar of our engines was mingled with the growl of a German fighter, bah!, even the clatter of his heavy machine guns. The sergeant kind-heartedly set my mind at ease by telling me that I'd only be sure that's what I was hearing when the rounds started piercing the shell of the aircraft, and *really* for sure if they pierced our own bodies. Besides, if they made a lot of holes in the fuselage, then the moonlight would really dance around the plane.

"Ooh, look over there, Sir, at that wall," he suddenly grabbed my hand. "I think we've already been hit once, though I don't know when, but there's light coming through that hole."

"No, no," I calmed him down, and myself, after a moment of blank terror, "That's an old hole. I noticed it right after the Tatras."

"Aha! Well, all right then," he roared in my ear and put on the intercom headphones, paying no further attention to me or the danger of a plane shot full of holes. He listened for a minute, then stood up and went to the rear gunner's cabin.

The familiar little spot returned to take its rightful place over JHR's head. It still hesitated for some time; a few times it darted to the side, to the right and down, to the left and up, but somehow it seemed calmer and more fluid. It must have gotten tired with all that craziness, because it even lost a lot of its former luster. It got dimmer, weaker: the moon was going down. After a moment it stopped moving — the danger had passed. The plane got back its dignity and honor, and flew on smoothly, unshaken. The bouncer walked past us again, and returned after a while with good news from the skipper — "We evaded that fighter. We lost him in some clouds, somewhere between Radom and ... Warsaw."

"And Warsaw?"

"Yes. In a minute we'll be right over Warsaw. Buckle up."

I hurriedly checked the center latch on Salamander's parachute and tightened down his static tape, but I myself popped into the cabin to take a quick look at the city. I didn't see a lot: just a few little lights — besides, they all went out as if on cue.

"No doubt the alarms are going off in Warsaw. We'll give them a fright — our own guys as well as the Krauts," Lt. Szrajer shouted at me. Then he suddenly remembered who he was talking to and hollered:

"What are you doing here, Sir? Hustle back inside and buckle up! The landing spot's coming right up."

I figured he had to know what he was talking about, so a couple of seconds later, I was already seated across from JHR, next to the hatch, which hadn't been opened yet. I was ready for anything — even this jump!

Our landing spot was about halfway between Warsaw and Minsk Mazowiecki. The nearest accumulation of people: Dębe Wielkie. If this landing party should be unable to receive us, meaning if they failed for some reason to give the agreed-upon light signals, we were to turn back and head for the backup landing spot, somewhere in the Świętokrzyskie Mountains. That option was unappealing to us, as getting to Warsaw would be much more difficult from there, but — what can you do? — we were even willing to take the second landing spot, just so we wouldn't have to return to base. The skipper had categorical instructions to drop us only in one of the two landing spots. In the event that neither of them was on, a wild jump was out of the question. Return to base. This wasn't 1941 anymore, when various kinds of improvisation were possible — with more or less happy outcomes. This was 1944, bound by very precise regulations.

The Halifax must have gotten to the area of the drop zone.

The plane made a great arc somewhere up near Minsk Mazowiecki and turned back over Dębe Wielkie. The pilot leveled out the plane, then turned it the other way. We must have been just about over Grochów. And again, the turn, leveling out, and the drop zone. No lights. The skipper called me on the intercom and reported that drop zone number one is probably rolled up and there's nothing left to do but head for number two. After a brief exchange of views with me, he agreed to give it one more try, and turned toward Dębe Wielkie again.

"But this is definitely the last time," he declared with finality. "We can't afford to cruise around between Warsaw and Minsk like chumps, because either they send some Messerschmitts on our tail, or we lose so much fuel that we can't make it back to base."[6]

I gave the headphones back to the bouncer and sat back down by the hatch. My conscience was bothering me, for I felt that by being stubborn, I was exposing the crew to serious danger. Deep in my soul, for a second, I weighed which was more important: a more comfortable arrival for us in Warsaw, or the plane's return to base — and I didn't have any doubt. I got up and went over to the sergeant, and asked him to connect me with the skipper again, because I wanted to tell him that I agreed that we should fly at once toward the Świętokrzyskie Mountains.

He listened to my entire complicated opinion rather absent-mindedly, because his attention was focused on his intercom headphones, and suddenly ... he smiled broadly.

"Take your places, please!" he shouted with a booming voice. "There's the lights! Good lights — you'll be jumping shortly!" (Easy for him to say.)

In a flash, I found myself next to the hatch. Now I concentrated strictly on the jump and on Salamander. He had actually hardly moved from his spot during the entire flight. He behaved just like a container, totally unaware of the beauty of the flight, or of the danger of being chased by a German fighter, or of that uncertainty as to whether and when we were going to jump. I know that sometimes the old man would puff a little harder than usual and manage to get out his flask of whisky, but that had been his only movement thus far. He must have dozed off into dreamland pretty nicely from time to time, or maybe he was pondering his brittle bones and what a fine mess he'd gotten himself into at his age. I poked him in the side, and when he saw how agitated I was, he moved around kind of strangely and then loudly asked — "Is it time already?"

"Yes — very shortly. After the hatch is open, please move over to it right away and wait for a signal from the sergeant. Jump out and do a half flip, feet together, hands up. All right?"

"All right."

"After you land" — I was repeating his instructions for the last time — "don't move anywhere. Anywhere! Not until you're met by our people from the outpost, or by me."

He nodded his head and looked over at the bouncer, who was just approaching the hatch cover. The sergeant stood over it, set his feet far apart so that he wouldn't step on the edge of the cover, then firmly grasped the handle and yanked it open. We were hit at once by a blast of cold air, chilling the interior of the airplane and bringing on a fit of shivering and trembling for the two poor jumpers.

Time! The sergeant stowed the cover off to the side, strode calmly over the freezing black opening and leaned over us. He checked to see that the metal "D" rings on our static tapes were properly clipped to the hooks, then shouted:

"Remember, the first batch of containers goes out first, then we circle around, then you guys go. You still have a minute. You, Sir, the older gentleman, you'd probably better not look down — it's unhealthy!"

I remember, from my first flight to Poland in 1941, that in that brief bit of time between the opening of the hatch and the actual jump, my thoughts were most intense. Some kind of pictures, feelings, thoughts tumbling around my head, racing in a random stream, mixed with the words of prayers, interrupted with shivers of fear and emotion. It was the same this time around. I knew that I was seconds away from jumping — well, maybe even a minute or two — and that the time was short and there was no point in thinking about anything. I thought it would be best to send a prayer up to God for help in my hour of need, and yet the prayer just didn't come. Nothing but nerves, nerves, a choking fear, and the awareness that I had to control myself — and how hard it was to do that. And thoughts, whole swarms of fleeting, shallow thoughts that felt like a dilletantish accompaniment, trying to fake a few bars in order to catch up to the melody, which was running away — a melody of tired resignation, with a light harmony of some kind of stubbornness. Yes, and a little shame. This time I wasn't a novice any more; quite on the contrary, I was regarded by some as an experienced paratrooper. I'd been entrusted with taking care of Salamander, and furthermore I had an important mission in Poland. If this jump worked out, I'd be a record-holder of sorts. That's why I had to keep it together.

My thoughts sorted themselves out somehow. Besides, this business of jumping into an outpost drop zone had its significant upsides, but only one downside — and what a one! At that moment I realized clearly that what I was afraid of wasn't the jump itself but that one downside: if the drop zone had been discovered by the Germans and liquidated (entirely possible), then the lights below, signaling that they're ready to accept the drop, were being sent out by thugs with skulls on their caps and the stylized letters "SS" on their collars. And we would be dropping right into their hands — brrr! — but that must be impossible! For who among the Poles would betray us or reveal the elements of our light signals? As for a coincidence — that the Germans might have guessed our signals — that must be impossible! The bouncer had clearly said that the lights were all right; those had to be our guys. That one downside gets crossed off the list. Well then, what was I afraid of, if that's so? Hmm, must be that damn jump after all. To hell with it, this whole thing goes against the laws of nature, why had I agreed to this?

Me? Why had JHR agreed to this? I suddenly remembered that the person sitting next to me preparing to jump was someone who had never parachuted before, was weak and almost sixty years old. Dang! That really is a marvelous person. I cocked my head and looked at him again. He showed no trace of

Four. 4.4.44

unease, sitting there just as calmly as when we used to play solitaire in our post–Nazi cottage in Bari. Nary a tremble, though his eyes were a bit runny. I remembered my first training jump, from a cramped Whitley bomber,[7] during my course at Ringway in England, and my admiration for the old man grew. Back then, I'd had something like the hiccups brought on by sheer nerves; I couldn't swallow, or whatever. Jerzy Mara-Meyer bit his tongue till it bled,[8] and Franek was going bald right before our very eyes, he really was. That was a rare sight. I remember how he unconsciously took his comb out of his battle dress a few minutes before the jump and dragged it across his bare head (those rubber head guards got really warm and uncomfortable; that's why we would generally wait till right before the jump before putting them on), and his comb was full of hair he'd pulled out. He looked sheepishly over at me, Buka and Jerzy,[9] cleaned the hair out of his comb and ran it through his hair a second time. Once again, his fair hair turned that comb a lighter color.

"Cut it out, dumbass, or you'll go completely bald and that funny hat will fall off on your way down," I hollered in his ear.

"I have a lot of respect for that funny hat," he barked.

"But you'll be bald when you land, and Betty will die laughing," Buka called over.

"What do I care if I break my neck bald or with a head of hair? And anyway, Betty's only got eyes for Jerzy ... look, Jerzy's got blood pouring out of his mouth!"

That brief and — shall we say — jolly conversation diverted our thoughts from the jump a little bit. Without it, I might not have been feeling so great. Had it not been for our conversation, I'd probably be looking down, and I ... I don't like looking down. Up till then I had always suffered from a fear of heights. Dizziness, nausea, and a terrible fear accompanied every effort I'd ever made to look down, be it from the top of Mt. Giewont or looking from Kosciuszko's Knoll at the concrete courtyard onto which I used to throw up my dinner from Sikornik's. And here, suddenly these new experiences: my second time ever in an airplane (the first having been a fly-around, i.e., a flight without jumping, just to get used to being in the air) and right off the bat they're telling me to get out of the plane in midair.

Yes, yes — I was dreadfully upset back then. I guess the situation was saved only by curiosity, that first step toward knowledge. In spite of how nervous and afraid I was, I was fascinated by this experience which is known to but a few people. So then I convinced myself of the value of it, and that there was a lot of truth in what I was being told. For on the one hand, there were those who would frighten you and exaggerate the dangers associated with parachuting, and on the other hand there were those who trivialized the whole thing from beginning to end. Naturally, the truth lay somewhere in between, as it usually does. It wasn't as devilishly frightening a thing as they had described it, but then again I wouldn't do it for my own pleasure either, or to show off. The moment you jump isn't really pleasant, except insofar as it's the end of an even worse state of waiting. The moment the canopy opens and your whole body gets jerked is a painful one, but it has the virtue of bringing an end to the even more annoying feeling of flying without your parachute open. The actual descent, with the parachute wide open overhead, is very, very nice: you feel like a great big bird, gliding along above the mountains and forests and looking down at the earth with the feeling that everything as far as the eye can see belongs to you, and that everything that walks the earth but can't fly is very poor and handicapped. However, this pleasure is in turn spoiled by thoughts of the inevitable approaching landing, especially if it's windy: then you start to feel like someone who has to, absolutely has to, jump out of a third-floor window in a second. Sometimes it works out and you can easily land on your feet without falling or getting seriously shaken up; most often, though, your body slams into mother earth so hard she lets out a moan, and you start to black out and the wind gets knocked out of you. It's true that we were prepared for these violent collisions with the earth, we were tortured for hours with forced exercises, jumping, running, and above all with various kinds of somersaults and tumbling. Finally — and this was the worst part — to gain experience and get to know the taste of it, we were made to jump from a speeding truck, facing forward from a standing position or facing rearward from a sitting position. But all that dry training, although it did more or less balance out the flaccid muscles and general sluggishness of the patient, didn't help fight off that nasty fear of hitting the earth in the least, and that's why thinking about the landing was not pleasant and wrecked the pleasure of flying.

Of course, it wasn't really I who was thinking these thoughts, sitting across from Salamander now in the Halifax and circling over the drop zone; my thoughts took over my brain, born out of some sort of weird random associations, connected to the outline of the bouncer and my persistent eyeballing of the two little colored lights, which were dark and silent as yet, but in a second....

The light signaling "action stations" went on. JHR twitched as if someone had poked him. With a quick motion of his body, helped by his nervous hands, he moved over to the hole, put his legs in and ... he would have jumped without an order if the bouncer hadn't grabbed him by the armpits and pulled him back. The old man looked indignant — here he was, raring to go, and they're holding him back! Seeing that the sergeant wasn't going to be able to subdue my subordinate by the hatch until the "go" light went on (which might happen considerably later), I jumped to my feet, got closer to JHR and grabbed his arm. The bouncer grabbed his other arm, and in this comical position — the little old man practically sitting in midair, the bouncer and I standing over the opening on either side of Salamander with legs spread — we waited for the signal to jump. The bouncer raised his head and observed the signal lamps, and I looked at Salamander with a look that combined curiosity, anger and amusement, while he leaned his head far out over the opening and serenely studied the earth speeding by below us, divided into dark patches of some little forest and lighter areas of fields and meadows, and speckled by the lights of the drop zone, looking like fireflies.

The old man's wrinkled, camel-like countenance didn't betray any fear at all, nor even a whit of irritation, but rather some kind of intense, childlike curiosity, mixed with a generous dose of impatience at the fact that all of this, this introduction to the dance, was taking so indecently long. At one point, he raised his head in my direction. A slight smirk passed over his narrow lips, something almost disdainful about it. There was a flash of cheerfulness in his lively eyes. He moved his lips as if he wanted to say something, which was written all over his face in any event:

"So you see, Marek, I told you. I'm not afraid."

The bouncer's raised right hand abruptly came down, and his left hand let go of JHR's arm. I feverishly let go of his other arm, and out of the corner of my eye I saw the "go" light signaling the order to jump.

"Let's go!" I roared at the little old man.

It turned out that this encouragement was superfluous. Salamander had already disappeared through the opening. He got tossed around a little, and his parachute line grated and rattled against the metal. I couldn't delay for even a moment. I shook hands quickly with the sergeant and as soon as I had let go, I charged into the opening head-first. I didn't have time to ponder the fact that while this might be a good way to jump out of a side door, there might be other dangers involved with going out a bottom opening, such as smashing my brains out on the side of the frame. The only thing on my mind was to jump right after JHR and land as close to him as possible. In my mind's eye I could picture him already, lying in a ditch with a broken leg.

I was lucky — nothing happened to me. The hum of silence getting louder in my ear, and the wicked blast of air that I felt in every shred of my body — almost in every shred of my uniform and parachute — swallowed me whole and held me with an iron grip. I tore myself away from everything that was normal and real. The jolt of the opening canopy finally brought me back to reality. I don't know if that's when I opened my eyes, or if they were already open and I started making out the surroundings, because I was never able to tell if my eyes closed at the moment I jumped, or not. Suffice it to say that the first thing I noticed below me was a dark patch of forest, followed by the blinking lights of the receding plane; and between them was its shadow, as the plane's cross-shaped outline got ever smaller against the dark blue sky. Finally, turning around, I saw the enormous white canopy of a parachute, rocking gently and gracefully, carrying beneath its silk the crouched, ungainly figure of Salamander. He wasn't very far from me, and a little bit below my altitude.

I concentrated fully on this figure. I decided not to take my eyes off him if at all possible, unless and until it was absolutely necessary in connection with my own landing. That way I could determine as precisely as possible where the old man had landed. If I was supposed to take care of him, then I was going to take care of him!

However, I quickly became aware that even though I had jumped later, I would be the first to stand on the ground. My descent was clearly faster than Salamander's. After a few seconds we were at the same level, and after that I had to look up to see him, and after that ... I fell into some bushes and birches, slammed my knee against a branch of some sort, and sat down on the ground. For a moment I sat there without moving, just trembling with the sheer joy of having firm, immovable ground beneath me. All those thoughts that had eerily tormented me before took on the shape of memories now — and in that form they're a lot more colorful, I even love them. Making a successful parachute jump — what a wonderful feeling! It even sidelined the joy of returning to my country, only letting it in as a later, secondary feeling. To get to this feeling, you need to start with the sheer elation of a person who is free of physical fear and the pressure that's so uncomfortable to the mind and soul.

I got up. I quickly took care of getting free of the parachute, then felt my hurting knee and convinced myself that it was nothing serious. I was just trying to pull the parachute out of the branches of a medium-sized birch tree when I heard the sound of running feet and human voices. I whipped out two giant Colt nines from the front pockets of my jump suit, leaned against the slim trunk of that tree and waited.

Forewarned is forearmed, you might say. My eyes pierced the grey darkness of the night and the forest, and zeroed in on the people running toward me. After a second I could make out two figures who were quickly approaching my little forest from the meadow or from that great field on which, according to my calculations, Salamander should have landed. At the same time I made out the words, quickly spoken in breathless Polish:

"This way, Pietrek, this way! He must have come down not far from the edge of the forest."

"Be careful, 'cause there's a ditch full of water right before those trees."

"I know. You have to jump over it."

I could hear breathing and faster footsteps.

"Stop!" I shouted sharply, seeing that they were speeding up to hurdle the ditch. One of them fell flat on his face out of sheer fear, and the other one fell in the water up to his knees. "Password?!"

Silence. I could only hear their tired breathing, then some whispering, and finally one of them mumbled sheepishly, "We forgot."

"Who are you guys?" I called out again, holding back a laugh. I was already sure that these were our guys.

"We're looking for you, Sir."

"From the outpost?"

"From the outpost. We're here to help you. Home Army."

Now they both started talking at the same time. After a moment, I jumped over the ditch and we got acquainted right away. The boys were young, they'd probably been tending cows until just recently. They were shaking with excitement, and looked with unmasked admiration at the giant figure I cut in my jump suit, packing two pistols. I told them to get the parachute out of that tree and bring it over to the gathering place. I asked them if they might know where the other jumper had come down.

"Not far from here, in the meadow. This way."

"Did you see him?"

"Yeah. One of our guys is with him."

"Did anything happen to him?"

"What could happen, when his parachute opened all right and the air was still?" one of them answered resolutely.

"You didn't catch his age and physical coordination," I thought to myself.

I wanted to run over to Salamander as quickly as possible, but not before promising the boys that I wouldn't tell the outpost commander about the forgotten password. "The fellas would laugh," they pleaded, "and some delegate from Headquarters arrived today, so it would be a shame." When they'd calmed down, they got to work untangling my parachute, and I jumped over the ditch and ran in the direction one of the boys had indicated earlier. After a moment I was talking to JHR.

The little old man (now definitely the world's oldest combat paratrooper) was completely hale and hearty.[10] He hadn't even fallen down when he landed, but stood straight on his feet and only sat down when the parachute covered him from above, the way the sexton's snuffer covers the candle's flame. JHR was incredibly fortunate: the weather conditions were so good, you couldn't have asked for nicer conditions for a parachute jump in your dreams — not the slightest breath of wind. The guy was born lucky. Of course, JHR's successful jump wasn't just a matter of luck. We had taken every conceivable precaution. Salamander was equipped with a parachute of the largest dimensions, the kind used for heavyweights over 220 lbs., and besides, all of his equipment (pistols, ammunition, first aid kit, shovel, food, flashlight, etc.), heavy as hell, was carried not on his shoulders but on mine. Out of all his equipment, the only thing he actually had on him was a little flask of whisky, all of which he had already tossed back in the plane. So that's the way it was with his load. And if you take into account that the old man weighed about 120 lbs. where I weighed about 165, and that I was using a regular-sized parachute, then it's easy to understand the curious fact that I had won our air race and landed first, despite having left the plane later.

Salamander was standing there, relaxed in the company of several Home Army soldiers, carrying on a conversation with the Outpost Commander and delegate from Headquarters.[11] Like any parachutist, especially one who's just made his first jump, he was lively and talkative, spilling out all of the things he'd been silently going through back there. I had to deprive him of his audience in order to take care of the formalities of the mission. I had the weirdest conversation with the delegate from Headquarters: specifically, the first words out of the delegate's mouth were,

"Aren't you by any chance the brother of Władek Chciuk, Sir? You have a totally similar voice, and your face looks a lot like his, too."

Of course, I didn't know how to react, and had to lie for all I was worth. Salamander was hugging me and jabbing my ribs with glee. It turned out that the delegate from HQ had been buddies with my brother at the Air Force Academy in Dęblin, indeed they'd gotten to be very good friends.

I gave the Outpost Commander a list of the containers and their contents, and forwarded all the intelligence and orders from base. We saw to it that the containers, parcels, and parachutes were collected and painstakingly loaded onto the waiting carts. They drove off with some of the soldiers, the others quietly walked away in twos. It was all over in a jiffy — magnificently organized. We two, plus the commander, the delegate and guide, were to head in the opposite direction to a nearby safe house. After I'd finished taking care of my duties, I got back to Salamander to tell him we were about to set off very shortly. He was standing rooted to the same spot. When I said something to him, he asked,

"What were those vehicles I heard back there?"

I wondered why he was saying he had *heard* them, since those carts and horses had been plainly visible. But I didn't have time to ask him, and just replied,

"Those carts belong to farmers from around here, who not only give their sons to the Home Army but also lend us their equipment when we need it. They use those carts to evacuate the equipment we air-dropped. In a minute there won't be any trace of the drop zone. And we'll be gone, too. We're going to a safe house."

"Hmm," JHR pondered. "This underground movement is really no bunk."

"No bunk!" I confirmed, then quickly added with a note of pride, "and this is just a little fragment of that wonderful Underground Nation that you'll see."

The sky was already starting to take on a milky color, the stars grew pale and the air got noticeably cooler. When our guide gave the order to start marching, Salamander suddenly called over to me.

"Marek, Marek, please hold on a minute."

The note of urgency in his voice puzzled me. I went up to him, and he grabbed me by the arm the way a blind man would. He smiled and said softly, so that no one else could hear,

"Please don't be angry, but I need your help during the hike and I'm going to need to hold on to you."

"Why?" I whispered, alarmed. "Do your legs hurt?"

"No, it's just that I suffer from night blindness."

I didn't know if I should laugh, start cussing like a sailor, or just admire him.

"What's that now?"

"I never told anyone about this," he went on quickly, "because I was afraid they wouldn't let me jump, and you might not want to take on the job of taking care of me. But now..."

"Now," I said, still not quite able to snap out of my amazement, "you can count on me more than ever, Sir."

"So you're not angry?"

"Quite on the contrary. I honestly admire you."

We moved off in the direction of the Home Army soldiers, who were waiting for us. We couldn't move very fast, because JHR was clinging tightly to my arm, stumbling at every other step, planting his feet like a child who's just learning to walk. Patiently, but a little helplessly, I helped him take his first steps on the path of being a Silent Shadow, but in my head the feeling of amazement was fighting the feeling of admiration, and admiration was battling with my inability to believe what I had just heard. After a long while I finally realized quite clearly that JHR was not only the world's oldest combat paratrooper, but also a blind one for good measure. He had a new world record. The feeling stopped me in my tracks.

"You see anything?" I asked.

"Almost nothing," he replied. "Everything sort of blurs together in these shadows."

"So that's why you sat so still during the whole flight, and never moved from your spot by the wall?"

"That's why."

"And that's why..." I bit my tongue. But JHR smiled, the way always did when he was sure he had read someone's thoughts, and he said cheerfully,

"Yes. And that's why the open hatch made no impression on me. I could have looked into it for hours — I didn't see anything anyway."

We could have gone on chatting like that for a long while, except that we heard the voice of the Outpost Commander from a distance, telling us to pick up the pace. When we caught up with them, the commander started moaning good-naturedly about how these parachute boys could never do anything on time: first, they kept everyone waiting from November to April, then they finally came, but an hour late; and now they're dilly-dallying to such a degree that it wasn't even certain that we'd all get away from the drop zone before the Gestapo showed up. But seeing the frankly crushed expression on JHR's face, he added cheerfully,

"Well, everything's going to be all right. The Germans aren't eager to get out into the terrain at night, and besides, what could happen to us, since we pulled the whole thing off with a clear head, and even with a date like today's? You'll have to wait over eleven years for another one like that."

Indeed. It dawned on me that ever since midnight, spent somewhere over the Tatras, we were in the fourth of April, nineteen forty-four: 4.4.44.

Five

Salamander, the Conspirator

Much to Salamander's visible relief, we arrived "at home" at last.[1] Our hosts were unbelievably cordial and hospitable without a trace of anxiety or calculation. They were just happy that the wait was over — and they'd been waiting since October.

We were both very moved. We could see pure, authentic service to Poland. Remembering my previous stay in Poland, I promised Salamander that we'd be received this way everywhere we went.

"Well, let's eat something and get some sleep!" But it was hard getting to sleep. So many vivid impressions — and Salamander couldn't stop talking. Our beds were right next to each other; we covered up tight in our blankets, looked at the ceiling and talked till it was almost dawn.

It wasn't until morning that it fully dawned on us that we were really in Poland and ... under German control.

Breakfast — scrambled eggs and milk. Then it was time to get rid of all incriminating material — we gave the delegate from HQ everything that we weren't allowed to have on us, and reviewed the details of the trip to Warsaw. The horses were harnessed and ready. Our young hosts, Jolanta and Jerzy, would travel with us, guiding us in our first steps, helping with everything.

We found out that two hundred armed policemen were out hunting for the parachute jumpers, and looking for the equipment that had been dropped in. Our hosts were laughing about it. They knew perfectly well that everything had already been stashed away without a trace. We were laughing too, because we had to — and because we trusted them. Off we went, in a little buggy with two brown horses, snug in our blankets on a frosty ride of several kilometers' length. The marvelous Polish air! We could take deep breaths and fill our chests with it.

We got on an electric train for Warsaw. Lots of people. With greedy ears and eyes, we took in the Polishness of every face, every sentence, every curse uttered against the Germans. With a smirking kind of disbelief, I recalled the previous night's car trip from Bari to Brindisi and the flight over the Adriatic, the Balkans, the Hungarian plain and the Slovakian mountains, last night's fairy tale above the Tatras, escaping the German fighter, and ... the jump. Could this possibly all be true?

I was abruptly brought down to earth when someone right next to me said the word *desant*. (It's curious that the Polish word *desant*, meaning "parachute mission," was used to describe not the mission itself, but rather the person taking part in it — rather similar to the way that, ever since 1939, the word *Soviet* meant a Soviet soldier.) After a moment of feeling very uneasy, but also distinctly amused, I listened in on the conversation about our parachute mission. Next to me a "well-informed" guy from Warsaw explained to several people that the "Polish Carpathian Parachute Brigade," or at least one division of that brigade, had landed last night near Dębe Wielkie. A lady sitting across from him was telling her younger companion that parachute silk made the most beautiful and longest-lasting lingerie. Our guardians, the nice young couple that was guiding us to Warsaw, gave us broad smiles, elbowing each other and quite pleased. Finally our guardian angel couldn't stand it any more and leaned over to tell us, "You gentlemen can find out a lot of interesting things here!"

Our other guardian angel couldn't stand it any more either; she butted in on the two ladies' conversation — "What are you talking about, ten square meters! A normal parachute has a surface of about fifty square meters — and there are larger ones!" She blabbed out everything she'd learnt over breakfast from the "parachute theoretician." And as pretty as she was, she had learnt a lot.

* * *

We were in Warsaw at noon. We beat every record in getting from the drop zone to the capital. JHR can relish setting one more record — maybe it's only in the Polish Underground, but still....

Of course, the credit goes not to us but above all to the base in Italy, which really gave us the very best drop spot and took care of the logistics at the outpost — admirably organized. And then these two, who steered us right to Marszałkowska Street. Just think of it! Yesterday we were in Bari and Brindisi, last night above the Tatras, and at noon today we're in Warsaw. JHR remembered me telling him about my first mission and the ensuing "Concerto for Four Colts," and about how many days and nights it had taken us to get to Warsaw that time, back in 1941. He talked about it and added, "Quite a difference, wouldn't you say? It's going pretty smoothly."

Five. Salamander the Conspirator

At the train station in Warsaw, we said good-bye to our kind, brave hosts, the first we'd met from the ranks of the Polish Underground. We went to our contact point. I left Salamander on Marszałkowska Street and went alone to such and such a floor. Everything was in order, the password and response worked out. I went back to get JHR, and together we got settled in our first secret Warsaw room. There was a brief conversation with the lady of the house.[2] Her eyes radiated joy. After a moment I made a phone call and raced off to the corner of Koszykowa and Niepodległości Streets, to one of my former safe-houses, to be with my family.[3] Everything was OK, thank God. I stashed all the things there that I had kept secret even from our own guys (for fear of the eternal rivalry between the army and the civilians — including encoded elements of the things I was supposed to relay from the government in London to the Chief Delegate and the National Unity Council) and returned to Marszałkowska Street to see Salamander.

Miss Marysia treated us to a magnificent Warsaw luncheon. She'd been waiting with it since the previous autumn in a state of action alert, but even so everything was great, fresh and tasty in the best Polish style. Both of us were feeling fine, although I suspect that our kind hostess, enthused though she was that her "birdies" had finally landed, had a hard nut to crack during that luncheon. I saw how she kept looking furtively over at Salamander out of the corner of her eye, and I felt that she was doing every imaginable mental exercise to try and guess who this unusual paratrooper might be. She couldn't do it, and neither could "Aunt Antosia,"[4] the unforgettable specialist handling parachute teams, who had come running over during our meal after she'd been notified by phone. We had proof that they hadn't figured out who he was when, a couple of days later, we heard about a rumor making the rounds of the Warsaw underground, to the effect that Professor Kot had been flown in. JHR got mad as hell and wanted to write a letter of clarification on the spot, addressed to the underground press of every political persuasion; he wanted the BBC to run a story about the "world's oldest paratrooper," but we talked him out of it rather forcefully. He would come back time and again to these magnificent conspiratorial ideas — more about this later — but always without result. I suspect that at moments like those, he thoroughly detested me.

After our lunch at Miss Marysia's, "Auntie" split us up. We were set up in different parts of the city: Salamander in the city center on Wilcza Street, I in the Mokotów district on Narbutta Street — for a quarantine of several days, to get acclimated, get some rest and a little relaxation after all the excitement we'd been through. He would be taken care of by his "auntie," and I by mine. Both of the hideaways were magnificent — such extraordinary people!

My little den in Mokotów was at the apartment of three orphaned sisters, the Wiśniewskis. The eldest of them, Hanna, was unfortunately at the concentration camp in Oświęcim (Auschwitz) at the time. The head of the household was the middle sister, Eugenia (Dzida),[5] and the youngest, Zosia, was a student at the secret university. Dzida worked in some small firm and ... on the enormous black market. But the main occupation of both young women — or rather girls — was the Underground, the patriotic struggle. An unusual family, without parents but with a Polish motherland for which they were prepared to sacrifice everything.

Salamander and I got divorced, so to speak, but only temporarily; I visited him two days later and from that time on there was hardly a day that I didn't see him, some days for several hours or several times. And that's how we started a new underground life together — at least as far as I was concerned, but "not too very" underground on JHR's side. And that's how we came to spend several magnificent months together, filled with adventure as well as hard work, worries and joys, difficulties, undeniable dangers and the feeling of a job well done.

* * *

Blessed were those days, beginning with the lovely date 4.4.44. Blessed were the people who helped us: relatives of mine or not, friends and acquaintances and total strangers — the Polish people.

* * *

I started getting stage fright anticipating my meeting with the Chief Delegate, code named Sobol.[6] Would he be as cordial and direct as Wartski, his predecessor?[7] Would there be any sort of closer contact between us, which might make it easier for me to fulfill the difficult assignment "Stem" had given me? The task at hand was to convince the Chief Delegate, and through him the other leaders of the political underground, that they needed to get engaged in "saving part of the farm, if it's absolutely impossible to save the entirety, so as not to lose everything."

Waiting for my contact with the Delegature, I was constantly evaluating the notes I'd first made in London and then added to repeatedly in Bari. I couldn't rely solely on my memory; the subject I was carrying to Poland was at once too important and too broad. This is why I risked taking those notes along, even though it went against all the principles of the Silent Shadows. I had the scripts with me at all times, hidden under my socks on both shins, held down with garters. While writing them, I used something like a code, with abbreviations and such, to the point where I was sure (or maybe only deluding myself) that no one else could figure it out. And no one would ever get anything out of me against my will, with God's help, and even if they should ... brrr!! Anyway, there was no other way to do it. In spite of all my training, I hadn't had enough time in London to study the subject to the point where I could navigate it easily, using only my memory. I had to make a note of numerous dates, many names (even so much as an initial) of people I'd be talking to, the authors of memoranda, articles, names of places. Above all, I needed notes of the agreements reached at the Teheran Conference, and commentaries on that theme. I kept reliving my feeling of how tragic it all was, the things I'd been told in London and that I was now supposed to relay to people here. How were they going to cope with this? Would they prioritize the matter of saving the nation, of conserving its strength and its unity for the future? — or might they push for *non possumus*, with "history's judgement" of them on their minds?[8] In London, in circles describing themselves as purely independence-minded and as defenders of the entirety of the republic, terms such as "sellout" and "appeaser" (referring to the old Targowica group, who had been in favor of appeasing the Russians during Poland's partition) were being bandied about in reference to those who were looking for a way out of the snare into which the three great powers had pushed us. Wouldn't these arguments resonate deeply when they were brought up in the Underground? Wouldn't the political parties in the National Unity Council be afraid of that resonance? Would the leaders of the Underground be able to summon enough fortitude of spirit to weigh all the real facts *sine ira et studio*,[9] and then come to the best possible conclusion for the Polish nation — or at least, the least awful one? Would "Stem's" arguments get through to them? Would their talks with Salamander carry sufficient weight?

Now, staying at Dzida's, isolated in the farthest room of the safe house on Narbutta Street, I repeated to myself endlessly the lessons I'd memorized, checked my abbreviation codes and enciphered words, and ... waited. And grew impatient.

The first evening went by, and the entire next day — a day of isolation, as Antosia had said — and ... nothing. Well, not nothing, because there was the great hospitality of the two sisters, Dzida and Zosia. But as far as my business as a Silent Shadow, there was a lull; time was wasting and I was getting irritated. The morning of the following day went by, and again: nothing. I was sitting on pins and needles. When was somebody finally going to show up and take me to my contact with the Chief Delegate?

Antosia showed up in the afternoon. I breathed a sigh of relief. I told her on the spot that I was ready, and asked to be taken wherever I needed to go, or be given an address and a password. I joked that I had been sufficiently isolated already. But Antosia cut me off right away:

"You're not going anywhere, Sir. Please write a report of your flight from Italy to Poland. The leader of the courier cell at AK Headquarters wants it from you as the team leader of the Salamander mission..."

"Oh, so that's what it's all about! Perfect. I'll write that report right away."

"I'll wait here and take it back with me."

Handing her a sheet of ripped-out notebook paper with my hurriedly compiled report, I asked Antosia again for some contact with the Delegature, but she answered curtly that it wouldn't be today. Isolation! Rest!

I remarked with a snort that I had been doing nothing but resting in isolation in Bari for a whole month, but that didn't make any impression on her. She hadn't had any subordinates since October of the previous year, and she liked giving orders. She put away the sheet of paper and got ready to leave.

"And how's my subordinate?" I managed to ask. "Is he in isolation all the time, too?"

"That's right. And while he's resting in isolation, he's doing a fair job of drinking," she laughed. And then she was off.

I was disconsolate. How come those guys at the Delegature were in no apparent hurry? We're wasting time, day after day. They are! And it's not just me waiting, but Salamander as well, and he's so much more important than all the people sent over previously by the government. Could it be that they didn't know about him being here? Impossible! Surely there must have been a telegram from London in the matter of our mission — that it had finally happened. Or maybe there were some sort of technical obstacles? I hardly thought so. It seemed, as I noted with approval, that from the technical standpoint, the Underground was in far better shape now, in 1944, than it had been two years back — it had matured, so to speak. The organization of our reception detail, codenamed Clock; the transfer of the Silent Shadows from the outskirts of Minsk Mazowiecki to Warsaw; the rapid and seamless integration of Salamander and myself into the Underground — all these things bore witness to great progress on our side. There was no comparison to the period of 1941–1942. And there was something else: various messages from the Underground to the government indicated that they were resentful in Warsaw of the London side, for keeping the Delegature informed too rarely and too late about the current political situation. They felt that the laconic (by necessity) radio messages weren't enough, that they needed more frequent live contact with well-informed emissaries. Well, please! Here are your live contacts, two of them at once, it's even the first all-civilian parachute mission in the annals of the Underground, with two political emissaries, and they can't seem to score a clandestine meeting.

I decided not to wait any longer. The next morning, pretending that I was just going to the church of the Holy Redeemer (it was Good Friday, after all), I hurried right after Mass to that first contact point of ours, on Marszałkowska Street, not far from the Alleys, as Warsaw's biggest thoroughfare is known. I know it was against regulations, but I decided to risk it. And it worked out! The nice, smiling woman who owned that apartment was at home, and received me graciously. Surely without knowing that she was going to annoy the dreaded Antosia, she gave me the address where Salamander was staying, as well as the password.

I went there right away. It wasn't far. A slightly tipsy Salamander cheered up when he saw me. He, too, complained about the time we were losing, but he didn't see any other way out other than to wait. He even advised me to get back to Mokotów, because there could be a contact from the Delegature at any moment, "and they'll surely show up at your place sooner than mine."

He was right. Right after noon, someone came over to Dzida's and said when and where "that man" was to report, and what he was to ask about at the door. The "when" was that same afternoon. Finally! I reported there with my heart pounding. And as for the password, I didn't need it, because the door was opened by none other than Marta.[10] I was overcome with joy, deep in my soul and mirrored on my face, and she was quite thoroughly pleased to see me, too. From her joyful smile, I thought I could foretell an auspicious future for our conspiracy.

I knew Marta well, from my first sojourn in the Underground in 1942. She worked in the Delegature, back in the time that Wartski and his Chief of Staff, Roman, were in office.[11] They weren't around any more, but she — thank God — was at her post. Wartski, I knew, had gone off to the Great Hereafter. Roman, on the other hand, who had been unkindly viewed even during Wartski's tenure as a busybody and meddler, resigned (or rather, was made to resign) after Wartski's successor, Wernic,[12] took over, and returned to his work in the Triangle, i.e., the Peasant Party. He was hardly missed at the Delegature.

Marta and I talked about these and many other matters while waiting for her new boss, Grabowiecki, the Chief of Staff.[13] This man, the successor to Roman, had been his deputy in 1942, so I knew him a little. I was counting on him to set up a meeting with the Chief Delegate at once for Salamander and me. He let me down.

Grabowiecki was admittedly happy to see me, but when I asked him for a meeting with the Chief Delegate, he spread open his hands. He asked me to be patient; he made promises. Mainly, though, he asked about Salamander. He was awfully curious about him, but he didn't find out much from me. Looking a little lost, he invited both of us over for lunch the next day. For the meantime, he recommended that I discuss all strictly technical matters with Marta.

"I know from the telegrams, it must have been back in February or March, that you will have lots of such matters, Sir," he said, "scouting, the Northern Route, Outpost W, well, I don't remember it all...."

"But the most important thing," I said, "is to bring the Chief Delegate and the National Unity Council up to date on the talks we've had with the Allies on the subject of Polish-Soviet relations. This is why I'm so keen to meet quickly with the Chief Delegate."

"Yes, yes! We'll set it up as quickly as we possibly can. And in the meantime, so that you don't lose any time, take care of technical matters with Marta. And you can start your, ah, activities."

This wasn't difficult, because everything was easy with Marta. I relayed all the messages from London to her, gave her the elements of our new and more sophisticated code, and discussed a lot of matters that were meant to improve radio communications between London and the Delegature.

Marta promised me she'd line up contacts with the political parties, the Boy Scouts and Girl Scouts of the *Szare Szeregi*, scouts from regular Boy Scout troops across Poland, and the *Wigry* units[14]; she hinted at a possible helper in the "construction of the Northern Road," having the "stealth" pseudonym Drogowski.[15] She told me that as soon as the Army had transferred to the Delegature all the items I had brought over and deposited at the landing outpost — money belts, the exploding can lined with mail, and so on — I would be summoned at once to help open up that dangerous can, and then we'd talk about the rest of it.

Marta and I didn't get to take care of everything in time; someone was already waiting for her. To be continued the next day, fairly early in the morning. And maybe I'd be able to get through to the Chief Delegate more quickly after all, through Marta.

The way it worked out, I wasn't able to meet the Chief Delegate, but someone else was able to meet me. Marta had been asked to set up a contact between myself and Nowak.[16]

Two years earlier, I had been in close contact with him and with his kindhearted, bravehearted better half, Zosia. Buka and I had had numerous conversations with him back then; we were even invited to some well-attended

Bogus work permit made out to "Marek Jurkiewicz" and identifying his occupation as "office employee" (courtesy MHPRL Warsaw).

dinners. Nowak was always curious about all things underground; he liked to be — and was — well-acquainted with what was going on. As the chief of the Directorate of the Civil Resistance, he had his own radio contact with London. And among other things, he supplied news updates from inside Poland to Radio Station Świt, thereby confirming the widely-held belief that that radio station was operating out of Poland and was indeed a secret underground broadcast.

My conversation with Nowak was a long one. We walked along Koszykowa Street, then Wilcza, then Chałubinskiego, until my legs hurt. Of course, we talked about "Anusia" (meaning Radio Station Świt), since I was the only member of the editorial team in country, and was therefore able to tell our most important supplier of news from Poland how things were going in England, and how we valued the underground element of our station. I told him about our work over there in England; I connected individual editorial comments to their authors (first names only, no last names), told him who was responsible for which section, bragged shamelessly that the Świt station signal (the song "*Bartoszu, Bartoszu, Don't Lose Hope*," played on a block flute) was my idea and my performance ... but Nowak was listening only as if out of courtesy; he must have been absent-minded, or something? Finally, he said that we'd discuss matters pertaining to "Anusia" separately some other time, "preferably in the company of Zosia," and that maybe we'd even listen to a broadcast together and then.... Other matters were also left for later, because right then he wanted to find out about Salamander. That was why he had come.

"Stem" had authorized me to relay his opinion about Salamander to trusted individuals in Warsaw, and that list included Nowak's name. So I told my partner in conversation everything I knew from the Prime Minister, and also described my talks with

Bogus travel permit, authorizing "Marek Jurkiewicz" to travel to Minsk Mazowiecki for "important family matters" (courtesy MHPRL Warsaw).

JHR in Bari, our flight, the jump, his unmatched boldness, night blindness, everything. He listened voraciously, constantly asking new questions, and finally he asked me to arrange a meeting somehow between him and Salamander. I promised to do so, knowing that this was something Salamander wished for as well, for he'd already known about Nowak in London and had asked me about him, too.

So it came to a meeting — and not just once — between Nowak and Salamander. Several of them took place in my presence, but that was later — let's not get into the future.

Salamander and I had an appointment to see Grabowiecki, the Chief of Staff, at noon. I was looking forward to this meeting, since I promised myself it would lead at last to a speedy contact with the Chief Delegate. I had gotten hungry anyway, and tired from my long conversation on the march with Nowak. But I still had to drop in and pick up Salamander, so I hopped into a bicycle rickshaw, and it was by this same means of locomotion, much to Salamander's delight, that we rode off in the direction of ... lunch.

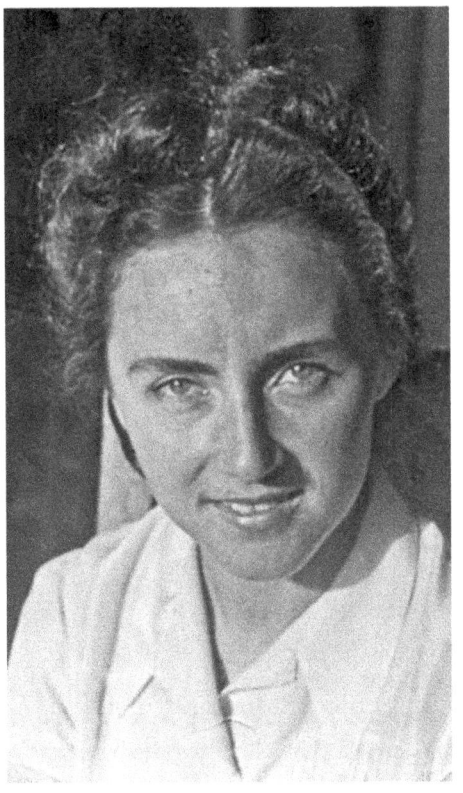

Hanka Śpiewakówna (later Mittelstaedt), the author's cousin, in Warsaw, ca. 1943 (Chciuk-Celt Family Archives).

The restaurant was cozy and quiet, the food was excellent, but from the point of view of the two emissaries, our lunch was not a success at all. Grabowiecki was interested in Salamander and London. Salamander asked him lots of questions about Warsaw, and I was like a fifth wheel, and a squeaky one at that. I was very unhappy when Grabowiecki told us right at the start that our meeting with the Chief Delegate couldn't happen until after the Easter holidays, meaning the day after tomorrow at the earliest.

During the holidays, I twice met with Salamander alone. Among other things, I led him to my family safe house, to my real aunt, Rela, and my real cousin, Hanka. They got to like "Uncle" on the spot, and agreed — to his great joy — that "in case anything happened" he would have a *pied-a-terre* at their place. And after that we often shared that magnificent family hideaway. It was located close to just about anywhere, the quiet was ideal, and no one in the Underground knew anything about it — unless I wanted anyone to know about it. I gave out the address and password only in exceptional cases. In 1942 this had been my House of the Quiet Conspiracy — now it was ours — at the corner of Independence and Koszykowa. I had two secret stashing places there — one close to hand, in the sofa; the other more substantial, specially built by the wall under the floor in "my" room. It was opened using a thin, stiff flat wire, which was placed into a virtually invisible opening in the corner floorboard; upon turning the wire, a small hidden lock would open and the floorboard could be removed with ease. There was a fair-sized hole underneath, with room for a file folder full of papers, and a package of cash, and a small camera, and even a Colt with a spare clip. Salamander saw it once and couldn't stop marveling.

With the help of the Delegature — in spite of the holidays — a new apartment was prepared for Salamander which was "legal" from the Underground's point of view. He used it rarely, preferring our House of the Quiet Conspiracy, where I, too, would often stop by, and where I spent the night with him more than once. He really liked the friendly, homey atmosphere that prevailed there.

I was counting on a meeting with the Chief Delegate on the Tuesday after Easter. Nothing came of it; he wasn't in Warsaw. During this time I was only put in contact with the head of the courier cell at AK HQ, and he interrogated me in connection with the report I'd submitted about the team on Operation Salamander, the flight, Outpost "Clock" where we'd landed, and so on. And the ever-dependable Marta gave me the contacts she'd promised, consisting for the present of the Girl Scouts and the "Triangle," i.e., Peasants' Party.

Salamander and I didn't get our meeting with Sobol until the 12th of April, or eight days after we landed in Poland and got to Warsaw. But I only took part in this conversation briefly, at the very start, upon which the Chief Delegate turned me over to Marta, telling her to set me up with vital Underground contacts connected to my mission, after which he stayed on with Salamander alone. They didn't talk for long, though. The Chief Delegate asked me to take Salamander wherever he needed, take good care of him and bring him back in two days' time for further talks, and that I should come back the next day to "finalize my work schedule."

So, on April 13th, I finally got to have what was basically my first conversation with the Chief Delegate. Right at the start, I told him about the ten days' lost time. He looked at me a little surprised and replied, "That was the way circumstances worked out." And then he proceeded directly to the main point of our meeting (in his estimation), namely to the person of Salamander. I wanted to start with the subject that "Stem" had placed closest to my heart: the consequences of Teheran. But Sobol put that off "until later." He did, however, ask me to bring Salamander by that same afternoon ("so as not to lose any more time") and in the meantime he wanted to know as much as possible about the man.

I spent a long time relaying "Stem's" thoughts on this subject to him. He had plenty of questions. Evidently he wanted to prepare for a second, longer conversation. At the conclusion of our meeting, he said, "Well, if that's the way it is, then it's a good thing that this Salamander has come here. And I see from all this that malicious tongues have been doing him harm."

Finally I could move to the subject of Teheran. To get the Chief Delegate to hear me out in this regard, I attested that I had more up-to-date news from London than did Salamander, and that the news was very unsettling. So he asked me for a brief report. With a visibly gloomy expression, he listened to my (or rather "Stem's") post-Teheran account. At times he asked questions, mostly relevant but sometimes almost naïve; then he'd get up from the table and pace nervously around the room; then he'd sit back down and hold his head in his hands.

He said: "Here, on our land, on the very heels of one invader, another one comes riding in; we don't know but that he mightn't even be worse, and those guys in the West are washing their hands of it. They sing songs about their Eastern Ally, forgetting all about their ... First Ally."

"That's exactly why," I replied, "the Prime Minister feels that we should ... more than that, he calls on us, over there and over here, to think about what possibilities we might still have, how to proceed so that we choose the lesser evil."

"There's nothing good left to come up with?"

"The Prime Minister is afraid we're pinned to the wall..."

"But it's the Anglo-Saxons who are pinning us to the wall, too ... can't we appeal to them? Could we not stir up the sentiment of the entire free world? Surely the West must know what Bolshevism is?"

"They don't want to know, so long as they need Soviet soldiers, so that American and British soldiers don't have to die."

I told Chief Delegate Sobol about the efforts of the Polish government, the countless talks with politicians in England and America, articles in the press, speeches (both *pro* and *contra*) in the House of Commons, Churchill's brutality, Eden's evasiveness, and the poorly masked indifference of the Americans.

I went on: "In their countries, they easily manipulate public opinion with the argument that, thanks to the Soviets, less Anglo-Saxon blood will be spilled, so we should stroke Stalin and pet him, and not oppose him in any way unless the immediate national interests of Great Britain or the United States are at stake. In this context, Poland doesn't count, nor even our whole part of Europe; in this context, the voices of our British and American friends, the ones who bring up moral arguments in our defense, can scarcely be heard at all."

"And how can I choose the lesser evil here," Sobol said, "when there's nothing but the worst news from every side?"

"Sir, the Prime Minister has requested that you have a thorough discussion of this whole matter as soon as possible with the leaders of all the political parties in the Underground, and let London know how the country stands. This will help the government in its talks with the Allies, in looking for solutions. In order to familiarize the leaders of the Underground political parties with the post–Teheran situation, I'm prepared to work up a detailed briefing — I have my notes — and present it to a meeting of the National Unity Council or possibly to your Council of Ministers."

The Chief Delegate didn't answer those words for a long time. He paced back and forth in that smallish room; sometimes he'd look at me as if with sightless eyes. Finally he stood still and said:

"I'll still want to hear what Salamander says. And you, Sir, please prepare that presentation in full detail and give it to me; after that we'll have a talk about your participation in a session of the National Unity Council."

Unfortunately, I never did get to participate. It wasn't until the 18th of April that I handed Sobol the first part of my presentation — I couldn't get to see him any sooner. The first part was an account of the post–Teheran talks that Mikołajczyk, Foreign Minister Romer and Ambassador Raczyński had with Churchill, Eden and other English statesmen. He read through the script quickly, then was silent for a long time; he returned to reading my presentation and then asked me to prepare the next part of the report, placing particular emphasis on talks between the Polish government and American politicians (Biddle, Schönfeld)[17] as well as the plans for Mikołajczyk's trip to Washington, which Roosevelt kept putting off. After immersing himself anew in my script, the Chief Delegate acknowledged my "detailed presentation" and asked for details of the Moscow and Teheran Conferences, as well as our public discussions with the Soviets in January of that year. But he never did say another word about my taking part in a session of the National Unity Council or his Council of Ministers.

Sobol didn't get to read the second part of my document until the 26th of April, and I still had the third part to put in order. That one contained a detailed account of the Polish government's talks with the Czechoslovakian President, Beneš,[18] as well as Mikołajczyk's remarks pertaining to Beneš' trip to Moscow, which he considered tantamount to splitting up Poland and Czechoslovakia before they ever got together. Sobol didn't get a chance to read that third part (and discuss it with me) until the 4th of May, or exactly a month after my arrival in Poland.

I was awfully frustrated by the slow pace of the Delegature's work, and this at such a crucial point, at such a dangerous bend in our road to freedom. I got into bitter conversations on this subject with Salamander, telling him that I was getting the impression that the Chief Delegate kept putting off dealing with this problem, not knowing where to start or how to manage it. He very clearly didn't want to bring it up at the National Unity Council. He praised me *ex post* for my detailed post–Teheran treatise, but he was in no hurry at all to study it in depth and discuss it, and hadn't as yet set up any participation of mine in a meeting of the National Unity Council or a session of his Council of Ministers. A whole month had gone by since we'd arrived in Poland. The Underground was still unaware of the real situation; they didn't know what position the western allies were really taking concerning our future, in the face of the Soviet Army's entry onto Polish soil. What kind of independence were the countries in our part of Europe supposed to have, the way the Allies saw it, when they had been relegated by them to the "Soviet sphere of influence?"

Salamander shared my unease. The Chief Delegate talked to him, sure, but he gave the impression that he didn't understand the gravity of the situation. Perhaps he felt that we were portraying the situation in overly dark colors, and therefore he didn't even register what he was being told? Salamander accepted the Delegature's opinion as to the Polish Worker's Party (PPR), that it was a small party without popular support, but close-knit and operating with powerful propaganda. His opinion differed from that of the Chief Delegate in so far as JHR felt that the PPR should be absorbed precisely because it was small, whereas the Chief Delegate felt the opposite, because the moment the true situation was revealed, Russia would in any case have to rely on a cohesive and well-organized clandestine movement centered on the Delegature and the Home Army.

Luckily, during that entire month of "hunting for Sobol," I wasn't wasting any time. I set forth into ... the Underground. Some of my old contacts from 1942 were still intact. Two magnificent and unforgettable young women — Black Wanda and Nika[19] — brought me up to speed quickly and ably: the former with Scouting matters, the latter with the Peasant Battalions and the farmers' concerns. Grabowiecki was very helpful in getting me to the political parties, but Marta was the most helpful of all, whenever she was needed.

But there were so many gaps now in underground Warsaw compared to two years back, so many chipped spots and losses! During these first steps of mine, it seemed like with every step I was running into ... emptiness. People would say, that one's not around any more, that guy died, that woman's at Auschwitz. Wartski had died; the fearless Nestorowicz (Colonel Alojzy Horak) was gone forever;[20] the head of the Polish Boy Scouts, Father Jan Mauersberger, had died; the magnificent leader of the *Szare Szeregi*, Florian Marciniak (known as Krzemień) was gone, no one knowing whether he was still alive in some Gestapo dungeon. The same was true of the top Commander of the Home Army, General Stefan Rowecki (aka Grot), and many, many others. There were losses among my Silent Shadow colleagues, political couriers. Filip was killed in a street battle, Andrzej was lost en route to London,[21] Wera was never found.[22] No one had any news yet concerning Włodek, who had been arrested in Hungary in 1942.[23] And what about Buka, my concert buddy in the *Concerto for Four Colts*? We were pretty sure that the Germans had hauled him off to Berlin and murdered him there. In the *Szare Szeregi*, a whole column of the bravest Boy Scouts was gone; they'll go down in scouting history (and Polish history) as "Stones for the Rampart."

A wasteland was left — that was the way I felt at the start, time and again. But later, with time, I began to see more clearly that wonderful new plants were appearing in this desert landscape: flowers, bushes, trees — a new, young, green forest was popping up, reaching toward the sunlight of freedom.

* * *

JHR was able in short order to liberate himself from the care of his Home Army "Aunties" as well. And since he hadn't broken his legs, he climbed right into the thick of the Warsaw conspiracy with both feet. As will become clear later on in this story, his prediction that he would be holding talks while in bed wasn't entirely baseless.

For the moment, however, this was not a threat. For now, his legs were in good standing order and it was a good thing that nothing had happened to him during the parachute jump. He surely would have lain there, somewhere in the vicinity of our reception outpost, and that wasn't a particularly safe place to be for the first few days after we got there. Despite mounting scrupulous searches and sending out a gang of informants, the Germans didn't find anything and didn't catch anyone. The valuable equipment that we had brought over from Italy had been masterfully hidden and secured by the AK, after which it appeared in Warsaw, delivered in its entirety into the hands of the addressees. The Army took the weapons and ammunition, radio gear, parachutes and enormous sums of money. The Government Delegature received a major amount of mail, as well as radio equipment and money, too. JHR and I got our own things, and money for ourselves for our stay in Poland. With a feeling of great relief, I took a large lacquered briefcase from the distribution point and carried it to the nearest safe house. It was filled with my hieroglyphic-like notes from London, taken during the time I was preparing for my flight to Poland, as well as a package with money that all kinds of people had given me before leaving England, entreating me in the name of all the Saints not to refuse them and to give the money to their impoverished relatives back home. I didn't refuse them. There was plenty of drudgery and even danger involved, but I was elated that fate had allowed me to take part in "doing good deeds" like that.

Literally and figuratively, I had dropped out of the sky bearing gifts. What a wonderful feeling, to be the Good Witch from the most marvelous of fairy tales! Saving people from material poverty, bringing them hope, pouring out whole golden handfuls of good news about their nearest and dearest — about whom they had only known that they were alive somewhere in the wide world, and sometimes even that hadn't been confirmed in years. When I got back from my trips to the country and told my acquaintances in turn what those meetings with their families had looked like, they showered me with thanks. Now, looking back on those wonderful moments of bringing people joy, I think that I should thank all those people who simply placed their trust in me personally and thereby gave me the opportunity to be noble and good and a bringer of happiness.

Although my role as Salamander's guardian officially ended the moment I handed him over to Antosia, I didn't stop being vividly interested in his fate and safety. I helped him figure out where the safe houses were, I made it a little easier for him to meet certain important people in the Underground, I was his go-between in some black market money-changing operations (we got our pay from Headquarters in dollars, which we'd change step by step into the current currency). JHR not only asked me — in the name of friendship now, not duty — to remain in permanent contact with him, but also stuck to me tightly, the way a kid holds on to his mother's skirt. He considered me an indisputable authority on the Underground (at least at the start), and would only occasionally get indignant when, worried about his safety after all, I would chew him out the way a professor might chew out an unruly student — for disregarding the matter of his own safety as well as that of others by revealing his identity to people we weren't sure about, by arranging lavish dinners at the finest restaurants, by rambling around all over town, and so on.

He himself knew how many stupid things of this sort I had talked him out of, how many extravagances I was able to persuade him to forgo or cancel. And only I myself know how many times I straightened out his twisted path in Warsaw, without his knowledge and contrary to his intentions.

Unfortunately, that didn't always work out. The farther you get into the forest, the more trees there are. You truly couldn't see the forest for the trees! The deeper Salamander delved into the Underground life, the more he started to meddle in it. He had always been something of a prankster, and although he wasn't willing to sacrifice everything, he was willing to sacrifice a lot for the sake of a good laugh. Once, you see, he came upon the highly dangerous idea of gathering about fifteen people from the highest levels of the Underground in one tavern. He declared to each of the invitees that the luncheon would be "a threesome with my young parachute guide, Marek"—so no one suspected him of calling together a major Underground meeting. And when he invited me, he declared innocently,

"You've got to come, Sir, we'll have the greatest time ever."

"What are we going to be having such a great time with?"

"Looking at the faces of the revelers."

"Does that mean you looking at my face, and me looking at yours?"

"No, Marek. It means you and I will get a kick out of seeing the expressions on the faces of these guys:"—and here, laughing merrily, he started listing the code names of all the invited guests.

A chill ran over me, all the way down to the roots of my hair. I listened in horror to the familiar code names, and made a mental note that if the Germans should happen to drop in at that restaurant and arrest this *congressus vivorum*,[24] the entire Polish underground machine would screech to a halt for a fairly long time, and then would only slowly return to its previous level of efficiency. So I tried with all my might to prevent this dangerous (and utterly unnecessary) undertaking, using every argument I could think of. And even though I think I managed to convince him in the end, he still wouldn't admit it (he rarely liked to concede that someone else was right). He simply declared that the luncheon couldn't be called off anymore, as it was meant to take place in a few hours and that meant there wasn't enough time to warn everybody, even if he knew all their addresses.

"So I can stand in front of the restaurant and give our apologies to the guests one by one, and tell them the luncheon is off," I said.

"You don't even know them all."

"So you do it, then."

"I wouldn't dream of it. This luncheon is going to be a great event in the annals of the Polish Underground. People will get together in a larger group, they'll be able to speak more freely, they'll be rid — if only for a few hours — of the trauma of always having to speak in whispers, and ... of the custom of answering certain questions with only silence or the one word: secret!"

"But in that restaurant they'll speak even more softly, or be all the more silent — that is, if they don't leave that dangerous meeting at once, as soon as they figure out what's going on."

"They won't leave, and they'll speak with normal voices. Marek," he added, with a note of feigned sternness, "please don't forget that I'm an expert at these underground meetings."

"?"

"Oh, yes! Because I know plenty of authentic waiters here in Warsaw, from before the war. And that is the most discreet creature under the sun."

"Well then, what is this all about?" I asked impatiently.

"I ran into just such a waiter, and together with him I'm organizing this reception."

"Together with a waiter?"

"That's right, with a real, authentic waiter. The height of elegance, combined with the most select Underground contacts. A separate room, just like for lovers; ring the bell for service; magnificent eats and even better drinks. And I'll vouch for it that nothing happens to anyone, and everyone will feel great. Including you."

"I won't be feeling any kind of way, because I'm not coming."

"Aha, my dear Mr. Marek, fear has got a hold of you. Scared shitless!"

"I'm in no way scared shitless, it's just that this whole thing doesn't make the slightest sense. Do you really not understand that, Sir?"

"I only understand this much, that my fearless parachute commander, my guide to every underground alley and dungeon, has gone and chickened out, and that's that!"

I was furious with the little old man. I was silent for a long time, debating in my mind whether I shouldn't stand in front of the restaurant after all and "uninvite" the invited guests. However, I had to ditch that plan since Salamander would reveal neither the place nor the exact time of the luncheon, despite some pretty crafty questions from me.

"I'll only tell you when you give me your word that you won't pull any stupid numbers like stopping the guests in front of the joint."

Finally, I got an idea. It seemed to me that Salamander's own eccentricity would knock him off balance and force him to call off this orgy himself. I declared that I would indeed come to the luncheon out of concern for the lives of the invited guests, but that I'd be armed from head to toe and accompanied by an armed escort. Even so, that nasty geezer enthusiastically accepted my project.

"Great!" he shouted, "excellent idea! Just make sure our distinguished guests don't notice your arsenal. As for your armed cowboys, we'll seat them in the main room at a separate table."

Seeing that I had gotten serious, he added soothingly, "Well, don't get too worried. I know I'm an illiterate as far as Underground matters are concerned, but even so, it seems to me that I've thought the whole thing through in the most minute detail. So please listen now and give me a proper assessment..." and he proceeded to roll out the entire plan for the banquet.

The waiter was fully reliable and devoted. We'd have a separate room with a second exit to the courtyard, and through the courtyard to a different street. The guests were asked to be strictly punctual, with their arrivals scheduled in 3- to 5-minute intervals. They'd be directed to the room by the waiter, and be greeted there by Salamander as well as the growing group of guests, etc., etc.

"But if you think it's indicated, by all means set up the bodyguards. I'll be treating them to lunch, however many of these cowboys there will be."

The luncheon was a stellar success and no one had so much as a hair hurt. And there were VIPs there: party leaders such as Marcin and Michniewski (code names),[25] various dignitaries from the Delegature. The bodyguard detail, put together by me and consisting of nothing but killer paratroopers, had absolutely nothing more to do than to eat lots of good food and drink a fine little toast to their unknown benefactor. The lads didn't ask a lot of questions, they ate as quietly as they had arrived, and on a signal from me, they marched off, each to his own work. But for all that, the invited guests did have really sheepish expressions at first. However, none of them wanted to expose themselves to accusations of being overly sensitive — just as it had been in my case — and everyone stayed. It was awfully Polish. We all showed a lot of military courage then, though none of us were guilty of displaying that more important, civilian kind.

Salamander was also right as to the conversations at the table. They really were interesting, sincere, even a little stormy at times, a little apprehensive; but in the end, they gave Salamander what he wanted: a cross-section of Underground thinking and the "averaged out" answers to a lot of his questions. And he construed his questions in such a way that it would be hard not to give a sincere answer in the presence of so many other matadors of underground life, who could correct any inaccuracies as to the conspiracy anytime, or even simply give an ironic smile. In a way, then, if it wasn't quite an Underground Sejm (that would be the National Unity Council, which had just been freshly formed, even if it was so long overdue — and they only did business behind closed doors) then it was at least something like the corridors of the Sejm.[26] And JHR had felt great in those corridors, practically since his childhood, and he could run the show *non plus ultra*.[27]

"I stripped the guys bare," he bragged later. "Did you notice, my dear Marek, that no one hid behind the veil of the Underground a single time, no one used the words 'top secret,' or 'confidential' or 'classified.' Thanks to that, I was able to find out more in two hours than I would have in two weeks of individual talks. We should organize little meetings like this more often, don't you think?"

"*Apage Satanas!*" ("Begone, Devil!") I replied, stepping back with my hand held out like a fortuneteller. "If you dare to do something of this sort another time, I'll disavow any knowledge of you, I'll disappear from your sight and send a telegram to Headquarters about the way you've been carrying on, and that's quite apart from the complaint I'll lodge at the very top of the Underground pyramid. And there, they'll find the appropriate way to ground you."

I had hit his weak point. I knew that the Chief Delegate had declined to take part in this luncheon meeting, and that he limited his contacts with Salamander to "strictly business" anyway. The same was true of the Commander of the AK (Home Army). That went for several others as well. Salamander knew that he couldn't use his backroom methods with everyone, every time. In any case, the truth be told, every one of his guests at that memorable luncheon told him only as much as they wanted to. It was only Salamander's impression that he had found out more than he normally would have. He'd simply found out faster.

When I told him that I was categorically opposed to any further tempting of fate and exposing of third parties to danger, when I demanded of him that he swear not to organize any similar luncheons or dinners, he made a long face and snorted:

"Well, then how many people will you allow me to see at one time?"

"Two at the most, with yourself as the third."

"Then that's the way it'll be, Mr. Dictator. I have a weakness for you and I surrender."

Both of us were busily getting increasingly active in the Underground. We both went underground. We blended into Warsaw life, not only in that not-quite-real, hard-to-understand wartime Warsaw, but also in that extraordinary place that never ceased to amaze us — seemingly carefree, a little like Wiech's popular column in the paper used to describe it before the war, a little bit of "what are you gonna do to me" and a little "leave me alone" —

and that truest Warsaw of all: fighting, giving its all in order to hold on, pull through, not let the enemy annihilate it, and win its freedom.

Sometimes we'd brush against each other, then again at times we both took part in this or that conversation. But for the most part, JHR took care of his business and I took care of mine. My assignments on this mission were substantial and varied, they took a lot of my energy and required making inquiries, contacts and so on — I didn't always have time to accompany Salamander and help him. Even so, we did meet often, mostly at the House of the Quiet Conspiracy, and when we did it was good, usually agreeable. He'd almost always bring some kind of treats — cakes, chocolates, a Burgundy or a Bordeaux — you could get anything in Warsaw if you had money, and the Dollar was trading high at the "Old Man on Narbutta Street" exchange. I would bring more concretely useful things to the family hideaway: bread, sausages, ham, cheeses. After "feasting with Uncle," as Hanka called it, JHR would smoke cigarette after cigarette, talking to the ladies, asking about this and that — about everything really, because he was interested in everything. Sometimes he'd play solitaire, and I'd take care of my encoded notes or — just to relax — I'd play the piano. Then JHR would shuffle over in my direction, stand next to me and say seriously:

"Rubinstein played that Waltz in C Sharp Minor a little better. You know how? In the second section he'd play it slowly at first, kind of thoughtfully, and then he'd speed it up."

"Yes," I'd say from the keyboard, "Rubinstein is a bit of a better pianist than I."

JHR would pretend not to catch the sarcasm, and after a while, listening to another little piece by Chopin, he'd go on: "That Etude in C Sharp Minor — you seem to like the key of C Sharp Minor, Marek — Rubinstein played that one better than you, too. After the reflective section, he'd get more songlike — there's supposed to be a storm!"

Hanka would crack up out loud, Rela would smile delicately (the way she does) and then Hanka would get deadly serious and say,

"I keep telling Marek the same thing, Uncle, that he'll never be any kind of Rubinstein or Paderewski, but he just keeps on banging away on those keys..."

It wasn't always so carefree with us, though. Often, Salamander and I would lock ourselves into a separate room and exchange views on general themes, mainly connected to our conversations with the Chief Delegate. With regard to the things we were both telling him — each of us separately — he behaved the same way, putting off until later the most important subject, Teheran, and "Stem's" urgent appeal to the National Unity Council and the

Five. Salamander the Conspirator

Council of Ministers to make a statement as to the current political situation, the concept of "saving part of the farm" if it was absolutely impossible to save it in its entirety, and saving the living substance of the nation. I was unsuccessful in my requests of Sobol to take me to a meeting of the Council of Ministers, so that I might read them my presentation. At first, I couldn't even get a meeting with the Chief Delegate's deputies, to wit, the Ministers Jasiukowicz, Bień and Pajdak. I did meet with them very late — too late — and that wasn't thanks to any contacts from the Chief Delegate. And they couldn't tell me anything binding or concrete. They wondered — especially Bień — why Sobol hadn't alerted them before.

Salamander had similar experiences in his talks with the Chief Delegate.

"It seems to me that he's waiting the Polish way — hoping that it'll work out somehow — and so he keeps putting everything off till later. He doesn't want to think, he won't allow himself the thought that our fate lies in the balance here."

The Chief Delegate let us know that he had some kind of information that would not confirm our bleak view. The Allies are going to give us up to the mercy of the Soviets? Well, how is that possible? The Allies aren't coming here with their armies to help us? Well, how come? They won't give any support to their first ally? You're telling me that not even our own Parachute Brigade is going to fight here? Because it'll be needed over there? How's that? And where are those assurances of theirs, the "shortest route"...?

One day I dropped in at my aunt's place. Salamander was sitting in the easy chair, holding his chin up with one hand. He looked at me and gave a sign for me to close the door to the other room, where Hanka was working at her workshop (she made money for survival by weaving homespun cloth) and said:

"My dear Marek! They want to murder me here."

"What? Who?"

"The Deuce."

"What deuce?"

"Section Two of the Home Army Central Command..."[28]

I couldn't believe what I was hearing. JHR had often made schoolboy jokes, but in the end I figured he wouldn't deliberately be making a fool of himself.

"Where did you get this information? Maybe it's a rumor?"

"It isn't a rumor. The report comes from a serious source."

"From what source? We need to inform the Chief Delegate."

"Exactly. And maybe you might find out something more from him. That's what I want to ask you to do, Sir. I know," JHR went on, "that various people from London have been seeking to have me liquidated in Poland — people who keep thinking I'm an English agent, or maybe a Soviet agent, and that I've flown to Poland to disarm the patriotic Underground and get them to toe the Communist line. You know what I've come here with, and the Chief Delegate knows it, too. And the Commander of the AK. They all know that I only want to convince them that in the future we're going to have to cooperate with the Communists, because the English aren't going to come here, but the Russians are. If we don't work something out with them somehow, it'll be a dreadful tragedy, because we know who Stalin is and what the NKVD is. The point is to get people here to try to understand that fact. And they want to murder me for that! For telling the truth, for warning them..."

I contacted the Chief Delegate without delay. Sobol confirmed the authenticity of the report of a planned hit on JHR.

"I've already taken steps to counteract this crime. I would never allow such an ignominious deed."

When I asked what those steps were, he replied that he had urgently requested a meeting with General Bór.

"When I presented the matter to him, he got mad as hell. He told me curtly that he would certainly and immediately put an end to this. This is impossible — Poles taking out ... Poles..."

After a while the Chief Delegate ordered that JHR should be informed — by me — that the Commander of the AK had taken the appropriate decision in this matter. He gave decisive orders — that is, a strict prohibition in this case — and threatened a court martial. Both Sobol and General Bór confirmed that the idea of killing JHR was born in London and had come to Warsaw in a telegram to Section Two.

After this failed attempt — luckily — on JHR's life, the Chief Delegate wanted to send him back off to London as quickly as possible, taking advantage of the new "air bridge" possibilities. Operation Bridge I (Wildhorn I), for which we had waited so long in Bari, had in fact been carried out: in the night of April 15/16, 1944, a Dakota had landed in the Lublin area with two Silent Shadows, and taken off again for London via Brindisi with five people, consisting of three officers and two political activists. JHR was also eager to get back quickly, to give people a picture of the situation in Poland.

Having to continually watch over Salamander's every step, and practically spying on him in order to protect him and others from the effects of his escapades — and simultaneously having plenty of my own time-consuming work to do — I started to lose some of my energy after working non-stop like this for a while. This is why my sadness over JHR's return to London was tempered significantly by a feeling of relief that he (and other people) wouldn't be in constant danger, and that I might get a little rest.

Salamander was to leave to country in the second half of May as a passenger on that famous (because it was to be the second in a row) "air bridge." He tried to convince me and my superiors that I should fly with him, but I was categorically opposed to it for what might be called fundamental reasons. First of all, I still had enough of my own regular work to last me at least a month; secondly, I was right in the middle of organizing the "Northern Road," i.e., a permanent route for couriers and mail through Pomerania (which had been added to the "Thousand-Year Reich") to Gdynia, and on from there to Sweden by coal-fired boat. So Salamander was given a different guardian angel by the AK — one who later turned out to play the role of a rather rotten angel. We said our heartfelt good-byes and agreed to rendezvous at the Dorchester at Park Lane,[29] and JHR drove off to Kraków, from where he would go to the Tarnów area, where they were building the bridgehead for the Second Bridge.

Six

The Tragedy of the Jews

Note: *This passage is excerpted verbatim from* By Parachute to Warsaw, *the author's 1945 English-language account of this mission. Used by kind permission of the original publisher, Dorothy Crisp & Co., Ltd., of London.*

The disappearance of the Jews is one of the strangest things about life in Poland today. Poles who left Poland in 1939 can hardly realize what it means. And even those who, like myself, went back during the war and were struck by their absence, could not conceive at first what lay behind it.

The Jews, who once formed such a typical feature of the Polish scene, simply do not exist. It is a fact. You cannot see them. And you will not find them, for they have been "liquidated" by the Germans in a way too terrible for words. By thousands on thousands, in the death trains, the extermination camps, the gas chambers and the gaping common graves, in Treblinka, Oświęcim and Majdanek, they have perished — until now almost none remain. Words are too weak to describe this kind of barbarism.

There are some survivors, of course. Some were in concentration camps like that at Łódź, where the prisoners worked for the Wehrmacht; but far more were in hiding among the Poles. People in Poland tried to help the Jews in every possible way, and the occasional cases of hostility towards them, occurring mostly among the so-called *Volksdeutsche*, were punished by the Underground immediately and severely.

Before my departure last spring, I talked with the chief of the Jewish Socialist organization, the *Bund*, and also with the chief of the United Zionist Organization, now called the Jewish National Committee.[1] They both asked me to stress that the Jews who were still in hiding were saved and could survive thanks only to the help and sympathy of Polish people throughout the country.

One of the Jewish leaders said to me:

Six. *The Tragedy of the Jews* 115

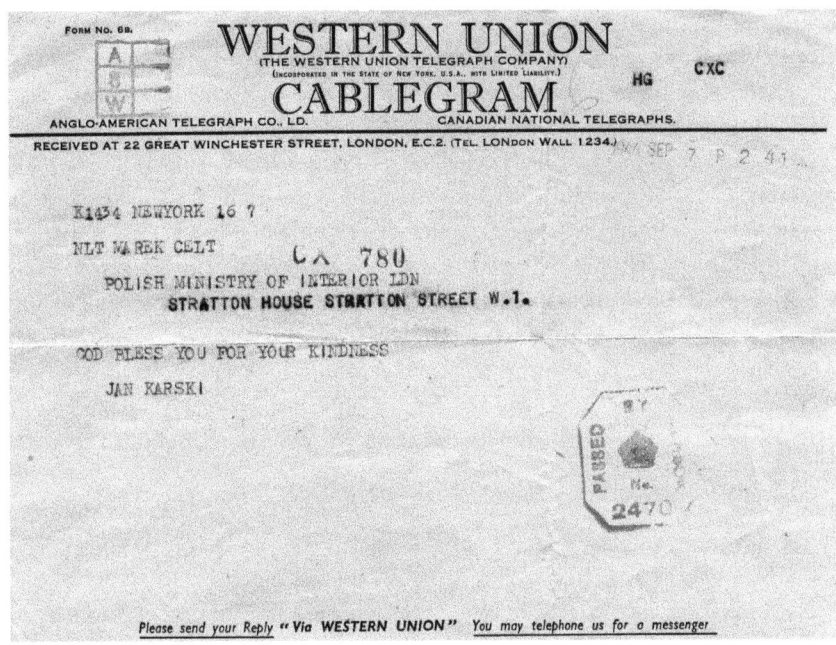

Personal telegram from Jan Karski to the author, dated September 7, 1944, with the message: "God bless you for your kindness." Both Karski and Celt had relayed first-hand reports of the Holocaust to the Allies (Chciuk-Celt Family Archives and MHPRL Warsaw).

"The Germans have killed almost all the Polish Jews and very many others from all over the world. They did not do it in one day, one month or even one year. They started in 1942 and they are still going on with it. It is total annihilation. All the time we have implored the world for help. And there has been no response, at least no effective response.[2] Help from outside did not come."

"And help from inside?" I asked.

"The help of the Polish people was limited by circumstances. As far as possible, it was given. We are the best proof of it, we," he pointed to his companion, "and all the others who remain."

He paused for a moment, and looked out from the window of the half-destroyed house where we had met. There lay the ruins of the ghetto.

"But what has been done will never be made good. It never can. So many lives! So many lives! ... "

I looked where he was looking. I had seen the ruins of the ghetto before, many times, and still I could never believe my eyes. This time again I was overcome by the horror of it. Ruins lay as far as the eye could reach, and around the ruins stretched the ghetto wall, still guarded by Germans.

Even now no one was allowed to pass it. The Germans had various reasons for this. From within you could often hear the thunder of mined houses crashing to the ground, and also the crack of rifle salvoes. You could see palls of smoke rising from the ruins; and when the wind blew the smoke towards you, you could smell the unmistakable odor of burning bodies. My meetings with the Chief Delegate and with the Jewish leaders were often interrupted by these sounds and these smells. I cannot easily forget the expression in the eyes of people about me at such moments. And they were accustomed to it. The Chief Delegate would stop talking. He would look at me, and his glance seemed to say:

"Listen, young man from the outside world! There, behind the wall, people are dying."

Once when the detonation of a long salvo had been followed by some twenty or more single shots, he actually said:

"You hear that? They are finishing off the wounded."

My first stay in Warsaw, in 1942, was before the destruction of the Ghetto, and twice I penetrated into its forbidden streets. On one of these occasions I saw the following incident — my own small eye-witness's testimony to the tragedy which preceded the Ghetto's final destruction.

A German patrol was walking along the street.[3] It stopped in front of a house. Some went in, and the rest remained outside. I was standing not far away in the company of a Polish policeman then on duty in the ghetto. He had a secret mission from the Underground to escort me there. Thus I could watch the Germans safely and undisturbed.

I do not know what happened inside the house. Suddenly a window on the third floor burst open, and a young Jewess, with two small children in her arms, flung herself out, uttering a terrible cry.

If I shut my eyes now, I can see the three bodies in the air. One of the children slipped from its mother's arms as it fell. The German nearest to me lifted his rifle, aiming so quickly and neatly that the sound of the shot merged with the thud of the bodies hitting the street.[4]

Seven

Patient Józef Brzoza

Right after JHR left, I returned to the normal treadmill of Underground matters: meetings, contacts, pumping information out of one place and pumping fresh information into another. From time to time I'd try to find out what was going on with Salamander, but I kept getting the same answer: "The bridge isn't built yet." Evidently the little old man had to endure anew those Italian days of waiting for a flight, only Polish-style this time. "Your little operation is off," he was told on a daily basis, and he'd get furious and pace around his hideaway fuming, in a futile search for a conversation partner and an even more futile search for those other specialties he'd had in Bari: fresh fruit, wine…. In one respect, he must surely have acknowledged that the wait was more bearable in Poland: the clear home-made firewater, or moonshine, which none of his whiskeys, gins or wines could ever replace in spite of it all. For if I haven't stated it clearly so far, then I'm telling you now that the old man enjoyed a drink, and this of all things was the area where he should have sought the record-breaker's laurels. But I must apologize, it's true that I've already compared him to Zagłoba….

After about three weeks, I got the news that the air bridge was a success. I even got word from Brindisi that everyone had arrived at the base safe and sound. My joy knew no bounds. I calculated the estimated length of JHR's flight from Italy to London, and arranged to be able to listen every day to the BBC's evening communiqués, in which JHR was to send me certain agreed-upon coded messages concerning my "Northern Road." Imagine, then, how astonished I was, how awfully stupid I felt, unable to believe my senses, when early the next morning there came a knock on the door of the apartment where I had my little family hideaway, and it was none other than JHR himself. My Cousin Hanka, who opened the door for him, yelled out for the whole house to hear, as if there was a fire: "Marek, come quickly, step on it, Uncle is here."

I knew that Hanka was never one to play jokes on people, even though she didn't mind being kidded about — that's why I leapt out of bed, quickly threw a coat over my pajamas and tumbled out of my room into the hall. I stopped dead, as if nailed to the spot. Standing calmly in the doorway, leaning against the frame, was Salamander, with a somewhat embarrassed smile, looking at me with tired eyes. In general, a deathly fatigue had carved its mark strongly on his wrinkled countenance. He looked much older. What's more, his eyes, which had always been so lively, now showed something like disappointment, something like shame. I could tell right away that something evil had happened — his very presence in Warsaw didn't indicate anything auspicious — and a deep sorrow gripped my heart. Then the thought crossed my mind that I was saddled once again with this defiant subordinate. But our friendship, my great human attachment to this magnificent old guy, and some kind of affection mixed with sympathy, all took the upper hand now.

"Where did you get here from?" I was finally able to croak out.

"Where? What do you mean, where? I got here on the train from Kraków."

"How can that be? You mean you didn't *go* over there?"

"If I had *gone,* then I wouldn't be *here.*"

When the old man started mumbling something about the mindlessness of certain dictators, I recovered completely. I stopped asking him questions in the open doorway in Hanka's presence, and took him to my room. I asked Hanka to fix us two breakfasts, and gave the little old man time to wash his face and unpack the contents of his little suitcase. Once he was lying stretched out on the sofa, I started asking questions, listening and not believing, feeling astounded, laughing in my heart at this strange adventure, clenching my fists with rage at his "guardian angel" and all the other people who had caused this disaster. I had to cancel all my meetings that morning, running the risk that it might be several days before I'd get to talk to those people again — and explain my failure to appear, calm them down if they were friends, maybe worry them if they weren't quite friends — and finally set up a new time for a meeting. My pocket appointment book or "train schedule," which had returned to some measure of order and normality since Salamander's departure, was once again plunged into chaos. I wasn't able to tear myself away from the house until that afternoon, to go and report Salamander's return to Warsaw in the right places and tell them the things he'd spent half the day telling me about.

His adventure had been simply unbelievable; funny and horribly sad at once. But in spite of the tragic moments, I would have laughed myself silly, if only it hadn't been about Salamander. Even as he told me his story and I looked him in the eyes, I couldn't restrain a few fleeting little smiles, especially because JHR made his story funny in spite of his fatigue, and told it with a kind of impersonal malice.

He had gotten to the "air bridge" outpost without any obstacles or adventures in the company of a certain Rudy, the "guardian angel" assigned to him by the Home Army HQ.[1] They were both lodged in a nearby village, arrangements were made for them to wait, and there they waited. Rudy, himself a Silent Shadow paratrooper sent by London and a high-ranking officer at that, was only supposed to see to it that Salamander was put on that "air bridge" plane, and then return to Warsaw.

So they waited, drinking moonshine, playing games of cards. JHR was cussing up and down because he wasn't allowed to stick his nose out of the cottage. Rudy bravely kept him company, only leaving once a day to go to the outpost commander for news. He'd come back and say, "not for a long while yet," and *da capo* the next day. However, after a week had gone by he announced to his companion (in a suspicious tone of voice, as JHR said) that he was to transfer to another hideout and that Salamander would stay by himself for some time. This clearly displeased our little old man.

"But you were supposed to take care of me and make sure I got put on that plane" — he insisted on his rights.

"Orders are orders," the other guy weaseled out, "so I have to follow them. The outpost commander, although lower in rank, is my superior right now. And as for being taken care of, you don't need that anymore."

"And who's going to let me know about the flight, who's going to take me to the outpost, who's going to help me run up to the airplane and get on board?"

"That's all been figured out. You'll be taken to the outpost by a Home Army soldier on special assignment, your duty is simply to be ready to fly every evening at seven o'clock. There won't be any trouble by the plane because everyone will be there, including me, and everything will work out all right."

Still, several more days went by. During this time, Salamander sat in total solitude, cut off from the world, denied any news of the air bridge.[2] He was immensely worried by Rudy's breach of faith, and he was getting a bad feeling about the whole thing, but there was nothing he could do to help himself, because no one came to see him and he was forbidden from showing his face in the village. Anyway, even if he had gone out of the house, nothing would have come of it because he didn't know which way to turn, where to go looking for the commander of the outpost or his people. Finally one evening, a little horse-drawn chaise pulled up outside his cottage, and a young lad named Wind hopped out, entered Salamander's room and reported for duty, army-style. He had come on the commander's orders and was to take Salamander to the place where the airplane was supposed to land.

The ride through the darkness took a long time, and then finally the chaise drove through a little forest and stopped at its edge. Salamander and the soldier got out and went off a few hundred paces. They sat down in a prearranged place, on a pile of wood or felled tree, and waited for the airplane which, according to the soldier, was supposed to land on the field at a distance of about 100 meters from the edge of the forest. He could hear voices in the field, some kind of hushed conversations. Of course, with his night blindness, JHR couldn't see a thing. He just guessed that the crew at the outpost were making final preparations for receiving their winged visitor.

JHR wanted to get closer to the people talking in the field, but the soldier was opposed to that, having clear orders to wait with Salamander at exactly that spot at the edge of the forest. That was the spot from which they'd be summoned to the airplane. Meanwhile, the conversations in the field quieted down. The voices moved away from the forest, and only rarely carried across the dewy nighttime field from afar.

Into the silence of anticipation a new voice was thrust: the drone of engines. At first it was like a distant yell, barely audible, buzzing like a fly behind double-glazed windows, like a bee in the upper branches of a linden tree in bloom. The sound would fade away, then flow back; break off and come back with a stronger resonance. Finally it roared without pause, growing stronger by the second, growing mighty, surrounding the listeners completely, taking over entirely the silence of the spring night. For JHR there could be no doubt that this was the "air bridge" plane looking for its landing spot.

In the field, a few hundred meters from the forest, the landing lights went on. The plane lowered one wheel and then the other and descended, after which it pierced the dark with the bright beam of its headlights and settled down on the field. It rolled along on the grass for a little while yet, evidently positioning itself into the wind for immediate takeoff, and turned off its headlights.

"Let's run over there, man," Salamander said feverishly. Up to this point, even though it was as if he'd been sitting on hot coals, he'd managed somehow to fight back his ever-increasing suspicions, as he had expected after all that the plane would land quite a bit closer to the forest. Now he knew that the plane, which was to take off at any moment on its return trip to Italy, was several hundred meters away and even a fast runner might not make it in time.

"We're not allowed to," the soldier replied. "The orders were to wait here. They will come for us here."

"You can take your orders and shove 'em!" The old man was getting really mad. "I'll miss my plane because of them."

And he ran off on his own. He tripped on some kind of little ditches and molehills, and he slipped on the wet grass. He got as muddy as some ungodly creature, soaked through from the outside, sweated through from the inside, to the point where there wasn't a dry thread left on him. And since JHR was, as I've already said, anything but an athlete of track and field, he was weak and clumsy and, last but by no means least, he suffered from night blindness — this particular run of his was an uphill battle.

After a while the soldier caught up with him. He started feeling sorry for the old man, who kept tripping and was breathing hard like an old blacksmith's bellows. In spite of his orders to wait, he grabbed Salamander under his arm and pulled rather than led him across the lawn, carrying his little suitcase in his other hand. With their last ounce of strength, they managed to hobble over to the group of people on the lawn at the very moment the airplane, moving faster and faster over the grass, began to fade away.

"Stop him, stop, stop!" Salamander croaked out in a stifled voice, out of breath. "But I was supposed to ... but..."

No one answered him. The shadows, in their silence, gazed in amazement at the distraught little old man. In the eyes of those who weren't in on it, there was surely sympathy; in the eyes of those who knew the score, there was nothing but irony and satisfaction.

"Maybe he's just circling? Maybe that wasn't the take-off?"— Salamander tried to cheer himself up — "I have to run after him." He tore himself away, wheezing, and ran off in the direction of the receding airplane.

"Yeah, sure, he's circling..." someone replied. "No use talking now, he's already lifted off."

Salamander stopped. His legs shook under him, he was trembling in his whole body as he watched the little lights on the wings start to lift up. After a while, high in the air already, they went out. The plane dissolved into the darkness, its roar diminishing, fading, finally disappearing completely. The place got really quiet. Salamander wiped the sweat from his forehead and dragged himself over to the people standing in silence.

"Were you supposed to go?" someone finally asked.

He just waved his hand. The soldier who had come running over with him answered for him.

"So where were you guys, that you didn't make it on time?"

Salamander shook himself alert with some effort. His thoughts were far away, getting ever farther, just like that plane. His entire organism was still not quite able to accept that he was here on the ground, and not there in the air, on his way to the free world. He answered in a resigned tone of voice,

"We were sitting over there, at the edge of the forest."

"Why so far?"

"Because those were the orders."

But JHR wasn't one who could be kept down for long, neither by despair nor by resignation. In spite of his weak body, this was a man of action *par excellence*, a fighter. He was, as they used to say in the Boy Scouts, a natural leader who could be counted on in crucial times — those times when people usually lose their heads and make use of only the slightest fragment of their intelligence — not to lose his clear judgement, nor waste time on any fruitless wailing and hand-wringing. That's why he got to work on the spot, doing what was doable in this situation: trying to shed some light on the matter. He calmly started asking questions:

"Where's Rudy?"

"Who's that?" — he was answered with a question.

"Kind of short and chubby, came over from Warsaw."

"Oh, that guy. He's on the plane."

"But he wasn't supposed to be flying."

"I don't know about that," one voice said.

"Evidently he *was* supposed to be, since he got on board and flew off," a second voice added.

"Where's the commander of this outpost?"

"He drove off with the guys who arrived, and the mail."

"What about his deputy?"

"He's around here somewhere."

"Where?"

"We'll call him over right away."

The deputy commander came over. He was greatly astonished to hear that there was some passenger who hadn't been taken; he expressed regret, but this was mixed with a feeling that surely the unfortunate "bridge passenger" only had himself to blame for not making it on time. Finally he declared that there was nothing he could do about it.

"Oh, I know there's nothing you'll do now," Salamander replied coolly, "but you might save your opinions as to who was at fault, if I was late, or the plane took off too early, for the regular investigation. Please just tell me why I wasn't brought to the landing strip in time, and why you gave the signal to take off when there was a passenger missing?"

"The plane was on the ground for five minutes," the officer replied. "In that time, all the passengers from over there got off, we unloaded the mail, the new passengers got in with the mail, and the plane took off. The regulations state that the length of time the plane is waiting on the ground must be kept to a minimum. There were supposed to be five passengers, and there were five. I didn't have a duty to know them all or check their names against a list. I also had no duty to try and figure out that there was some passenger who was graciously waiting at the edge of the forest, since everyone had been given clear instructions to wait right here, where we now stand."

"The soldier who brought me here had orders to wait with me at the edge of the forest until you guys sent someone to me. If I hadn't decided to run over here in violation of his orders, we'd be waiting there yet."

"I can't do anything about that."

"I've already heard that. So maybe you could be so kind as to explain to me just what you can't do anything about? About the fact that the plane took off, I know about that. But about taking responsibility for your own orders..."

"I did not give that order."

Salamander turned to the soldier. "Wind," he said, "who gave you the order to wait with me at the edge of the forest?"

"The man who was together with the commander."

"You mean Rudy?"

"The short one, chubby, a little older, the guy who first lived in the village I picked you up from, and then moved in with us."

"That's him. And did the commander hear what he told you?"

"That I don't know. I thought it was an order from the commander. I knew that someone was supposed to come for us at the edge of the forest."

These questions and answers were sufficient for JHR to form an opinion on the matter. Section Two of the Home Army (the Intelligence Department), of which Rudy was a pillar, had accepted that JHR's departure, and hence return to England, were contraindicated, and that's how they knocked him aside — and his place on the airplane was taken by Rudy himself.

It turned out that this business of knocking him aside didn't end with merely keeping him off the plane that had actually come principally to pick him up.[3] For the outpost detachment had packed up their gear quickly and ably, and the deputy commander hadn't really thought about the fact that Salamander was to be delivered back to Warsaw in one piece. Only the soldier, Wind, had mercy on him. He led the dead-tired old man to the cart, in which he was driven to the nearby village. There was no trouble with the Germans; however, there was a spot of trouble of another kind, which was to have tragic consequences. While fording a tributary of the Dunajec River, the cart turned over and Salamander took a bath in the icy cold water.[4] Several hours elapsed before they got to the people they knew and the little old man had a chance to dry off and warm up. The next day, he was taken to the nearest train station, from which he took a train to Kraków by himself. The same evening he boarded a night train to Warsaw, and although it was horribly overcrowded and he spent most of the time standing, he arrived in Warsaw in the morning.

All the while as JHR was telling me this, I couldn't believe my own ears. I felt so sorry for the little old man, I understood so well how he'd felt when the airplane landed and he ran to it in a hurry, only to get a good look at its taillights as it flew off. I didn't know how I could cheer him up. Finally, totally without thinking about it, I began on the most appropriate note.

"Don't worry about it, Sir," I said. "As soon as I organize my Northern Route, we'll both go that way."

"When can that be?" he asked excitedly.

"Hmm, it's hard to say, but probably in early August."

"Ohh ... that late," he said with a tired voice.

"You must be well and truly exhausted," I said, seeing how tired and discouraged he was.

"Yes, of course. All of this has really wiped me out. I have to rest. But above all, I also have to travel as soon as possible, in June still."

"I don't know if that can be done. Unless ... unless we can quickly organize another air bridge."

"Exactly. That's what I keep thinking about. Please be so good as to take my message to the Doctor.[5] Please tell him everything and ask him urgently to send a telegram to 'Stem' in the matter of a new air bridge."

I didn't get back till evening. I'd asked JHR not to get out of bed, to get some decent rest and get warmed up, because he gave me the impression that he wasn't just tired, but had a cold. I let him have my hideaway until we could find him a new place. Imagine my astonishment, then, when Hanka let me know that "Uncle" didn't want to eat lunch at home and had gone off to some joint.

"He phoned a minute ago, asking that you come see him. He's not feeling well."

"He's probably plastered," I said angrily. "He's been sitting in some joint since lunchtime, I've heard that one before. That ugly geezer..."

"You'd better hurry," Hanka interrupted me. "It'll be *Polizeistunde* (Police Hour, i.e., curfew) soon, and it's a fair distance from here."

I took a hackney to the restaurant the old man had mentioned over the telephone, fully sure that I was going to drop him off at home completely drunk. I was so sure of it that I asked the hackney driver to come into the restaurant with me. I already had a little speech ready for my incorrigible subordinate.

JHR was not plastered. He sat all alone in a corner of the large room with his arm leaning on his cane, looking at people. He wasn't even reading a newspaper, nor was he drawing anyone into a conversation, as was his habit. I was struck by this unusual behavior of his, especially as I knew that he'd been sitting like that for several hours already.

I was even more alarmed by his dull look and utterly dejected facial expression. He'd never resembled a camel more than he did at that moment; but I'd also never been so moved by the sight of him. This lively, bold, bright person seemed to be ... a mummy.

My emotional reaction was even stronger when JHR's gaze came to rest on my figure. Such great joy and relief were reflected in his face, such a smile came to his dark eyes and brightened his features, it was as though their owner had been driving a bumpy road with great effort and suddenly found himself on a motorway as smooth as a tabletop.

"Marek!" he shouted at the top of his lungs.

I went up to him quickly, already sensing some kind of calamity. I sat down at his little table and gave JHR a questioning look.

"I can't walk. I totally can't," he answered my questioning look calmly.

"How come?" I croaked. "What happened?"

"I don't know," he replied. "We'll have to ask some kind of doctor. I told you about my night-time bath in the river. I was all sweaty, and then suddenly that cold water. It must be from that."

"Does it hurt anywhere, Sir?"

"No, nowhere. It's simply that my legs are refusing to obey me. They don't want to walk. I was on the street, you know, I got out of a streetcar and wanted to walk toward the Saski Garden, but suddenly I felt like every step was becoming damned difficult. Just like that, out of nowhere, I almost fell over. Then it got worse and worse. I was staying close to the wall, people were starting to look at me. I'd stop, my legs were shaking, it's a good thing I had my cane. I made it to this joint and here I sit."

"Such a long time! Couldn't you get anyone–"

"But who? You're the only one I have left. I'm very grateful that you came, because I couldn't get from table to table on my own anymore. I'm telling you, Marek, what a problem I had making that phone call to you. I put on a show for the whole restaurant. They thought I was smashed ..."

"It was just lucky that Hanka was home to answer the phone."

"It sure is. I don't think I'd have made it a second time."

"Let's go," I said. "We'll help you get to the hackney, and from it to the house. You'll get to rest overnight and warm up, and tomorrow I'll call a doctor."

The cab driver and I practically carried him, holding him up by his armpits. He could only drag his helpless legs behind him. He was wheezing and muttering, very unhappy with himself.

By morning, his arms had also ceased to function. He couldn't hold up a cup or even a spoon. Walking was completely out of the question. He could only be carried, and already had to be fed. For several days, various doctors visited him and studied him, making contradictory diagnoses and prescribing various medications. Since he couldn't move his arms or legs, we sent him to the countryside so that he could come back around. In the end we requested a council. At that time it was finally determined that it was paralysis. We took him to the private Omega Clinic, where a normal treatment was begun.[6] It could take ... a year.

I was in despair. My concern that the Gestapo might discover patient Józef Brzoza — for it was under that name that he was operating at the time — at the Omega; my feeling sorry for the little old man and feeling responsible for his fate, with which I had already willingly burdened my soul all the more: all of this robbed me of sleep and peace of mind, and made me start getting nervous and inattentive in my work. Dedicating a lot of time to "Mr. Brzoza," I had to limit the hours of my other work. To top it off, my work organizing the Northern Route was going pretty roughly. One guy somewhere was caught carrying money, another couldn't find the contact address in Bydgoszcz, a third guy was arrested in Warsaw. I had to change my hideout and cover all my tracks for fear that he might give me away.

The old man accepted his fate with unusual good humor and calm. His relationship to his disease alone was enough to give a person the best possible impression of the man. No one heard a single word of complaint from his lips, he never was angry about anything other than his loneliness. He made fun of himself at every opportunity, whenever his disability was particularly severe. He couldn't even dream about lighting up a cigarette; just holding a cigarette was enormously difficult for him. I bought him a very long silver cigarette holder. This would be placed in his straightened, stiff hand, between the index and middle fingers, right at the base. When he wanted to take a drag, his hand would cover half his face, and when he held the cigarette in the resting position, he laid his hand on the bed covers, palm down, and the cigarette in its holder would stick out like a chimney between his fingers. The ashes fell wherever they fell.

JHR was a pure-bred chain smoker who just couldn't get by without puffing away non-stop. I was constantly drawing his attention to the dangers of nicotine poisoning. This didn't help, of course, for this generally agreeable person was absolutely unyielding on the subject of cigarettes. It was about him that I first heard a joke that was to make the rounds later, that if he weren't a widower he couldn't live with his wife anyway, because she would have run off with a fireman on account of his constant smoking. When doctors came to visit him at the Omega Clinic, he'd tell them right away that he would be well-behaved and obey them like a Boy Scout obeys his parents and superiors — except for any ban on smoking cigarettes.

A separate problem for "Mr. Brzoza" was the matter of pressing the button for the electric bell that summoned someone from the nurse's station for help, which consisted most often of lighting a cigarette for him. To do this, he'd turn over on his side so that he could more easily reach the wall, then he'd move his hand along the bed covers until it touched the wall, after which he'd raise it along the wall and use the outside of his hand, or his forearm around the wrist area, to press the button. This wasn't easy at all. Many times JHR would have to go to quite a bit of trouble before the button would decide to give in and make contact with the bell. Watching him go through this bell-ringing ordeal, in which "Mr. Brzoza" was trying to show me how well he was managing, I had to choke back tears. This man was more helpless than an infant. The long fingers of his magnificent hands seemed lifeless, and the weird way they were folded made his hands look like stumps.

Reading was even worse. At first, we would lay the book on his bunched-up blankets at such an angle and at such a distance from his eyes that he could read. But he would have to call for help to turn the pages. When someone would come to visit him, he always preferred carrying on a conversation, of course — a fanatic for conversation, and a master of the art — and he wouldn't allow anyone to sit next to him just to read a book aloud or turn pages for him. And so he read only when he was alone, and at first he would ring the bell after every two pages, to have someone come turn the page for him. Then, seeing how much bother this was for the staff as well as himself, he learned to turn the pages with his tongue. A lot of time went by before he got to be any good at it, and many times the attempt to turn one page forward ended up with several pages turned back, or the book closed or flipped with the cover facing up. Then he really had to call for help.

When I allowed myself once to express aloud my admiration for his sunny spirit and the magnificent way he was tolerating this awful disease — especially for such an active person — he answered unexpectedly:

"As long as it hasn't paralyzed my eyes or made my tongue go stiff in my mouth, I'm a living person and I won't give in to any depression."

The fact that "Mr. Brzoza" still had the faculty of his tongue was also the cause of my constant worries. At first, no one knew about him staying at the Omega, other than myself, Hanka, and one messenger to the underground authorities — we were also the only three people who had access to him. I was decidedly opposed to any and all of "Mr. Brzoza's" requests that I should invite this or that person to see him, and I categorically forbade the others who were in on it to reveal the sick man's address. I considered it the cardinal rule of his security. Too many people in the Underground were already talking about JHR's stay in Poland. He himself talked more than anyone, of course. He even wanted, in defiance of all logic — and he was such a highly logical person! — that the BBC should announce a communiqué about his arrival in country. I was most categorically opposed to this, and my protest was supported by everyone I talked to on this subject. The point was that the Gestapo, irritated by such a communiqué, would start searching for JHR even more zealously than they reportedly already were, and they would surely arrest all persons having his last name, regardless of whether they were related. Lately, people were even talking about his being ill, and from there it was unfortunately just a small step to the Gestapo becoming interested in sick people and starting to search every hospital and convalescent facility. I was enormously afraid of this, and I'd always enter the Omega Clinic with a feeling of considerable fear when I came to visit the little old man, not knowing if he'd already been caught and if I mightn't get caught along with him. The management of the Omega didn't know whom they had as a guest.

After all, reports would reach us time and again that the Gestapo were interested in this aged parachutist, even before Salamander's unsuccessful

Bogus doctor's note made out to "Marek Jurkiewicz" and dated April 13, 1944, ordering dental X-rays (Chciuk-Celt Family Archives and MHPRL Warsaw).

return flight. It was hard to tell, obviously, whether they were all based on the truth, but I never took them lightly, even if I wasn't always convinced of their authenticity. Once, for example, our counterintelligence reported that the Germans were looking for an older gentleman in Warsaw, wearing a brown hat and carrying a cane with a handle shaped like a dog's head. Salamander had such a hat and such a cane, so I immediately changed his hat to a cap and his cane to an umbrella. Another time, I was warned that the Gestapo were looking for some kind of highly important emissary from London, wearing a pince-nez. That same day I exchanged JHR's beautiful pince-nez for a cheap pair of wire-rimmed spectacles. The old man complained and got grouchy with me, defending his hat, cane and pince-nez with uncommon valor, arguing that I was full of fear, much too sensitive, butting into other people's business and believing any old rubbish — but I invariably got my way. I'd answer each of his cutting remarks, unmoved, with the old adage that "The Lord helps those who help themselves," to which he would reply with statements such as, "Adages are the last resort of the mentally handicapped," or that the Lord didn't have time to think about who was helping himself so that He could help him, but rather had His own criteria, unknown to us, to guide Him in extending His care over humanity.

"Exactly," I'd say, "and it seems that He sent me to you, Sir, so that I could do your Underground thinking for you, and take care of you, since you won't bother to take care of yourself on your own."

"Conceited little Marek," the old man would fume in jest. "He wants so badly to be the instrument of divine providence. The provident husband!"

"The reckless widower," I'd fire back at him, doing my part.

In the earlier days of our mission, before the disaster with the second air bridge, it had still been relatively easy to watch over Salamander. After all, he was an ordinary person, one of thousands in the Warsaw Underground; and although people talked about him a lot, they didn't say anything too very dangerous, and his description could have fit every third slightly older gentleman. Besides, he could always change his hideaway with ease. Now, however, lying gravely ill at the Omega Clinic, he was easy to identify and easier still to snatch. That's exactly why I did everything I could to make sure no one got wind of the old man's location, and my efforts consisted mainly of extending my control over what "Mr. Brzoza" said, and to whom. I knew that he would give himself away most easily, most quickly and most eagerly. There are people like that, who can't stand to be in the shadows for even a moment and who push toward the light like moths, never thinking that the light might also be their undoing.

To this day I don't know how it came to be that entire pilgrimages started making their way to the old man's bedside. First I found out from Hanka that she had encountered two unknown gentlemen visiting "Uncle," with whom he was carrying on a half-political, half-social conversation with great animation and verve. Then, I once dropped in at "Mr. Brzoza's" private room myself at a completely unexpected time, and I, too, encountered one of the real matadors of the Underground with him. Getting mad didn't help this time; the old fellow not only wouldn't reveal his secret method of getting people to meet with him, he didn't even intend to promise any improvement. And since the circle of people who were in on the whole Omega business was clearly expanding, I decided to effect a change of location for "Mr. Brzoza."

There were, unfortunately, two cardinal flaws in the workings of the Polish Underground: the unnecessary writing of whole tons of paper notes, and the unbelievable gabbiness of the worst kind — strictly in confidence and spoken softly in your ear. These two deficiencies cost us a lot of human existences. I was only able to change his location thanks to the influence of the top level of our Underground and the great kindness of the director of the Dermatological Clinic.[7]

As much as the old man surprised me with his lengthy chats and his way of calling together entire processions of the most incredible people to come see him (one time I encountered a greatly distinguished lady in his room, who was at that time the co-owner of a great tavern; she was known throughout half of Warsaw for whispering everything into everyone's ears), that's how much I surprised him with a change of premises. I arrived at the Omega early one morning in a hackney with a trusted friend, took care of everything at the administration office, and "dragged a dying person out of bed at dawn, in the rain and wind" — as JHR put it — in other words, I carried him out to the hackney at nine o'clock, as carefully as if he were an egg; and on a sunny and windless summery day, I drove him at an easy pace, right to the Dermatological Clinic. The old man complained the entire way, saying he had a whole series of appointments for that day and the next, but I wouldn't let him get to me. I told him that the new place would seem more remote after the Omega Clinic than the convent of the Barefoot Carmelites might seem after the tumult that reigns in Bielany at the Pentecost.[8] The strict rules in effect there wouldn't allow him any more of his disregard for discipline.

"You forgot yourself in that Schaffhausen Clinic, despite the fact that nothing more was asked of you than to lie there as snug as a gear in a watch.[9] Presently you will be squeezed in among nothing but syphilis patients, you old disabled soldier, and you'll not only be unable to move your hands and feet, you won't even be able to move your tongue any more. Other than the sworn doctor and the sworn nurse and your sworn friend, which is to say your parachute commander, the only faces you're going to see will be on photographs, unless you enjoy gazing at faces without noses, without lips and so on, belonging to your syphilitic neighbors. I kind of doubt that you'll be wanting to strike up a conversation with one of those half-faces."

"So I won't even be seeing Hanka?" he asked sadly.

"Not even Hanka. Even so, the old disabled soldier should be happy that he only got confined to barracks for what he did, and not a couple of days of hard time."

"Cheeky dictator!"—the old man cried out in despair—"You'll be the third one, behind Adolf and Benito, with whom an angry people will want to get even."

"The people can settle down."

"Somewhere, the people have..."

"If the people don't get busy cutting out their revolts and won't listen to their proper leaders, then some very important news won't be told them."

"What news? What?"—his eyes flashed. I knew that it was all the same to him if I told him about Himmler's sudden death, or about a new Monte Cassino,[10] or about how Hanka had a thing for this dentist when her mother would have preferred a pharmacist for her. He mainly wanted to hear any kind of news, just so he could chat and gossip on the subject a little and then switch to ever more distant and irrelevant topics and never stop talking. The poor, poor man, cut off from the world, denied control of all four extremities, wanted to devote himself entirely to conversation. Once a master of the art, now he became a fanatic for conversation, and its slave.

I kept him in this state of uncertainty for a long time, making him try to guess what important matter I had to tell him. I laughed as I said the word "important," which totally threw him for a loop, and during the entirety of our ride in that hackney he was unable to guess the nature of my revelation. Finally I told him, without meaning to:

"No, no, you surely won't guess it, Sir. And what it's about is a completely ordinary revelation: it's simply that in two weeks there's going to be another air bridge."

The old man went dumb. He looked at me quickly, blinked his eyes a couple of times like a person who comes out of a dark place into the sudden sunlight, and shouted:

"Well, then we're going together?!"

But then he looked sadly at his powerless arms and legs, sighed heavily and said:

"But will a cripple like me be able to drag himself over there–"

"He will," I answered softly and cheerily, "if he listens to all the doctor's orders, if he takes all his medications, gets massaged, light therapy, and so on, but above all if he lives in absolute peace, which will have a dual health benefit: first, that he'll recuperate, and second, that he won't fall into the hands of the Gestapo."

"And will you come with me?"

"I don't know yet, because there's still a chance of putting together the Northern Route. I'll know everything in a week. If my route doesn't work out, I'll gladly come with you, provided of course that the top brass agree to it."

"They'll agree to it — I'm involved in this. I won't make a move with anyone else, only with you. I won't let myself be made a fool of a second time. I mean, that air bridge is organized just for me, so surely I have something to say here."

"Well, well, let's not overdo it. The air bridge is principally organized for you, true, but not exclusively for you, and you can only make decisions about yourself. Anyway, it seems to me that the authorities will approve my travel. In a fortnight I'll be more or less done with my work, I'll gather up all my materials, and if the Northern Route doesn't stop me, then I'll fly with you. I'll have the pleasure once again of commanding a forbidden civilian."

"Please just do everything you can so that that whole Northern Route doesn't work out ... all right?"

* * *

Knowing already that I was to leave the country via the third air bridge operation, and wishing to get as much as possible done in the meantime, I concentrated more and more on my own assignment, which was a big one after all, and getting bigger. I had talks with the leadership committees of many unions, or with their individual presidents, and with the directors of individual departments within the Delegature, with priests, scouts, representatives of the Jewish community.... Most important were the political talks. The picture I was going to present to "Stem" was taking shape ever more clearly in my mind. I was coming to some conclusions that were, unfortunately, very sad.

The total lack of awareness of our international situation, in other words the political provincialism of the nation, was truly widespread. It was as much the fault of the old system, which tried to convince the Polish people of their power and glory while portraying Russia as a giant with clay feet, as of the fact that the nation was cut off from reliable sources of information. It was also proof of how very much the nation lived and wanted to live with its fervent wishes, and how very much it didn't even want to hear any bad news about our uncertain future. I think this provincialism of ours also contained a bit of the old self-preservation instinct, which doesn't allow a person's blackest thoughts to take hold, because they weaken the will to fight and even the will to live. Even among the people who were leading our Underground life, I could count very few individuals who were well-informed about international events, the global balance of power at the time, and our possibilities in this regard. And even those people who were well-informed seemed to mostly prefer rejecting any unfavorable news, basing their views, hopes and actions solely on favorable reports.

Basically, then, only good news was accepted. Important political deliberations were most often based on people's opinions of individual representatives of Anglo-Saxon societies, not their governments.

It's true that the underground press did occasionally run articles which could be said to set off "alarm bells" in Polish public opinion, and which poured the cold water of reality onto the overheated heads of the provincialists. Still, there were too few articles of this kind to allow the population or even the politicians to grasp the essence of the state of affairs; and all too often, they avoided such crucial topics as Russia's power, which was going to have to be taken into account in our calculations; the deepening discord between the Anglo-Saxon democracies; and the events in Yugoslavia and Italy, which were symptomatic of what could happen to us.

Even so, every article in the underground press, even the ones that were well thought-out, either ended with an unexpectedly over-optimistic assessment or arrived at the old Polish conclusion that "somehow everything will work out."

Not many people were capable of presenting the matter of the friction between Poland and Russia in an upright, logical way. There was widespread fear that the author of any such article would be labeled a Communist.

At times I was horrified to realize that it was hard for me to find a common language with the people I was talking to. For example, when I would draw attention to the fact that Russia was a great power with whom we'd have to reckon in our politics, people would reply categorically that these were her last death throes, that she had neither arms nor ammunition of her own and had to fight with American and English equipment, that she had neither an air force nor a navy and was entirely dependent on Anglo-Saxon food deliveries. "And you know, Sir, how the Americans handle Russia. They help her now so she can fight the Germans till they're defeated. But they don't want that help to be used in the future. The best proof of this is that the Americans are currently sending only sterilized grain to Russia, which means it's only suitable for milling and baking bread, but unsuitable for planting."

Perhaps subconsciously, people could feel Russia's power and the great danger connected to it, but instead of looking at the matter realistically, they tried to find instances of Russia's weakness. The stereotype of the barefoot, hungry Red Army soldier with his rifle slung over his shoulder on a string was still alive and well, even at a time when the Red Army was decisively pushing the Germans back westward at several points of the eastern front simultaneously.

Rumors and fairy tales, used to justify some pretty improbable ideas, popped up as if on demand. People figured out, for example, that the Western democracies had come to the conclusion that Warsaw had already been so heavily damaged in this war by German and Bolshevik bombardment, and as a result of the destruction of the ghetto and the general German terror, that it couldn't be subjected to any further destruction. That's why ("I heard it myself on the radio") the Americans had sent out an ultimatum (!) to the Germans and Russians (!) demanding that the former not defend Warsaw and the latter not attack it. In exchange for that, Königsberg wouldn't be bombed (a concession to the Germans) and the flow of military supplies to Russia would be increased. ("We have clear proof that it's so. A blind man could see it. The Germans have aborted their construction of fortifications around Warsaw.")

Every time England acted submissive toward Russia, it was explained that they were just lying in wait for them; every time Russia humiliated England, it was treated almost as a *casus belli*.[11] Even Churchill's February speech wasn't treated appropriately, and when it was debated in the House of Commons, only voices friendly to us (such as Allan Graham) would be quoted in the press and in people's discussions.[12] Unfavorable articles in the British press were rarely mentioned, but attention was drawn to the favorable ones, even if they were pretty obscure, such as in some of the Scottish press, the *Catholic Herald*, articles by Voigt,[13] and things like that.

Everyone was totally convinced that as soon as Germany fell apart, the Allies would order the Russians to leave our soil, under threat of war. Tremendous significance was ascribed to the Polish-American community. People thought that if only because of them, America wouldn't allow Poland to get hurt. Russia would have to give up its ambitious plans, because the Anglo-Saxons would support us, and finally — here we get to the crux of the matter — if the Russians refuse, there will be a war between the Anglo-Saxons and Russia. On many occasions, I felt a pain in my heart as I took part in talks where this kind of argument would be made, listening to opinions of this kind and contrasting them in my thoughts with the things I'd brought to Poland from London. But — to oppose them? On a daily basis, in ordinary conversations, that was impossible. I couldn't even do it at the top levels of the Underground. I was able to convince myself of this on several occasions, and Salamander had similar experiences.

There were even those (serious people, including university professors) who demanded territorial concessions from Russia, because Poland should once again extend "from sea to sea." (From the Baltic to the Black Sea.) When I asked them what kind of forces we had at our disposal to reach this goal, they'd answer, "Faith."

The paramilitary Combat Organization "East," which had set a goal for itself of fighting the Russians (or anyone else) for our eastern territories, took the basic stance that it was the duty of every Pole not to yield a single square meter of ground in the east.[14] When I asked the leader of this organization what kind of support he would have in such a battle, he answered that he'd have the support of the entire Polish nation. When I then asked if that would be enough, he answered, "It'll have to be." In its proclamation entitled "To the Citizens of the Republic of Poland," the Combat Organization "East" wrote as follows: "The great Western democracies will understand the validity of our position and its significance not only for Poland but for all of Europe; however, we must chiefly count on our own forces. When, in spite of the disasters and destruction that have touched us, we distill all of our efforts into one, then the fate of our Eastern Territories, and indeed our independent political existence, shall not be decided by a unilateral land grab by the Russians."

No one could understand that Poland — the "First Ally" and the one fighting the most faithfully and with the greatest casualties — might get a large piece sliced off. No one allowed the thought that Poland might lose the war to enter their heads. This is why even serious politicians made unexpected miscalculations — or at least very one-sided ones — utterly failing to anticipate the possibility that matters might take a turn for the worse, and utterly failing to prepare for it.

The Chief Delegate was often unhappy with the Prime Minister's position. Speaking of the conversation "Stem" had had with Professor Oskar Lange,[15] he looked truly bent out of shape, and asked me quite clearly to draw the Government's attention to the fact that in the matter of the Home Army and the underground administration coming out into the open, Lange was very heavily exaggerating. It was not helpful, for example, that Minister Banaczyk told all the world about the Underground coming out into the open, because governments of nations should be notified of things like that by means of diplomatic notes and not radio addresses. And here in Poland, the persistent announcements of the Underground coming out into the open produced only dislike of the government and a bad atmosphere, as people were finding out at the same time about ever more incidents of the Russians' scandalous behavior toward the Home Army with which it was meant to be cooperating. "We come out into the open. Russia leaves us to the Germans, not even notifying our division of the withdrawal of their units, which our division had been helping (as in Wołyń); or they arrest the AK officers outright, and conscript our soldiers by force into their columns. And we, instead of strongly condemning this, go bragging again about how we're coming out into the open."

When I approached the Chief Delegate with "Stem's" suggestion that he should sharply curb the anticommunist propaganda and persuade the press not to publish overly flagrantly anti–Russian articles, he said he wouldn't do that, because he considered it a mistake. Communists needed to be isolated from society. Then I asked him if he didn't anticipate that it would be necessary to recognize the Communists in Poland — to which I heard him answer that that's impossible, because public opinion would never agree to it, since they thought of the Communists not as Poles but as Russia's lackeys. I replied that that's exactly why we needed to mitigate somewhat the anti–Russian statements of our propaganda, especially because the actions of the underground movement against Russia and Communism were being skillfully played against us by the Russians. To this, Sobol replied that he wouldn't do that, and that if the government ordered him to do it, he'd resign from his position.

The Chief Delegate also didn't even want to hear about any talks with the Polish Workers' Party (the PPR, i.e., Communists). Many people had suggested such a thing to him. One time, when I reminded him of this, Sobol replied that he, as a representative of the government, couldn't jeopardize the prestige of that government by entering into talks with people who didn't stand fundamentally for Polish nationhood, and who were in the pay of a foreign power. When I drew his attention to the fact that the world was going through deep changes and that we needed to be well aware of them, treating the events in Italy and Yugoslavia as symptomatic — he replied that our situation was entirely different, the Communists were isolated from society and the people would immediately react negatively to any kind of attempt to come to an understanding with them. Consequently, the Chief Delegate could neither jeopardize the authority of his legal political power, nor "personally hand the Communists and their henchmen a trump card." In the National Unity Council, aside from the somewhat shaky stance of the Peasant Party members, everyone supported the Chief Delegate.

When I asked "Michniewski" (code name), the leader of the Anticommunist Committee, if he thought it useful to continue their anticommunist actions, using billboards, flyers, etc., (along the lines of "PPR is the enemy" and "PPR = Paid Pawns of Russia") in view of the fact that we might soon find ourselves in the situation of being forced to recognize the PPR immediately as the legal communist party in Poland — and it would be hard for society to accept that, since society was very strongly set against the PPR as a direct result of his group's activities — he told me that it was precisely because of those actions that the PPR was so isolated from society and had such a minor influence, and that his group's anticommunist actions should not be interrupted on any account.

When I expressed the opinion that it would be a good thing from the point of view of international politics to include the PPR in the National Unity Council (the PPR would recognize the legal authorities, the prestige of the Delegature would be enhanced, it would be a demonstration of good will on our part, etc.), Michniewski replied that that would be impossible, for if we were to give the PPR even one mandate in the National Unity Council, that would be a threat to all our Underground authorities, since a Communist in the National Unity Council would be nothing other than a hidden propaganda cell.

And that was the general attitude. "The PPR is the enemy" — we mustn't enter into any agreements with them — we must totally isolate them from society, and by doing so, we'll expose how small and ridiculous they are. People didn't want to agree with the idea that in spite of the PPR's isolation from Polish society, they would always be kept strong by Russian power, especially if the Russians should take Warsaw; and that an anti–Russian conspiracy (even without letting a PPR man into the Council) had a very slim chance of success, or let's just say no chance at all, since the PPR was already familiar with all our Underground channels. Besides, the NKVD were far and away the masters of their craft, whom that poor pupil, the Gestapo, could never equal. Moreover, the Russians had vastly improved their technical ability to liquidate the Polish nation once and for all.

People didn't seem to realize that it was impossible to achieve national unity and a strong, monolithic anti–Soviet front (the way there had been an anti–German one) in Polish society. Impossible because there were Communists in Poland after all, and because plenty of people could be found who would go for cooperation with the Russians — not just as rats fleeing a sinking ship, but as supporters of the ideals of Communism.

The error in their thinking resulted from the fact that the Polish Workers' Party was considered weak and isolated in Poland, and that actually the national bloc was strong, when in reality, the closer the Red Army came to Warsaw, the more the Party grew in strength. The deeply divided Polish political parties weren't showing any real initiative in the direction of national unity, continuing to treat each other with suspicion and continuing to attack each other vehemently over relatively trivial matters in the face of truly total danger. The error was also due to the fact that people didn't fully appreciate the degree to which Polish society was exhausted, nor the degree of skill shown by the Bolshevik propaganda, which was bound to be successful when striking at such an exhausted society.

In spite of what the Chief Delegate had said about Polish society not recognizing any agreement about coming to an understanding with the Communists, I was of the opinion that Polish society kept believing that the government ought to finally take some decisive action that would lead to some results. The atmosphere, which was by turns filled with uneasiness and optimism, full of the certainty of victory and the uncertainty of our fate in the coming months, urgently demanded some kind of discharge. People wanted to heave a sigh of relief at long last. Of course everyone dreamed the Polish Army would come, the real one, meaning the one from the West; of course they yearned for this to happen as soon as tomorrow, or even today; but if people would sometimes allow themselves more realistic thoughts, namely, that the Bolsheviks would unfortunately get to us first, then a great feeling of unease would come over them, and they saw their only hope in the government — and they were even prepared to accept compromise solutions. The concept of a demarcation line, as put forward by "Stem," had many supporters. It was simply regarded as a *malum necessarium,* a necessary evil. For one thing was sure, and that was that Polish society would never willingly agree to give up Lwów and Vilnius. They would fight for those two cities in defiance of logic, in defiance of the factual reality, and against the whole world. People simply didn't consider it right and decent to live in a Poland without Lwów and Vilnius. They couldn't imagine that kind of life.

If, therefore, we can accept it as an exaggeration that the claims made by various groups, to the effect that the basic stance of Polish society (with the exception of overt Russian agents) regarding our Eastern Territories, could be summed up in the words "Not a single inch of land" — nonetheless it has to be said, without exaggeration, that in spite of our exhaustion and our enormous losses, and in spite of our future shaping up in the saddest possible way, no one would willingly agree to give up Lwów and Vilnius, and a government that would go that far in its concessions would find no support among the people.

The political provincialism of our society, if regarded from a different point of view, could be called the purest form of patriotism. It could also be called a self-preservation instinct, for who can say if our people would be capable of such a stubborn fight against the Germans if they were clearly aware of our position in the world. People fought on, despite the fact that the advancing army wasn't composed of their brothers and loved ones, but rather the ominous Red Army of our "Allies' Allies," and that behind the first column, there might not be any others, only the NKVD, only an empty expanse with a clearly marked road to Siberia.

* * *

I said good-bye to the Chief Delegate in the early afternoon of the 16th of July, strolling along Wilcza Street. I heard out his final directives, and noted the things he was asking me to relate to the Prime Minister and the other ministers in London, as well as those specific problems which the people "in country" most urgently wanted to solve. I told him what steps I had taken to ensure the success of my trip with the ailing Salamander; told him that I had put Drogowski in charge of setting up the "Northern Route;" told him I had wrapped up various jobs and conversations, and had gathered an enormous volume of mail headed for London. As we were saying good-bye, feeling an atmosphere of some sort of extraordinary excitement in Warsaw — having to do with the advancing front and various decrees made by the occupiers — just as I was leaving him, I asked Sobol a direct question:

"What do you think, Sir, about a possible uprising in Warsaw? People are talking about it a lot."

Jankowski's verbatim reply was: "An uprising in Warsaw would be nonsense."

Eight
The Third Bridge

We left Warsaw on the 17th of July. The road was dangerous and very difficult. Our whole trip could be described as one continuous streak of good luck, a chain of miraculously avoided dangers.

First, we took a hackney from the Dermatological Clinic to the East Warsaw train station, for it was from there that the train to Kraków departed. The director of the clinic had assigned a medic to help us, so we were able to manage. We were at the station several hours before the train was to depart. I left JHR in the medic's care, and went to find the chief conductor of the train. I went around to everyone from A to Z, from Annas to Caiphas, from Polish railway employees to the Germans and back, until at last I was able to get rid of four 500-złoty banknotes. In other words, for a 2000-złoty bribe I managed to buy one whole compartment for our exclusive use.

As we were carrying JHR into the compartment, the train was still empty. By the time it moved, though, you couldn't have squeezed a pin in there. Scenes right out of Dante were playing out in the corridor next to us; someone fainted, someone was squeezing a child against the wall. We couldn't bear to look at that from our empty, comfortable compartment, so after a little while our compartment was full. I let people in gradually — here a mother with two small children, here some little old man, here a lovely lass who had been assigned to observe our travel from the adjacent compartment, so that in case of any kind of disaster the right people would be notified at once. I announced to one and all that I was letting them into "Paradise," but that they would have to adhere strictly to military regulations, the main point being that the bench on which JHR was lying was not to be touched.

We traveled all night, calmly and without incident. JHR would doze off, or strike up conversations with people. As a patient in the horizontal position, his behavior was outstanding. We pulled into Kraków at dawn. My com-

Eight. The Third Bridge

panion was to assume an upright position, and that's where the trouble began. There was no hope of getting a porter to help me with my living baggage. I tried to talk one of the travelers into helping us, tried offering money, but that was no good, either. Everyone was rushing for the exits in order to get outside the station as quickly as possible, since there was the ever-present danger of a German raid. What to do? I carried JHR in my arms, like a child, and that's how I moved along, step by step, along the platforms, the underpasses, the stairs. Fortunately, the lass was able to carry our briefcases and coats. In this manner, we managed somehow to make it right to the station exit, but that's where we were confronted with an insurmountable obstacle. The *Ausgang* (exit) was barricaded by black uniforms, either the *Bahnschutz* (railway patrol) or the Gestapo, and they were scrupulously inspecting the travelers. Was it standard procedure, or were they hunting for someone? I couldn't tell, but I was certain I couldn't endure a long wait with JHR in my arms. Somewhere in my subconscious I had the feeling that they might be trying to catch the two of us in a German dragnet. My decision came all by itself, somehow. I simply gave our messenger girl a signal with my eyes, indicating that she should leave the station via the regular exit, while I — still carrying JHR in my arms — headed for the exit marked *Nur Für Deutsche* — "Germans Only."

Luckily we managed to make our way through the crowded waiting room, between Wehrmacht officers, Gestapo men and various other Germans in and out of uniform. Some of them got out of our way, others had to be asked. My skin was crawling at the thought that they might stop us. There was no turning back, we had to keep pushing forward. How we managed it, I don't know. When we were sitting in a hackney in front of the station, in relative safety, waiting for our lass, JHR smiled and said:

"Well, you certainly are a gambler, Marek. You bet the fate of the world's oldest paratrooper on one lousy card. I was really curious to see how that would work out."

We spent a full day and night in Kraków. JHR spent the night with his relatives, and I stayed with some people I knew. Every joint in my body ached from carrying the world's oldest paratrooper around, and I knew that I was in for several further workouts of that sort.

The next morning we said good-bye to Kraków, our relatives, the messenger girl, people we knew — and by noon we were nearing Tarnów. At that point, an air bridge detachment of the AK was to take charge of our safety, so I was waiting for that Tarnów station as eagerly as a man possibly could.

Things worked out better there than they had in Kraków. While we were still in the train, which was unusually empty by *General Gouvernement* standards,[1] one of the passengers offered to help me. We carried my paralyzed "Uncle" to a hackney quite efficiently.

I was tired, not only from the physical exertion but also from the constant awareness of the danger we were in, yet somehow a new spirit got hold of me then, at the train station in Tarnów. The weather was wonderful — although, judging by the sound of distant rumbling, a storm was on its way — and the stranger's good deed, combined with JHR's sparkling good spirits, all somehow raised my own spirits and filled me with hope that our contact here would work out and that my hard work and heavy responsibility would soon be over.

And yet some kind of uneasiness gripped both of us. Something wasn't right here. How come Tarnów seemed somehow deserted, how come there were so few people on the train today? Finally JHR asked the hackney driver what was going on.

"Don't you hear it, Sir?"

"Hear what?"

"Well, the Russkies, you know, the Soviets. They've already advanced to the outskirts of Dębica, and maybe even closer."

After which, turning completely to face us and looking us dead in the eyes, he added: "The Krauts are already on the run."

That's when we finally realized that the distant rumbling we'd heard wasn't caused by any heavenly artillery. In the course of the last few days, while we were traveling, the front line had moved quite a bit to the west. To our assorted worries about the Germans you could now add an uneasy feeling about the Soviets. Were we going to make it to that air bridge before the Bolsheviks got here?

I settled JHR comfortably on a park bench and set out to look for our contact. Walking away, I took a look at the little old man. He was sitting there calmly, leaning on the arm rest of that bench and looking behind me. Some kind of grimace passed over his face, he moved his lips, he may have said something I didn't hear. But I knew exactly what was on his mind. "Don't worry, old man, I won't leave you here." I made a friendly, reassuring gesture with my hand from a distance, to which he replied with a smile.

The little shop whose address we had been given in Warsaw wasn't far away, along one of the side streets. I strolled around near it for some time, checking out the situation on the street, and finally I entered.

As soon as I had closed the door behind me, I heaved a deep sigh of relief. A stone had fallen from my heart. Everything checked out: I recognized at once the two people whom the Chief Delegate's secretary had described in Warsaw — a woman and a man.

"Am I talking to Mr. Krzysztof?"—I addressed the man.
"Yes, I'm Krzysztof."
"Good day to you. I've brought a bouquet of flowers for Miss Zofia."
"Are there any violets in it?"
"No, just roses."

We smiled. I was invited into a room in the back of the shop. We discussed everything in a few short words, and an hour later my companion and I were already resting in one of the organization's meeting places. This is how we both got into the care of the local cell of the Home Army, which played the key role in getting a couple of travelers from southern Poland to ... southern Italy.

This was a huge relief for me. I didn't have everything hanging over my head any more, I could ease up on my vigilance, calm my tense nerves. During the luncheon to which we were treated at some AK person's private home, I must have got drunk. What happened next, up to the late evening, I don't quite remember. There was some sort of hackney in which we were sent to the vicinity of the village of Łęg, I think; we transferred over to a farm cart in the middle of an open field, were driven around on side roads, were ferried across the Dunajec River, and drove on. There were passwords and responses of some sort, which I neither had to know by heart nor call out; there were orders of some sort. This all just seemed to go right past me. JHR and I both took delight in the thought that we were in the hands of a skilled organization.

The last password and response were called out in the rectory of a church in the village of Zdrochec. That's where we were quartered. The priest, corpulent and very friendly, took care of us as if we were his nearest and dearest. He was seconded in this by another priest, a refugee from the East — probably from Wołyń — who was a guest of the Zdrochec parish, just the same as we were. In general, there were plenty of refugees hanging around in that area, displaced persons, runaways and others from the eastern part of Poland.

No sooner had I washed JHR and dusted him off a bit, and brought myself in order after our trip, than we were called for supper. In the dining room, besides the priests, there were two other men. When I carried JHR into the room, they both stood there thunderstruck. They must have been doubly dumbfounded. Finally they started firing questions at the old man.

"Is that you, Sir?"
"Mr. Brzoza?"
"And look at the state you're in!"
"Are you unable to walk, Sir?"
"My old acquaintances," JHR said to me with a smile. "The ones who

thought it appropriate to push me off the 'Second Bridge' in order to make room for a certain Rudy. Greetings, gentlemen, greetings. I think you'll treat me better this time around, especially since I'm a helpless cripple, as you can see."

"What happened to you, Sir?"

"What was supposed to happen? Nothing happened. I'm only paralyzed. Mr. Marek is acting on my behalf now. He's already washed me, combed my hair, let me go (begging the pardon of the clergymen) pee-pee, and now he's going to feed me, which you gentlemen will both witness, and then he'll lay me down in my cradle, for I can't move my little arms and legs."

"But for all that, you can still move your tongue all by yourself, without any help," the priest said with a smile.

"My tongue, yes, I can still move it. And I'm about to read these AK officers present a *pater noster*, father, the likes of which it might be better for clergymen's ears not to hear. What do you say, Marek? What's your order, Commander?"

That conversation went on a long time. It was both comical and stormy, but it ended with ... brandy. The antagonists drank away that previous Second Bridge, the one that hadn't worked out for JHR. They explained to JHR that they had been the victims of Rudy's intrigue, just as he had been. They beat their breasts, contritely declared their sorrow for their sins and firmly resolved to improve. When I lifted a shot glass of liquor to JHR's lips with my right hand, and a second glass to my own lips with my left hand to drink a toast to the success of the Third Bridge (never mind that Second Bridge), there was already a general feeling of "let's be buddies!" Under the influence of this feeling, I was even able to subdue a new sense of unease, which had been awoken at the moment when the Commander announced that the current Air Bridge operation was going to take place in exactly the same place as the previous one.

"*Ipso loco*, gentlemen, *ipso loco!*"

The officer was clearly proud that the AK Headquarters had entrusted him with such an important assignment a second time, and rightly so. This was proof of an enormous level of trust, faith in his organizational skills, and so on, but did it not go against the basic principles of the Resistance? Well, what of it, somehow we'll ... be buddies!

The officers still had some other business to tend to that same night, so they took their leave of us rather swiftly. They gave us our directions, more or less, as to the rules of waiting, and also several key bits of information. Our little village was several kilometers distant from the place where the air bridge plane was supposed to land, on an improvised airfield code-named

Eight. The Third Bridge

"Butterfly." Three other passengers were already waiting in neighboring villages. In all, there were to be five passengers on the Third Bridge. These were: two important political figures ("Stanislaw," meaning Tomasz Arciszewski, the old and distinguished leader of the Polish Socialist Party, who had been designated by the underground National Unity Council to be the successor of the President of the Republic; and Salamander), two military envoys (Captain Jerzy Chmielewski, a distinguished AK intelligence officer, and Colonel Czesław Miciński), and finally myself, an ordinary emissary from London, returning from Poland with a huge bag filled with mail, underground press, books, photographs, even musical compositions — and a head so crammed with information that "even the news of Hitler's sudden death wouldn't have fit in anymore," as one of the messenger girls had put it. Each of us was to arrive at the assembly point (about which, until then, we had only known that it was somewhere near Tarnów) separately and by separate paths, scrupulously laid out by the authorities. The only exception was made for JHR, who was to be under my care. I took upon myself the responsibility for getting his body to the waiting area in one piece, and then for packing him into the plane, watching over him during the flight and handing him over to the Commander of the airbase in Brindisi, hopefully not damaged any further than he already was. The Chief Delegate had also ordered me to take care of Arciszewski. He, too, was quartered in a parish church, in the village of Zabawa as I recall, and the AK officers were in Biskupice.

The most important thing was what Captain Chmielewski had with him, not only in his head, and in diagrams and documents, but also in several large bags. Of course, we didn't know the contents of those bags at the time. They contained the main reason for the urgency of our operation, which also lay in the fact that ever since the middle of June, 1944, these weird airplanes without pilots had appeared in the skies over England — flying bombs. The Germans had introduced their first secret weapon into battle: the V-1. The British had no time to lose. They wanted to see an intelligence specialist from the AK as soon as possible, and they were particularly interested in the technical description and components of Hitler's second secret weapon, the V-2. Polish intelligence had got their hands on one. They were afraid — and rightly so — that the V-2 would be even more destructive than the V-1. That's why the action called "Third Bridge" (Operation Wildhorn III) was given the highest urgency.

The local church organist was to act as messenger between ourselves and the commander. After the two officers had left, he showed up at our place, whereupon we couldn't get by without several drinks of brandy — at JHR's urging, naturally. All in all, that was a pretty drunken day.

The next day, I found out to my great relief that my bag, containing the greatest load of political mail in the history of the Polish Underground, was also in our vicinity. For security reasons, we couldn't transport mail like that by rail, so it was brought over in ... a German truck. The driver and his assistant were both dressed in German uniforms and equipped with documents stating that they had to deliver over a dozen bottles of oxygen from Warsaw to a little town in southern Poland. Staff units of the AK watched over the vehicle's entire route, in such a way as not to arouse any suspicions on the part of the Germans. When they arrived, the stamped and sealed packages were extracted from the oxygen bottles. They contained materials for the government in London as well as parts of a V-2 rocket gotten out of Germany. Getting this mail to our departure point was a magnificent accomplishment, and an excellent example of the abilities of our Home Army.

Other than eating, sleeping, secretly going swimming in the Dunajec and warming myself in the sun, I had absolutely nothing to do. I waited. For two days, I got plenty of rest after the arduous journey from Warsaw; after that I started getting bored and worried. I had all kinds of time to calmly think things over. I double-checked my thoughts, organized my impressions of being in-country, tried to settle on what I was going to say in London. It was really an enormous amount of material, my head was overloaded with information, and finally — perhaps most of all — I was thinking about our coming trip.

I was happy about it, and yet I was unhappy about it. I was a little afraid of the trip's dangers, but on the other hand I felt an enormous sense of relief at the thought that in just a few days I'd be able to sleep safely, walk down the street safely, and be entirely free. I would have fully accomplished the important mission with which the Government had entrusted me. I felt happy thinking about the happiness I would be bringing people.

However, on top of these feelings of worry, relief or joy, there was an overriding sadness, because I'd be leaving the country, leaving behind those magnificent people who fought on so bravely. I was sad because it would be impossible for me to actively take further part in the fight.

Every afternoon, the messenger would come to us. When we'd ask him if it was time yet, he'd invariably answer: "Not yet. The operation isn't going to happen today. Did you gentlemen need anything?"

There were various reasons for the operation being delayed; however, the leading role in this matter was played by the weather, which was driving us to despair with its variability. If we had sunshine, then there was a storm on the flight path. If we had good weather and the flight path did, too, then there was fog at the air base. Fair weather at the base as well as en route — a low ceiling of rainclouds where we were. And so on, in a vicious cycle.

Meanwhile, our local situation began to get severely complicated. Literally day by day, we could feel the danger growing — let's face it. The eastern front was rapidly approaching Tarnów. Day by day, the German units in our area were observed to be getting more densely concentrated. The Germans began mounting dragnets in the towns and villages, on a previously unseen scale. They wanted to snatch a sufficient number of laborers for the construction of new fortification lines to which their army could retreat, and to help in the evacuation of administrative offices and civilian families. About five or six kilometers from our landing field, in Radłów, the Germans began construction of a new airfield. They finished it in less than two days. Airplanes with black crosses were landing and taking off from that field every hour. They were constantly rumbling right over our heads. Most of them were transport aircraft, some taking wounded soldiers from the eastern front to hospitals in the rear, others supplying war materiel to the front-line units. And finally, to our great dismay, several fighter planes also appeared. Every few hours we received unfavorable news concerning the reinforcement of police and gendarmerie posts in our administrative district (Brześć) as well as the neighboring districts: Tarnów, Dąbrowa Tarnowska and Bochnia. There were reports of Gestapo automobile patrols prowling all the roads, and of a Kalmyk cavalry sub-unit (made up of Russian units collaborating with the Germans) being quartered in one of the nearby villages.

The impact of these reports was even reflected quite clearly on the otherwise indifferent face of our messenger. He was particularly worried about the fighter planes and the cavalry.

"Cavalry," he said to me, "that's a pretty unpredictable thing. They move quickly from place to place. They could screw up our business on the ground. And the fighters could do the same thing in the air."

One afternoon, the parish priest brought us a new and highly disturbing bit of news. A Hungarian transport plane had crashed in a field next to our village. It must have gotten into some kind of whirlwind, because it very suddenly lost a wing and crashed into the ground, smashed to bits. It was carrying mail to the front-line units. All of the crew members were killed. Some boys from our village immediately ran up to the wreckage of the plane and removed the weapons and anything else of any value whatsoever.

A couple of hours after the boys, the Gestapo showed up and naturally figured out that there had been looting. All kinds of military, medical and police commissions started arriving. The roads and villages — including our Zdrochec, among others — were crawling with German cars. The chief of the local Gestapo ordered that an announcement be made to all the village elders in the area, to the effect that if the items stolen from the airplane weren't found, hostages would be taken from each village.

With despair in our hearts, we peered through the curtains of our room at the German cars speeding by, and at the shouting gendarmes. They could enter the parish hall at any moment in search of hostages. Then they'd discover us: not registered in Zdrochec, carrying papers from Warsaw that didn't authorize us to stay in the village, and counterfeit to boot.

I pressed my burning forehead to the window, begging God to finally put an end to this see-saw of nervous tension and grant us the right weather to allow us to tear ourselves away this very same night from this cauldron, which was getting hotter day by day.

Every time the door to our room opened, my companion and I would look at the messenger or priest with a questioning expression. Regular as clockwork, we would find out about yet another German patrol, another dragnet, a new unit quartered nearby.

I finally went completely dull. I actually stopped believing that our trip was going to be successful. I even stopped believing there was any possibility of a safe return to Warsaw. The Soviet front was drawing inescapably nearer. The Germans were going crazy.

"I'm not going to get out of here," I said to myself, "It's like I'm trapped. My responsibility for the mail and my duty to render all basic assistance to the ailing JHR have got me nailed down to this village. And above all, the fact that the air bridge isn't being called off means I can't work on any other plan. The only thing we can do is wait: either for the airplane, or to get arrested."

In the event the Germans should raid Zdrochec — upon consultation with JHR — I devised a plan to hide away in the little church next door. The parish priest had given me the keys to the back door of the sacristy. One morning I had a look at the church's attic — I dusted off a few boards so there was someplace to sit down — and only then did I begin to feel a little bit safer. Surely they wouldn't search the church! JHR was pretty calm for his part. Who could possibly be looking for a little old man, and paralyzed at that?

We waited. The hours crawled on like days, the days seemed like years.

The only good news we received during those several days was a radio communiqué about an assassination attempt on Hitler. A hundred rumors started racing around, as usual, twisting the BBC report this way and that. Hitler was dead! Goebbels, Himmler and Göring were all dead! The war was over! When the priest burst into our room with bombshells like these, JHR

Eight. The Third Bridge

would interrupt his game of solitaire, ask the priest a few questions and return to his cards, calmly saying:

"Not even you, Father, are required to believe in miracles like these. What can we conclude from these reports? That there was an attempted assassination of Hitler, and that it failed."

The war kept on going — roaring with ever-closer cannons, rumbling with ever-more-frequent airplanes and cars, with those detested German uniforms coming and going, ever new and yet the same as before.

* * *

Then came the day of July 25th. In the afternoon, the organist gave us a different message than usual. He poked his head into our room through the window and quickly blurted out:

"The operation's tonight. Everything's ready. The passengers are to be ready at eight o'clock this evening."

And he was gone.

My hands shaking with emotion, I quickly packed my few things — some souvenirs for my relatives and friends, several books, a few German newspapers. Then I helped JHR pack his things and left the house.

In the empty church, full of flowers and greenery, illuminated by the rays of the westward-bound sun, which were broken up by the stained-glass windows, I made my confession to the parish priest. My confessor must have been even more moved than I. With a trembling, sincere voice he said to me:

"May God bless you, my son!"

He made the sign of the cross on my forehead with his finger and left the little church. I stayed, alone. I thanked God that the flight was going to happen, and asked Him to make it work out. I wasn't even aware of the fact that time was going by. I sat down at the reed organ and played something very softly, my thoughts wandering around the distant world; pictures flashed before my eyes, one after the other.

The sound of the cowbells on the cattle coming in from the field called me back from my reverie. It was getting to be evening already — the appointed hour was approaching. I slipped back into the parish house.

Punctually at eight o'clock, Mirosław and Młot showed up. Both priests came in right behind them.

"Good evening. Hiya!"

We smiled at them.

"We're fully ready," my companion said.

"Are we going?" I asked.

The two officers didn't answer at all. Their faces were solemn. They carefully closed the door and windows, and with a wave of the hand asked the priests to leave us alone. My heart tightened up in a weird way when Mirosław started talking:

"I can't, I won't, cover anything up. The situation is difficult, and the obstacles are very serious. The airplane is already on its way. We got the news not long ago that it has taken off from the base. However, I can't see any way of pulling off the operation successfully under normal circumstances. I'm not talking about the airfield at Radłów — with that one, under normal conditions, there's no telling how things will turn out. The Focke-Wulfs or other German fighter planes could wreck everything for us, but they don't have to. I mean something else. The conditions might not be normal anymore: today two German planes landed right on our airstrip..."

"Storchs," Młot added.[2]

"...people got out, walked all around the meadow, talked amongst themselves for a long time. We were already starting to think that the action would have to begin with a fight with those Storchs, so they'd make room for the Dakota. But after a while they took off again. What is this supposed to mean? It may mean — not necessarily — that the Germans know our operational plans."

"And in that case, the airfield at Radłów is already deadly dangerous," JHR interjected.

"Yes. But that's not all. Two hours ago, about a hundred Luftwaffe infantry soldiers were quartered about one and a half kilometers from our landing strip. I just got the report. They have heavy machine guns, anti-aircraft cannons, searchlights and over a dozen cars and motorcycles. Their guard posts are set up outside the village, which means they're only about 800 to 1000 meters from the landing spot. Between us and them there's just a smooth, even field. They'll have to see the lights of our outpost, the plane's headlights, they'll have to hear the sound of the engines, see the landing and the movement on the field. That would wake up even a sleeping guard. And finally" — the officer seemed to heave a sigh of relief, getting to the end of his sorry speech — "on the other side of the landing strip, in the village on the left, they've stationed a cavalry unit. Distance: not quite three kilometers."

He stopped. There was utter silence.

"So what do you suggest, Sir?" my friend asked at last. I knew I couldn't get a single word out, my throat was so tight. I felt something like a grudge against God for not hearing my prayer. I was so sure, back there in the church! Why, then? Neither the mail, nor the military shipment, nor the important envoys, nor I would make it to London.

Mirosław spoke:

Eight. The Third Bridge

"I can risk the lives of my soldiers, and my own, but I don't have the right to decide over your lives and the fate of the mail. In the event of a fight with the Germans, which seems inevitable, we will surely lose. Each of you gentlemen will have to decide personally, each for himself. And you, Sir"— he turned to face me—"will also have to decide about the mail. And I must ask you to decide quickly, because if the operation is to take place, I'll have to give the final orders in a minute and send my people out. And that's why I've just come to see you gentlemen."

I was in despair. Could I possibly say yes? If I did that, the important envoys could die because of me— the ones waiting here as well as the others, who were on their way to Poland right at that moment. Besides, the mail could fall into the hands of the Gestapo. I was furious with the commander for putting the responsibility for the decision on our shoulders. I wouldn't have hesitated for an instant if he had decided the matter in the affirmative. I'd agree to it, and that's that. But me? I was supposed to decide? I didn't know, I had no idea what to do.

For a moment none of us said a word. Night was falling. The officers sat glumly at the table. Młot was drumming his fingers nervously on the tabletop and looked us silently in the eyes—first the one, then the other. Mirosław lit a cigarette and looked at me through the smoke. I felt as if the whole world was watching me, at times maliciously, at times sympathetically, then again brutally, ruthlessly.

Each second was an eternity ... each second said to me, "Are you afraid?" I answered each second anxiously: "I wouldn't be afraid if it was only me." And again, they would ask, "Are you afraid?"

"Anyone would be afraid in my situation," was my feeble defense.

The priest came in. He brought an oil lamp, set it on the table, adjusted the wick, turned it on, and slowly pulled down the blinds on the windows. He, too, looked intently into my eyes. I realized that I must have had a weird expression on my face. When he left the room, JHR started talking, completely unexpectedly. He spoke quickly, but was also totally calm.

"I have three questions. First: if they capture us, will we have enough time to destroy the mail? Second, will we be able to evacuate the air crew and the people who flew in with them? And the third question: in the event of a fight, will the Germans later take repressive measures against the local population?"

What a magnificent man!—I thought. "He has not only kept his cool, he's also got his wits about him."

Mirosław looked at JHR approvingly and replied at once:

"My answer to your first question is: yes, there will be enough time. I think we can hold the Germans back for twenty minutes, maybe even for half an hour. Ten minutes ought to be enough to destroy the mail. The second matter: we're going to try to evacuate the passengers arriving from over there and the air crew, as well as you folks, the passengers departing from here. Whether it will work out, I can't guarantee. And then the third question, as to whether there will be repressive measures. I can't predict anything; however, I don't suppose that anything serious will follow. If there should be something after all, well — 'tough luck,' as we say."

The Captain, who had been silent up to now, added: "It's a clear, fundamental rule of the Resistance that if you have an assignment of truly outstanding importance, then even if it entails a risk to the population, it should nonetheless be carried out."

The thought ran through my head that these officers were decent and courageous men. I was aware of the fact that only a moment earlier, I had prejudged Mirosław to be cowardly and panic-stricken. I was wrong: he was simply loyal. The officers looked at me. Evidently they considered my companion's words a positive reply, and now they were waiting to hear what I would say. A thought raced like lightning through my head. What was that? Aha. I know. I could see it clearly: *The priest is making the sign of the cross on my forehead and saying, "May God bless you, my son."*

I started talking, as if from my subconscious. My own words rang in my ears as if someone else were speaking.

"My answer: the operation is to be carried out. Only, provided the terrain will allow it, maybe we should move the landing strip by a few kilometers; there's probably still time, and these meadows are reportedly pretty wide. Because the greatest danger has to be those soldiers from the *Luftwaffe*."

"Włodek is working on that right now. If it turns out that there's a level field without furrows and ditches, we'll move the 'swamp' over. If not, we'll have to stay with the existing one and ... defend ourselves."

"In any event, we'll put the strongest defense on the side of that infantry unit," the other officer added.

"Yes, near the infantry — that is danger number one."

"Because on the other hand, it seems to me" — JHR interjected — "that those German planes landing on our field today were just a coincidence."

"Quite right. I think so, too," I joined in. "If the Germans should know our plans, then surely they'd try to surprise us in such a way that they might get hold of our plane. They wouldn't give themselves away by revealing that they knew the details of our operation."

"You may be right, gentlemen," Mirosław agreed. "And the cavalry unit is set up at the opposite end of the forest. They surely won't realize what's going on in time, and if they do get involved in the fight, it won't be till after the plane has taken off."

"Sure. Obviously," JHR said, somewhat maliciously. "As the two of us know best of all, the last air bridge went very smoothly. A few minutes after landing, the plane was already airborne, right? Maybe things will work out just as quickly this time."

When the officers had already stood up, I added: "And you guys shouldn't have too much trouble retreating into the darkness. I feel that a fight will be unavoidable, if only because you'll have to safely evacuate the mail and the people who are going to be arriving on that plane."

"Please don't worry about us," Mirosław said, "we'll manage. Well, we have to leave now to talk with the other passengers, especially the oldest one. We'll send the horses around ten o'clock. See ya!"

After they had gone, I turned out the lamp and opened the windows. Lying on our sofas fully dressed, we waited in the dark and listened for the rattle of a cart. Somewhere in the distance a shot rang out, and then another. Silence fell, broken only by the distant bass notes of cannons, and sometimes by the whistled signals of the local resistance guards, who were on the lookout for any approaching German reprisal expeditions that night. The distant hum of an airplane finally jerked me to my feet.

I glanced at my watch. It was just past nine o'clock. I couldn't sit still any more, or even stand still. I paced around the room, bumping into various pieces of equipment. JHR must have been snoozing, because he didn't say anything. I was trembling from the chill air and the excitement. Finally, at about a quarter to eleven, I heard the rattle of a cart. It was getting nearer, and then farther away. The sound got nearer again, finally it was totally clear. The cart circled around the parish house and came to a halt. Together with the parish priest, I led JHR in front of the house and carried our briefcases out. On the cart, Stanisław's beard looked white in the darkness. Our traveling companions were to arrive at the landing spot by another route. Next to the horses were several armed people: our escort. Excited and full of hope, we greeted the people who had just arrived; sadly and very gratefully, we said good-bye to the priest. We drove off into the darkness. Would the Good Lord ever let us visit these parts again?[3]

Our ride along bumpy side roads was long and very difficult. Several times, we barely avoided landing in the ditch at the side of the road. The ceaseless shaking was making my head spin. We were stopped several times by Home Army checkpoints. Taking advantage of the directions they gave us, we avoided places where there were Germans quartered.

Just before midnight, we were in place. Gathered into a tight little group in a large field, we spoke in low voices with Mirosław.

"We're one kilometer from the Germans," he informed us. "We couldn't change the landing spot. There are all kinds of molehills, and besides, in the dark we might not have noticed some kind of ditch or other obstacle which could have turned out to cripple the plane. Security is good, but please be quick about loading into the plane, because I don't think we'll get off without a fight."

I looked around in the darkness. Our carts stayed behind, at the edge of the forest. They were waiting there for the mail and passengers arriving from the free world. A few silent, ominous shadows were lurking near us, appearing and disappearing. One of the soldiers, Kmicic, who had helped me carry the ailing man over, stood next to us, ready to be of further assistance. I checked for the mail bag; it was in place. Quietly, I greeted my remaining traveling companions. JHR was leaning on my arm with his entire weight. Tomasz Arciszewski stood at my other side. We all began listening intently.

We were surrounded by the soundless night. It seemed as though the whole world was asleep. Nary a sound, not from where the Germans were, not from the sky—just someone speaking in a hushed voice.

"There it is, there it is, it's coming in!"—the waiting, trembling group quietly whispered.

The hum of the engines was faint and distant. It would rise for a moment and then get farther away. It would get more distinct, only to fade away. At times I felt that I was hearing an airplane, then again it seemed that it was just the trees rustling. Finally the hum got stronger, started to grow, increase, become more powerful.

There was the clear, high sound of the lead officer's whistle, and all around the field the lights went on, glimmering like fireflies. They laid out a straight landing strip in the middle of the meadow, as well as a shorter cross-strip.

The luminous dials of my wristwatch indicated it was five minutes to midnight.

We were all trembling with emotion. Would the pilot notice us, but the Germans not notice us? Would he land without any trouble?

Judging by the sound of the engines, the airplane was starting to circle.

"He must have spotted us already," someone whispered next to me.

"Right there! The dark silhouette!" someone else shouted out loud.

"He's got his bearings! He's turning! He's coming in for a landing!"

I, too, finally saw the plane's silhouette. The agreed-upon signals began to flash from the Dakota. That was it for sure, and not some kind of surprise from the Germans. A second later, powerful lights came on, beaming out from the wings, slicing through the dark of night. They hit us! What an unforgettable sight! Right before my eyes were the silvery circles of two propellers, spinning in the powerful beams of the headlights. Ahead of them, the diamond dewdrops in the grass glistened with multi-colored light.

He's landing! But ... Jesus ... he's coming straight at us! He's gone off the path laid out by our lights, in a moment he's gonna crush our entire group, standing here rooted to the ground. There's no possible way to get away. There's a man leaning against me who can't walk. I can't leave him here.

On my other side, Mr. Tomasz Arciszewski grabbed my arm tightly. He stood there, thunderstruck. However, the others weren't running away, either. It was all happening too fast. A general paralysis of the will! The entire group, blinded by the lights, deafened by the roar, leaned to one side like a stand of wheat in a hailstorm. Several soldiers hit the ground — the wet grass.

The high-beams were drilling painfully into my brain, and yet I couldn't take my eyes off them. I couldn't think about anything.... The End!

But no! No! The pilot must have seen us and figured it out in time. Besides, Włodek was waving his flashlight like a madman. The roar of the engines increased strongly. With a terrific whooshing noise, the black monster stood straight up and climbed back into the air right over our heads, making an enormous racket. We were hit by a powerful blast of air.

The pilot turned off his headlights, circled around once, circled again ... as he made his circles, preparing for another landing approach, I felt like a person whom a firing squad had shot at and missed.

With unnatural and somehow guttural voices, we spoke of death, which had brushed up so close against us. I wasn't even thinking about the Germans at all.

"He's landing again."

"Yeah. Getting it right this time."

"Well, not exactly, go left a little, go left!" The deputy commander was unwittingly shouting out orders, directing the pilot with his hands.

The wheels touched down, the airplane hopped up once and then again, then rolled along and came to a stop right before the end of the grassy airstrip marked by the lights.

"A Dakota," I said to JHR. "I flew in one of those from England to Italy to meet you half a year ago, Sir."

The high beams were extinguished and everyone ran to the plane, going around the back end. The powerful airstream laid the tall grass neatly down in rows, knocked a few people over, tore a few caps off people's heads. With Kmicic's help, I carried the ailing man to the plane's door. Someone opened it. One after another, the people who had just flown into the country hopped out of the plane.[4] We were set up in a row, and they quickly passed us with barely a "hi" or a "howdy" before they were swallowed up by the darkness. Someone led them toward the waiting carts. The air crew and the Home Army soldiers carried out the equipment brought over from England. Parcels were passed from hand to hand. Others carried them to the edge of the forest, to the carts.

The engines kept roaring. We, the new passengers, waited for the order to board the plane. I checked to make sure the bag of mail was close by me. I felt relieved, thinking that everything was going according to plan.

I caught a glimpse of an airman's flight suit, with "Poland" on the sleeve and a familiar face. Who's that? Ah yes, Lieutenant Szrajer, the very same one who flew to Poland with us in April on the auspicious date of four fours. I called over to him. We exchanged a few hurried words.

"Ah, it's you, Sir," he shouted. "Bravo! And your bigwig is — what? — not wearing a mask?"

When he flew us to Poland, Lieut. Szrajer was on his seventieth combat mission; the current flight was his ninety-ninth sortie.

"It has to work out," he said with a laugh, "because I want to reach a hundred."[5]

"I'm sure it will," I replied, "but what's with the little shovel?" I asked, seeing he had a camp shovel in his hand.

"Oh yeah. I almost forgot, and then I would have caught hell from my friends back at the base. Excuse me just a minute."

He moved the shovel across the turf a couple of times and gathered some Polish soil into a little bag.

"A souvenir!" he shouted to us, running, and hopped into the plane.

"Passengers and mail, board the aircraft!"

I jumped into the middle of the Dakota. I helped those people who were entrusted to my care get in and take their places, then I pulled in the mail bag. I took a deep breath and wiped the sweat from my brow. Through the noise of the engines, I could hear the good-byes being shouted to us from outside. I made out Mirosław's stentorian voice:

"We'll see you in a free Poland. And remember! Send us more weapons!"

I waved at him. The doors were slammed shut. The air crew passed by us, disappearing one by one into the pilot's cabin. One of them, the mission commander, was a New Zealander; there were two Englishmen and one Pole, the deputy commander.[6] As he entered the cabin, he shouted to us:

Eight. The Third Bridge

"Hang on tight, and remember your seat belts! We're about to get going."

The roar of the engines got louder. The whole plane was shaking. In a moment, it would start rolling, get up to speed and climb into the air. There was a little window right next to me, through which I observed a Home Army soldier standing by the wing. In his hand, he held a flashlight, shining a pale green light. I could see someone's legs, standing in the slanting, waving, wet grass. In a moment, those legs would disappear and the little light would start to get smaller and more distant.

But what's this? The engines are going silent?!

The pilots got out, then after a second they returned; we were totally disoriented and didn't know what was going on. The engines roared once again, the tail lifted up slightly just as before, but the plane wasn't moving.

The engines went quiet. The door to the pilot's cabin was violently jerked open, and the excited New Zealander ran out, shouting in a high voice:

"All out! We're going to fire the plane!"

"Get out! Get out!" the Pole called out.

We were dumbfounded. As if in a dream, I threw the mail bag out the door. I helped the other passengers get out, especially the one who couldn't walk. The Polish airman had a forceful conversation with the Home Army commander, who shortly thereupon gave the order:

"Passengers and mail, to the carts!"

We walked toward the forest, trudging through the wet grass. Every few seconds I turned around, wanting to see them torch the plane. At first I felt something akin to curiosity, wondering what it was going to look like, but then I just felt a dull fear. What were we going to do with ourselves? If the Germans hadn't spotted us up till then, or hadn't figured out what was going on, then an airplane in flames would bring them over, without a doubt. We had to get out of there as fast as possible. However, the people I was accompanying were unable to run. One of them was very old, the other was utterly unable to move his arms or legs.

With chapped lips, I started praying feverishly. I don't actually know what I was praying for; first, it was to escape into the forest with the mail and my companions; then, it was to fly away after all and have everything work out; then I prayed for a machine gun in my hands, and finally it was for nothing in particular. I just kept repeating, "but deliver us from evil ... but deliver us from evil..."

Someone called to us from the direction of the plane. At first, I couldn't understand what it was all about, but then I heard it clearly:

"Passengers and mail, return!"

We were swept up. We carried the ailing JHR at a full run. The others were running after us. We got to the plane, feverishly asking:

"What's going on? What happened? Did...?"

"Get on board, we're going to fly."

"We couldn't move, the wheels were stuck too deeply. We've laid down some boards. It ought to work this time."

In a couple of heartbeats I was inside the plane. I looked around quickly to make sure the passengers were all safely seated, glanced at the mail bag, and the doors were slammed shut with a loud noise.

The Dakota's engines rumbled to life, one by one, and warmed up. The airplane was shaking, just as we were shaking with emotion; it was waiting for its great experience, just like us — uneasily, impatiently. Take off! ... Take off!

I felt all the blood in my body rushing to my heart, I could feel my whole body getting colder and colder. I was going pale, very pale.

The little green light outside didn't move an inch. Oh merciful God, not this again! And I was so awfully tired, so terribly weak....

The cabin door opened. "Stop feeling sorry for yourself!" — something within me called out — "Get to work!" I already knew what the crewmen were going to tell us as they ran out. I was already in the doorway when I heard the words, "We're going to fire the plane!"

We walked at a normal pace, following the clear trail we'd made in the grass the last time. For a moment, the world seemed so boring to me that I couldn't care less, to the point where I felt a chilly emptiness in my breast. Then I pulled myself together, took a look at my two companions and felt ashamed of my weakness. I felt a growing respect for them. Brave people. They weren't breaking down. One was marching spryly along, hatless because the wind had torn the hat from his head; he was calmly smoothing down his milky-white beard. We were carrying the other one in a four-handed seat carry. He must have been enormously weary, doubly so because of the pace of the unfolding events and his long, severe illness. However, he gave no sign of it. In his lively eyes you couldn't make out any apprehension; on his face, covered with wrinkles, there was a slight smile. Maybe he would even come up with a joke, but hardly any of us felt like laughing.

This time, we didn't get far away from the plane. We were told to turn around again, and ordered to wait about fifty steps from the plane. The engines went quiet, people were talking and gesturing, running back and forth. Somewhere up above, we could clearly hear the sound of engines, surely those of a German plane. This didn't make the slightest impression on anyone.

Eight. The Third Bridge

Soaked with dew and sweat, we waited impatiently once again to find out whether our efforts would be successful.

I couldn't stand still. I walked up to the front of the plane. With their bare hands, the soldiers were digging deep troughs in front of the wheels, which were sunk in the mud. The lead pilot was watching from the side with his hands in his pockets and a cigarette in his lips. I heard him say:

"Well, that's better. And besides, I'll cut the brakes altogether. That may do it."

"Return! We're going to try it one more time!"

Once again we boarded the plane. Once again I checked the mail. The door slammed behind us. This time, too, the Home Army commander shouted out, just as before:

"We'll see you in a free Poland! Remember! Send more weapons!"

What was he hollering like that for?[7] I got angry at this totally innocent person, thinking we bloody well weren't going to fly anyway. Once again, this whole thing just started feeling ugly to me, and I didn't feel like living. Dragging my feet, I got to my seat and sat down heavily. I was completely fed up.

But when I looked out the window at the green lights, I was suddenly overcome by the feelings of a gambler. Would the plane move, or not? Despite the enormous weariness, the tension was rising. Once again, I felt that my heart was in my throat and my face was on fire ... what? Was I dreaming? Was I in control of my senses? I was falling into a black abyss. Where was that green light? It was getting more distant, getting smaller —*getting smaller...!*

"It moved!"—I shouted out, finally realizing what had happened—it had moved!

The Dakota rocked back and forth, jumped a few times on the uneven ground, gathered up its strength, tightened up. I felt a slight pressure on my stomach. As if heaving a great sigh of relief, the airplane lifted off from the ground.

I looked at my watch. It was 1:30 A.M. on the 26th of July, 1944.

* * *

Our airplane had been on the ground for over an hour, raping the silence with its roaring engines and then going silent. The high beams of its headlights had torn open the dark of night. How had it happened that the Germans didn't attack us? I don't know. Maybe they were afraid, or perhaps they thought it was one of their own planes? I don't know. Had they noticed us or not? Oh, that I do know without the slightest doubt. They had seen us and heard us. They were only one kilometer away.

Be that as it may, up to the time of our takeoff, not a single shot had been fired. No lights came on in the distance. Maybe the fight was just starting now?

I looked out the window. It was black down there. I couldn't see anything, anything at all. Only darkness.

That's how we tore ourselves away from Polish soil; that's what the last moments of my stay in Poland looked like. Darkness — that's all. And yet there were people who stayed behind — women and men who would live and fight on in spite of the darkness, waiting for daybreak. For those people, freedom was the highest value in this world.

We had a tailwind and flew quickly. The landing gear was stuck, and didn't retract until we were over the Tatra Mountains.

The darkness surrounding us started getting grey, matte, pale. The stars disappeared like the candles in a church, extinguished one by one. Dawn came from out of the Balkans, and the golden sun brightened, arising as if out of the waves of the Adriatic. It drove out the last remnants of darkness.

All around us was freedom. We were slicing into it with the propellers of our powerful engines. The others, left behind in Poland, were soaking it up drop by drop, with their own blood. We needed to hurry as fast as we could, for just as we might run out of fuel, they might run out of blood.

Nine

The End of the Song

After we landed at Brindisi (with no brakes, coming to a stop at the very end of the longest runway, which had only just been completed) the people on the base were as happy as children, clapping us on the shoulders and practically carrying us to the canteen in their arms for a proper booze-up. Pouring streams of Black and White Scotch Whisky into ourselves, we were also shaking off all the fear and tension that had been our constant companions from the time we'd left Warsaw en route to the airstrip outpost, all the way up to the moment when we stood in the open door of the parked airplane and gazed upon the faces of our buddies from the base, smiling and tanned by the Italian sun. We, the passengers of the Third Air Bridge, had our specific reasons for the internal anguish we'd experienced, and even for our external trembling; so it was that we were met and greeted particularly joyously in Brindisi, and later in Bari, after our successfully completed Great Test. Based on the example of our third (and last, as it turned out) air bridge, one could clearly see what kind of gauntlet of difficulties and dangers had to be run, what a multitude of foreseeable and even more unforeseeable obstacles had to be surmounted, and what sheer dumb luck you had to have in order to pull off a show like that, even if it was buttoned down to the last detail, which it was.

Upon his arrival in Brindisi, JHR was enthusiastically received by the British. However, we were somehow separated, so that I wasn't quite sure what had happened to JHR. Later we were told that we were supposed to fly to London via Gibraltar in the same Dakota that very afternoon. Aboard the Dakota, JHR wasn't there anymore. Later on, I found out from him that after arriving in Bari, he held a long talk with the SOE officers: Truszkowski, Claubert and Holsworth. He stayed behind in Bari in order to fly directly to Cairo on the orders of Prime Minister Mikołajczyk. The rest of our team — Tomasz Arciszewski, the two Home Army officers with their shipment, and I with my mail — took off for Gibraltar in the afternoon. But Gibraltar turned out not to be Gibraltar, as the pilot had received a telegram in flight, instructing him to change course and fly to Rabat. We didn't know about this, and when we landed in the middle of the night we found ourselves wondering where we were. Where was the Rock of Gibraltar, where was the sea?

Only then did the pilot inform us: "This isn't Gibraltar, it's Rabat, in Morocco."

"Why?"

"I don't know. Those were the orders I got en route. There are hotel reservations for you."

Each of us got a separate room. Mine was adjacent to Captain Chmielewski's (code name Rafał). We had a shared balcony. Of course we couldn't get to sleep after all the things we'd just gone through, so he and I stayed up practically all night talking as compatriots, relaxing after the dramatic events of the air bridge and the further flight. We'd had a chance to talk a little on board the Dakota during the flight to Brindisi and on to Rabat, but at that time he'd been rather reserved. I had the impression that Rafał was a person who was: 1) cautious (it was only after I had told him quite a bit about myself that he described his underground activities to me, and I might add that he kept it to a few words — and I knew that he'd already been talking about me to Tomasz Arciszewski); 2) calm and truthful (he spoke almost impersonally, stressing the enormous contributions that other people had made; often, for example, he'd use phrases such as "I remember that exactly, since..." or "that is permanently etched in my memory, because..." followed by a point which confirmed the event he was describing; he was talking, among other things, about the time he sent his first report to London about a new weapons factory — shortly thereafter he'd been arrested, and spent a lot of time thinking about it at the Pawiak Prison and later at Auschwitz); and 3) sober in his assessment of political events (he

The author in London, 1944, after his return from Poland (Chciuk-Celt Family Archives).

Nine. The End of the Song   163

drilled me for everything I knew on the subject of our situation, asking very intelligent questions, colored somewhat by a certain pessimism caused by the overly submissive attitude of the Allies toward the Soviets). We talked for a long time on the subject of the V-1 and V-2, and only then did he confide in me that he was carrying fragments of a rocket.[1]

In the morning, we found out that we were to report for breakfast at the officers' casino. Upon entering the room, I realized that there was a pretty large group of people present, and I was astounded to see Prime Minister Mikołajczyk in the company of the chairman of the National Unity Council, Stanisław Grabski, foreign minister Tadeusz Romer, the journalist Marcely Karczewski, the Prime Minister's secretary Józef Żarański, translator Aleksander Mniszek, Colonel Markowski and the English Colonel Harold Perkins. Mikołajczyk invited us to his table, and during the course of our breakfast we found out that he (using his code name "Stem") was flying to Moscow. It became clear why we'd found ourselves in Rabat. Right there and then, in Rabat in the early morning, a talk lasting about an hour was held in which the participants were Mikołajczyk, Grabski, Romer, Arciszewski

Group photograph at the airport in Rabat, before departing for Cairo, July 27, 1944. Left to right: Tadeusz Chciuk, Tomasz Arciszewski, Colonel Harold Perkins, Stanisław Mikołajczyk, Marceli Karczewski, Tadeusz Romer, Stanisław Grabski, Aleksander Mniszek, Józef M. Żarański, Colonel Markowski (courtesy MHPRL Warsaw).

and myself. During this conversation I didn't say anything at all. Arciszewski did most of the talking, going off on numerous digressions completely unrelated to the matter at hand. He basically stressed that, speaking on behalf of the entire nation, he was surprised and outraged that Mikołajczyk, the Prime Minister of our legitimate government, "behind which the entire nation stands united as if it were the most sacred symbol," was flying to Moscow a mere couple of days after the Russians had created the puppet Lublin Committee, or PKWN, in Poland. Mikołajczyk grew impatient, although he didn't want to let Arciszewski see that, and he decided that since we wouldn't be able to comprehensively address such a major question in a short time, and it was already time to leave for Cairo, Arciszewski and I would fly with him to Cairo, where the actual conference would take place, including Retinger. The two military couriers would fly to London. After breakfast, Mikołajczyk spoke for some time with those two military couriers, after which he asked me to take a walk with him in front of the hotel.

Our conversation was brief: first, he recommended that I bring along the mail from the Chief Delegate and the political parties as well as articles from the press, and arrange them in such a way that he could look over the most important items in the airplane. Then he asked: "Are they going to badmouth me very severely over there as a traitor, because I'm flying to Moscow?" I replied that people in Poland were greatly depressed on account of the lack of any agreement with the Soviets, while at the same time the Red Army was making lightning progress — when they should be entering our country as if we were a friendly nation, not an enemy or an indifferent nation. Besides, I said that the creation of the PKWN (Lublin Committee) indicated that time was running against us and that this was really our last opportunity to try to come to some kind of agreement with Russia. Mikołajczyk asked if the Chief Delegate was going to come out into the open, to which I replied — on the basis of my talks with Sobol — that I thought he would reveal himself, along with a large part of his organization, but that he would leave a large part of it underground, in case that part that was revealed got arrested. I thought it would be a similar situation with the AK, except that the part that was revealed would be much smaller. Then Mikołajczyk said:

"The situation is very difficult. It would be best if I could come to an agreement with Stalin as quickly as possible, so that I could immediately go on to Warsaw, which should be free pretty soon. But I'm afraid that I won't be able to push my demands through. I don't have limitless powers from the government. And in the meantime, Stalin has really pulled a fast one on me by setting up the PKWN just as I'm on my way to talk to him. This problem will lead to arguments between Poles, while he will be in charge from above, unwilling to treat it as a Polish-Soviet problem. I fear that."

To this I said that Sobol, in refusing to talk to the PPR (Polish Workers' Party), had said that those talks should be held between the Polish Prime Minister and the Soviet Prime Minister, not the government and the PPR. I added that Polish society placed their hopes in Mikołajczyk that he would defend Lwów and Vilnius. Mikołajczyk replied: "As to Vilnius — I doubt it. Lwów — I think so, because Stalin will want to make a gesture. Anyway, I'm thinking positively in that regard, based on my talks with Roosevelt and Churchill." After that, Mikołajczyk sharply criticized the Chief Delegate for his position in the matter of talks with the PPR.

"The world is changing right before our eyes, the Communists are being honored everywhere as a democratic party, and they're playing an ever greater role everywhere, and he doesn't want to talk to them. He should look at Italy, Yugoslavia, France. By refusing to talk to the Communists, he's making my situation a lot more difficult, because when the British ask me why our underground movement isn't coming to any agreement with the Communist underground movement, I can't tell them that it's because we consider the Communists to be traitors."

Finishing up, Mikołajczyk said:

"Well, we'll talk some more later. Now tell me for yourself— not in the words of people in Poland, the Chief Delegate or anyone else — whether you'd think me a traitor if I agreed to give up Lwów and the oil fields."

"No," I replied, "and I'd do the same thing myself, even though I would consider that day of our life to be tragic, the blackest of all days."

A short time after that conversation we set out by air, on the way to Cairo. During practically the entire time of our flight from Rabat to a place in Libya called Marble Arch, where we spent the night, Arciszewski and Grabski slept, while Romer, Perkins, Mniszek, Karczewski and Markowski played bridge, and I handed "Stem" various items I'd selected from the mail. He would read them and occasionally tell Żarański to make a note of something. They were primarily excerpts from the secret underground press, as well as non-encrypted writings by the Chief Delegate and the political parties. Every other moment he'd ask me to explain various things. He was particularly sensitive to even the smallest attack on him in the press, or any article that decidedly took the tone of "We won't give up Eastern Poland." Then he'd say to me: "You see? And you keep telling me the nation wants an agreement."

When it was Perkins's turn to wait out a round of bridge, he came up to me and started talking, mainly asking me about the paratroopers, army couriers and JHR. After a while, Mikołajczyk butted into our conversation, asking Perkins to save his questions for later and telling him he'd soon be seeing Retinger personally, because he would like to ask me about something. Clearly embarrassed, Perkins respectfully withdrew.

During our flight, which took all day, the Prime Minister also spent three hours talking to Tomasz Arciszewski. In Marble Arch, after dinner, he continued talking to him, after which he summoned me and said:

"What did you bring him for? It's like we don't even speak the same language. I was very worried that Witos hadn't come. This guy's going to be grist for Raczkiewicz's mill, and they'll both return to the tradition of friendship between the ultra-right and the socialists, the way it was in 1926. When I tell him that we have a knife at our throats and an agreement is a necessity, he replies that we have our honor and we're going to fight the Russians the way we once did, and he starts telling me about 1905 and 1920. Is this the voice of the nation, or not?"

I answered that his was a voice from the nation, but not the voice of the nation, and that in my opinion this person was completely childish. He came with us at the express recommendation of the Chief Delegate and the National Unity Council, and he was to take up a position as the President's deputy. Witos hadn't agreed to make the trip, and this was the National Unity Council's second choice as a candidate.

Mikołajczyk replied, "This is going to make my situation a lot more difficult." When I asked how his trip to Moscow had come about, and whether Stalin had officially invited him, he replied with a smile:

"No, there was no official invitation and I haven't contacted Stalin at all. I owe this trip to a trick by Churchill. In one of his telegrams, he asked Stalin if he didn't think that in view of the rapid changes on the battlefront, he should settle the Polish matter and have a talk with Mikołajczyk. Stalin answered that it was indeed high time to take care of the matter of Poland. Thereupon Churchill told me, 'Get on my plane at once and go to Teheran. I'll send Stalin a telegram saying you're on your way and that he should send a plane to Teheran.' So I'm going, but I'm not at all sure that there will be a plane waiting for me. Perkins is supposed to contact London when we're in Cairo, and I'll know something more certain when we're there. There was no news yet in Rabat, and here in Marble Arch ... we weren't supposed to land here. But in the meantime Stalin has played a trick on me by creating the PKWN."

In a brief conversation with me in Marble Arch, Perkins attested that he was accompanying Mikołajczyk on his trip as a liaison to the British authorities, so that there wouldn't be any difficulties or misunderstandings. When I asked him if he was flying to Moscow, he replied — as if he were surprised at

Nine. The End of the Song

my naïve question — that he was only flying to Teheran, meaning that's as far as the British plane was going, and that's where he'd wait for Mikołajczyk to return from Moscow, in order to send him back to London on the very same plane. And he added: "But maybe that won't be necessary, because Mikołajczyk will fly to Warsaw and I'll return by myself."

In Cairo, after JHR's arrival and an early lunch (at which, in addition to the team on our plane and JHR, there were present: Major Truszkowski; the government's delegate for Mideast affairs, Henryk Strasburger; the Polish envoy to Cairo, Tadeusz Zażulinski; and a Polish colonel whose name I don't remember) there was a conference, attended by Mikołajczyk, Grabski, Strasburger, Romer, Arciszewski, Retinger and myself.

Mikołajczyk made the opening remarks. Laying out the situation, he said he still wasn't quite sure whether or not there would be a Soviet plane waiting for him in Teheran, as Perkins still hadn't had any news on that subject; nonetheless, he was flying there that same night and asked everyone in turn to say what they thought on the subject of an agreement with Russia. Romer began, as foreign minister, and after a general summary of the situation in the whole world and in Europe, he came out in favor of an agreement, with a forcefully emphasized reminder of the matter of Lwów.

"I am aware," Romer said, "that Stalin will under no circumstances want to begin the negotiations from the borders of 1939, but rather from the Curzon Line; but we must save Lwów by all means. This will allow us to not lose ground in our own society and it'll give us a moral advantage over the Communists, who have long since agreed to giving up Lwów."

Going second, Grabski got into historic deliberations, setting out to prove that if we lost our eastern territories but were allowed at the same time to shift to the west, then the nation would be able to live; it would simply be returning after the long Jagiellonian historical era to the earlier Piast era. He declared that, taking full responsibility for his words and speaking as a man standing over his grave, he was in favor of an agreement, because this was really the final hour already.

Arciszewski was asked to speak third, but he said he'd speak later on. Retinger was then invited to characterize the mood of the nation as he saw it, whereupon he launched into a speech about the heroism of the nation, about the excellent organization of the Delegature as well as the AK, and that they were looking to the West while simultaneously not wishing to dwell on the fact that the Red Army was already very close. After the second front was opened by the Allied invasion, people's enthusiasm rose enormously, principally because they expected the Germans to quickly break down on the western front while holding the eastern front. In effect, people were expecting the

PASZPORT DYPLOMATYCZNY	PASSEPORT DIPLOMATIQUE
W IMIENIU RZECZYPOSPOLITEJ POLSKIEJ	AU NOM DE LA RÉPUBLIQUE POLONAISE

Diplomat passport made out to "Marek Celt" at the Polish Legation in Cairo on July 29, 1944 (courtesy MHPRL Warsaw).

Anglo-Saxons in Warsaw sooner than the Russians, much the way they had counted on paratroopers coming into East Prussia in 1939. Hence, at the moment that the Red Army began rapidly approaching Warsaw while the front in France wasn't budging, people experienced a powerful feeling of disillusionment, and started thinking about reality in a different way, switching

Nine. The End of the Song

over to the hope that the Russians would behave like Allies. They knew that some kind of agreement would be necessary for that to happen, and that's why — according to JHR — they would accept any agreement that Mikołajczyk might sign in Moscow.

At that point, several protests were heard: what do you mean, any kind of agreement? — and if he agrees to attach Poland to the USSR as its seventeenth republic, the nation will accept that, too?

Retinger got confused, at a loss for words, then said that of course he meant any proper and reasonable agreement, since the nation did trust Mikołajczyk and his politics, after all. He went on to say that time was working against the Government-in-Exile in London, and that Russia was in a position of being able to present one *fait accompli* after another with ease (such as the recently created

Photograph of Józef Retinger, attached to his diplomatic paperwork from the Polish Legation in Cairo on July 29, 1944 (courtesy MHPRL Warsaw).

PKWN), and that if Mikołajczyk was going to form a government, then he had better do it quickly. It was his understanding that the British would give Mikołajczyk every possible support. At the conclusion of his speech, returning to the subject of the mood in Poland, he turned to me for support in his assertion that the nation wished to establish relations with Russia. Mikołajczyk interrupted, wanting to invite Arciszewski, and not me, to speak next, but he declined once again. Strasburger also wanted to wait, so I took the floor.

I questioned Retinger's account insofar as, even though I admitted that the nation wished for an agreement, I thought that people's thoughts were constantly with Vilnius and Lwów. I declared that when the rumor had started going round in June that Mikołajczyk was going to go to Moscow (at the time that he went to Washington), it had awoken a great joy among the Polish people, because the lack of established relations with Russia hung over us like a specter, and there was a general fear that if we didn't establish relations, the Soviets would start arresting everyone from the AK and the Delegature, just the way they were reported by sources in country to be doing in the areas around Wołyń and Vilnius. Hence the conclusion that an agreement was necessary. I added that it seemed to me that the perception of an agreement being needed was stronger among the younger generation than among the old politicians I'd been talking to.

Arciszewski took the floor. He spoke longer than anyone else, interrupting his speech several times by bursting into tears, so that people had to calm him down. Among other things, he went into the history of his own life, various details from various underground movements, tales of the heroism of the nation, and so on. His speech was chaotic and senile. Anyway, the conclusions that could be drawn from what he said were that an agreement could only be reached without the loss of our eastern territories, and that we couldn't agree to the Communists taking part in the government, because they weren't Poles. Then he turned to Retinger and said and said he didn't know on what authority Retinger could speak in the name of the Delegature, the National Unity Council and the AK; surely he, Arciszewski, had a greater claim to such authority, being in the resistance from the very beginning and being a member of the National Unity Council. According to him, the nation would not agree to any *diktats* from Russia, and would fight. He said this was the opinion of everyone from the right to the left, meaning from the SN (the Nationalists — not even mentioning the even more secret right wingers, who weren't represented in the National Unity Council) to the Polish Socialist Party, as well as the Home Army and the whole of Polish society.

There followed a moment of silence, after which I spoke up rather timidly, stating that the left in Polish society didn't end with the Socialists. The situation at that time, in my opinion, was such, and the political power system was such, that if we accepted the existence of the Centralization Party and the KRN, then the right would consist of the National Unity Council (possibly without the WRN), the center would be made up of the WRN and Centralization, and the left would be the Polish Workers' Party. We wouldn't even mention the secret far-right, i.e., the NSZ (ONR) because the Chief Delegate himself had told me that they were prepared to accept weapons and ammunition from the Germans to fight the Russians. We really couldn't admit people who were cooperating with the Germans.[2]

Arciszewski interrupted me several times, and finally declared angrily that we also couldn't admit people who were cooperating with the Russians, accepting weapons and ammunition from them and fighting the same kind of internecine battles. Anyway, he couldn't confirm that the NSZ were cooperating with the Germans, and after all, he ought to know best what matters were like under German occupation.

Retinger declared that he, too, had been told by the Chief Delegate that there was proof that certain groups within the NSZ were cooperating with the Germans. Arciszewski got hot under the collar, and alternating once again between crying and thundering, confirmed his earlier words. He treated JHR and me with obvious disdain.

Strasburger stated that people's voices from inside the country were very valuable, but that he nonetheless had to note that people in Poland weren't very clearly aware of the seriousness of the situation. Those who were outside the country had contacts with the whole world and could clearly see that the kind of power that Soviet Russia had become was such that you either get along with it or cease to exist. He spoke out in favor of an agreement and believed that Mikołajczyk would take care of everything all right. In the current situation, he didn't see anyone better suited to the mission.

Mikołajczyk thanked everyone and then, turning to Arciszewski, said with a smile: "Don't worry, Chairman, I'm not going over there to sell Poland out, I'm going to help." Arciszewski fell apart in tears again.

After this conversation Mikołajczyk talked for a fairly long time with JHR one on one, then with Perkins and JHR. When I asked JHR what they'd been talking about, he answered that he wanted to fly to Moscow with Mikołajczyk, but that he didn't agree to it, using Retinger's ailing state as an excuse, and that Perkins had supported Mikołajczyk. Right before flying off with his crew, Mikołajczyk asked me what I might know about the people involved in the PKWN. I replied that I didn't know much, since the PKWN was created during the time we were waiting for the plane to arrive from Italy, essentially cut off from all news reports. On the basis of talks I'd had with the Chief Delegate, I gave him a few names from the KRN, such as Bierut, Osóbka, Schwalbe, Janusz and Gomułka (I think), but I'm not sure if I already knew that at the time. Besides that, I thought they were all from the Union of Polish Patriots.

During all this time, not a word was said about the possibility of an uprising — not during the conference, nor in Mikołajczyk's conversations with me.

The day after Mikołajczyk took off, we flew to England in another plane, in the company of an SOE officer whose name I didn't know. When I sat down at the piano in Gibraltar and played the *Warszawianka*, a rousing anthem, Tomasz Arciszewski came up to me, having hardly spoken a word to me or Retinger during the entire trip, and said: "If you had spoken in Cairo the way you're playing now, things would have been considerably better," and then sang along: "Hey, all Poles, charge with bayonets fixed!"

We got to London on the 1st of August, 1944. The next day a press conference was called, with Arciszewski, JHR and myself taking part. During the press conference we found out that the uprising had begun in Warsaw. The situation underwent a diametric change. It was only now that I became convinced that all the things JHR had said about his contacts and relations in the world of politics were not exaggerations. I was still taking care of him, and witnessed how the most distinguished politicians, English and non-English, came to his hotel room or, more infrequently (due to his illness) he visited them: Anthony Eden, Richard Stafford Cripps, Ben Smith, General Gubbins, Brendan Bracken, Archibald Sinclair, Paul Henri Spaak, Mariel-Henri Jaspar, Curstins, Jan Masaryk and many others, to say nothing of the Poles.[3] At that time, JHR was a celebrity, a V.I.P. in the full meaning of the term. The main theme of his talks, as he told me, was the state of the Polish Underground and the matter of giving aid to the uprising, be it material or moral. He was one of the initiators of the Fund for Warsaw, which Lady Sinclair would head. He saw to it that an Englishman staying in Warsaw, John Ward, who had been sending dispatches via the Chief Delegate's radio transmitter, became the official correspondent of the *Times*.[4] Retinger also played a key role in getting the British to agree to airlift certain aid to Warsaw from their bases in Italy, and in getting the press to give more coverage to the uprising. I saw that Retinger could get a lot done in England and in several other, smaller countries, and I valued him immensely for the things he did.

I witnessed, among other things, Retinger's meeting with General Władysław Anders. They were friends. Anders came to the Dorchester, and I led him to the room of the ailing Salamander. "This is the guy who helped me in Poland, who saved me..." JHR said, pointing at me. Anders grasped my hand as if in recognition; I clicked my heels and withdrew. I could still hear:

"Oh, Recio, Recio, boy you showed 'em..." to which JHR said: "You're the one who showed 'em!" I'm sure the one was referring to the parachute mission of the "Oldest of the Silent Shadows" and the other was referring to Monte Cassino.

One day I was talking to JHR, he in his bed and I in a chair with my back to the door, when suddenly someone knocked at the door and JHR said in English, "Come in! Come in!"

The door opened, JHR looked in that direction, and I could see the anger in his eyes. I heard him say:

"You pig!"

It was Colonel Rudkowski — Rudy, the double-crosser of the Second Bridge.

"Recio, Recio, for God's sake! Do we have to go on like this with a third party present?"

Nine. The End of the Song

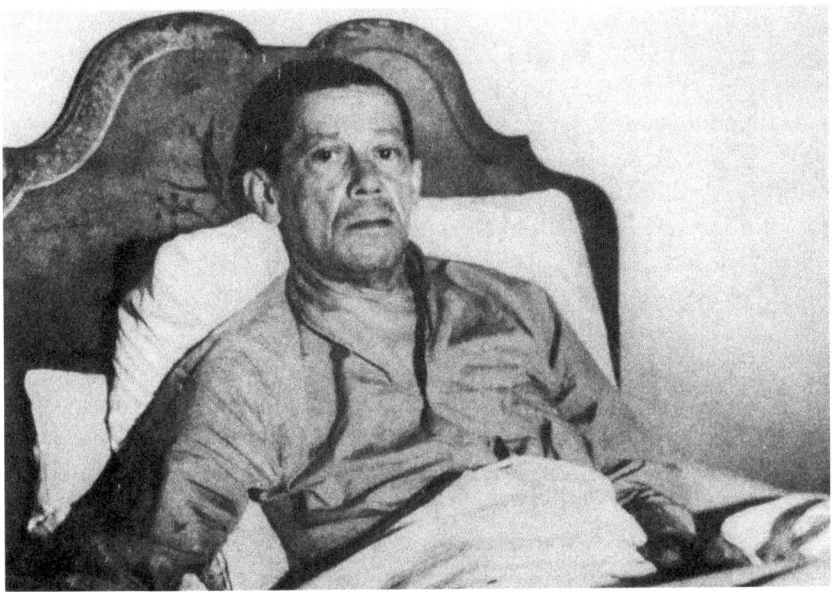

Józef Retinger recuperating from his poisoning, at the Dorchester Hotel in London, August 1944. Photograph by Datko (Chciuk-Celt Family Archives and MHPRL Warsaw).

"That isn't any third party to me. He's the first party as far as I'm concerned. It's you who are the third party, or even far more distant. You pig! And what, did you guys convince yourselves that I'm an agent? Whose agent? British? Soviet? Or maybe some other kind? You were convinced by those notes of mine, the ones you stole from me?"

"I handed everything over, Recio, everything..."

"But first you made some kind of photocopies of it all, am I right? You inspected those notes thoroughly. Were you convinced that I'm an agent? And you, who pretended to be such a great friend, had your hand in this dirty business. And my cigarette case with my gold sovereigns must have got stuck in your pocket..."

"Recio, here's your cigarette case, here are your gold sovereigns, your notebook ... I'm so very sorry, Recio, they ordered me to do it, I had to..."

"Yeah. Various criminals, such as yourself, always hide behind that. They had orders. You promised me that everything was going to be all right, you'd hand me my things at the airplane and I'd fly off. When I ran up to the plane half-conscious and soaked with dew, it was just taking off, with you and all my things. And after that I had another bath. And now I'm severely ill because of you, because of you guys. They didn't manage to kill me in the Underground, so they tried to rub me out this way, at least psychically, morally, by saying that Retinger's an agent..."

"Recio, I'm so very sorry..."

JHR interrupted him: "Ech, you know what, you'd better go. Leave whatever you were going to leave, I don't want to have anything more to do with you. And don't call me Recio anymore..."

Rudkowski's face lost its color; he was clearly beaten down to the point where I felt sorry for him. He went slinking away. And that was what the real ending of the Second Air Bridge looked like.

* * *

After Mikołajczyk's return from Moscow, I didn't have any contact with him whatsoever. He was busy all the time, wouldn't see me, and finally had Siudak relay to me his strong recommendation that I should write a full report, which I did. In the midst of my writing, I'd take parts of my report to the Presidium of the Council of Ministers in the hopes of getting through to see Mikołajczyk after all, which I was never able to do. It wasn't until the end of August that he agreed to a ceremony at which he'd be presented with a medal from the Officers' Candidate (Scout) School of the AK, which I'd been asked to see to back in Poland.

Scoutmaster Eugeniusz Konopacki, code names Trzaska and Gustaw, had played a key role in the Wigry resistance movement, and was also the commander of the Agricola Officers' Training Academy. At the time of my sojourn in Warsaw toward the end of May 1944, he had invited me to a secret ceremony marking the completion of a training course at Agricola, at which I gave a speech in my role as an emissary of the government. At that time I was given the school's medals, with a request that I present them to Mikołajczyk and the Commander in Chief, General Sosnkowski, upon my arrival in London. I was decorated with the same medal myself. I still have it to this day, and still get joy from that little souvenir: a white letter A on a bronze oak leaf, which signifies a year of service on a scout's uniform. The head of the *Szare Szeregi* had given Trzaska a real fight about that decoration, saying he had no right to create a medal like that, because decorations of any kind were antithetical to the *Szare Szeregi's* principles of secrecy and modesty, and so on.

I delivered the medals. I gave the one meant for General Sosnkowski to Scoutmaster Kazimierz Sabbat, Vice Director of the Supreme Scouting Committee, and he presented it to the Commander in Chief along with Olga Małkowska, who was Director of the Scouting Committee.

However, when Mikołajczyk found out that I had a medal from Agricola

Nine. The End of the Song

for him, he immediately came up with the idea of exploiting the occasion for the benefit of the people taking part in the Warsaw Uprising, whom the Germans still considered "bandits" who were not to be taken prisoner but executed by firing squad. It was difficult at that time to try to get the Allies to make the Germans recognize the AK fighters as combatants in the spirit of the Geneva Convention. An award ceremony was organized at the Presidium of the Council of Ministers, at which the Prime Minister was decorated with this medal from the Underground Officers' Candidate School, which was run by the Scouts. Dozens of the most distinguished western journalists were invited; there were Ministers present, the National Council was there, diplomatic envoys accredited by the Polish Government, the entire Executive Committee of the Scouts, reporters from the BBC and Polish radio. I handed the Prime Minister the medal and made some brief remarks about the people who had sent it to him through me, and who were at that very moment fight-

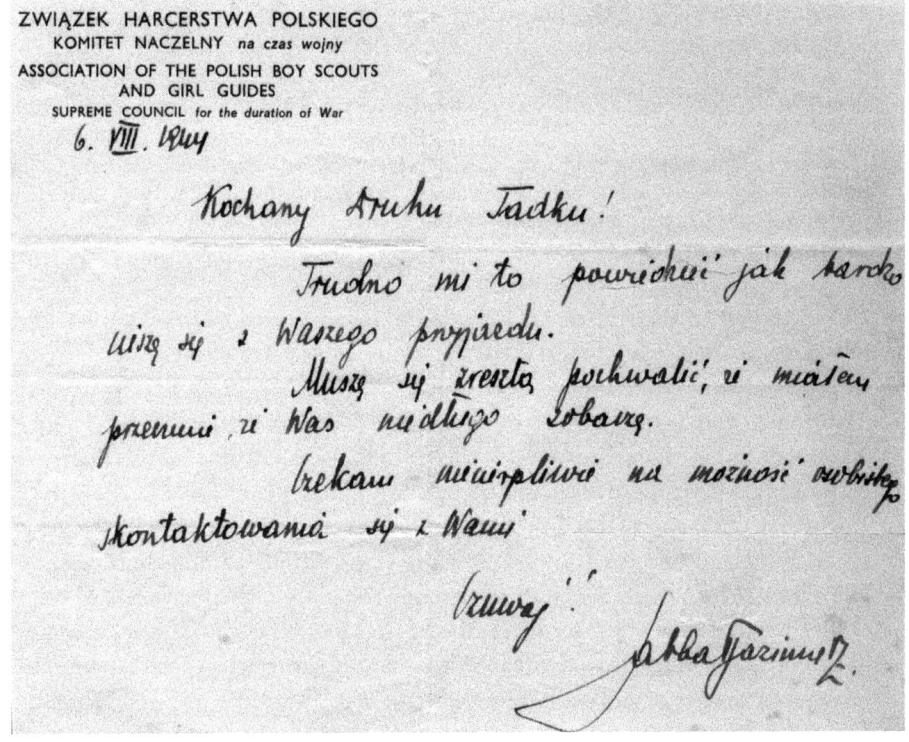

Note from Polish Boy Scout leader Kazimierz Sabbat to the author, dated August 6, 1944, expressing joy at his safe return and attempting to set up a personal meeting (courtesy MHPRL Warsaw).

Tadeusz Chciuk handing Polish Prime Minister Stanisław Mikołajczyk the Agricola medal, awarded by the Boy Scouts in Poland, in London, August 28, 1944. Left to right: Tadeusz Chciuk, Stanisław Mikołajczyk, Adam Romer, Władysław Banaczyk (courtesy MHPRL Warsaw).

ing bitterly on the barricades of Warsaw and being treated by the Wehrmacht not as combatants but as bandits. At that point Mikołajczyk gave a very forceful speech about the tragedy of the people taking part in the Uprising in the fighting city of Warsaw, who were executed as "Polish bandits" if they were captured, and the incomprehensible silence of the Western allies in this matter. He said that five tons of ammunition and equipment per day would allow the fighters to seize and maintain control of Warsaw. He concluded with a categorical demand that the United States and Great Britain should threaten the Germans at once with a death sentence for the most important cities of the Third Reich if they didn't recognize the AK fighters as legitimate combatants. The correspondents proved equal to the task: there were heaps of pointed articles in the press, and radio broadcasts went out into the world. The governments of the United States and Great Britain listened to the voice of the people. Hitler recognized the soldiers of the Polish underground army as combatants.[5] After the surrender of Warsaw, those fighters who wound up in German hands were no longer turned over to firing squads or the Gestapo, but taken prisoner. Among them were our fellow scouts from the *Szare Szeregi*, Polish scout troops and the *Wigry*; among them also were the people who had contributed with their Agricola medals to the recognition of AK soldiers as combatants, as well as some who begrudged them that decoration.

Time and again, I shed copious bitter tears in London at the thought of the fate of the city and its heroes, seeing what a tragic decision had been made, and thinking how much better it would have been not to follow through on that impulse, especially since the outcome of the war had already been decided. I spent sleepless nights in helplessness and sorrow as Warsaw, far away over there, rose up and fought while I could do nothing to help. There were so many people who were unable to give Warsaw their support, and so many who were unwilling.

Finally, one September night, even though Warsaw was already dying out in holy flaming ruins, I heard words of comfort whispered straight to my tired heart:

"Don't lose hope. Stay strong. No sacrifice can be in vain — especially a sacrifice so great."

Appendix 1.
Salamander's Report
(Operation Wildhorn II)

On or around the 5th of June, 1944, while still in Poland, "Salamander" dictated a report to the Prime Minister, describing the circumstances of his failed attempt to depart aboard the second Air Bridge, i.e., Operation Wildhorn II. The characteristics of the handwriting indicate that neither JHR nor Celt had written the report; "Salamander" just signed it. This is the earliest known source document concerning this event, translated here into English:

Report

The fact that I didn't make it onto the airplane on May 30th 1944 can be ascribed either to criminal negligence on the part of the operation's organizers, or else to their ill will. I couldn't have been late through my own fault since, in accordance with the standard procedure in these cases, I was treated as a "parcel" and complied in every way with the instructions of the operators. I must add also that I did not know, nor did I inquire even vaguely, where the airplane was going to take off from.

Since I've had the opportunity during my stay in Poland to observe repeatedly the unbelievable nimbleness, energy and precision of the people involved in these air drops, or indeed preparing an operation involving landing a plane, and having after all been specifically informed about the operation in L. by the Chief Commander as well as Rudy — it's hard for me to suppose that such glaring sloppiness could have crept into such an able organization.

I must add that as early as a week before the date of the 30th, I was unpleasantly puzzled by the fact that Rudy, who according to his own words was supposed to take special care of me, informed me unexpectedly after a conference held — without my being present — with Młot (the AK Commander on whose territory the airplane was to take off) that even though he was supposed to stay with me right up to the last minute, he was going to have to disconnect himself from me. Moreover, he claimed that our living together would be impossible in the future, due to security requirements. This seemed to me to be highly suspicious, all the more so because his female messenger was to stay with me. I expressed to Rudy in very sharp words my lack of confidence in this new setup, stating that if I should fail to make my flight, I would consider that to be his fault alone.

Moving now to the matter at hand, it presented itself as follows:

Mr. S., the owner of G., drove me away along with the female messenger, on Młot's instruction. On the way, we were joined by the Outpost Commander, Mr. W., a teacher from G., under whose specific care I was placed. At the appointed hour of 22:30, we arrived at the appointed spot, from where, according to our agreement, Młot was to take me to the take-off point. Not until about a quarter to midnight did one of the young boys under Młot's command arrive for me, and he took me and Mr. W. to the place that Młot had indicated for us, as he himself said.

Mr. S. and the female messenger stayed in the horse-cart on the road.

A few minutes after our arrival at the appointed spot, I spotted an arriving airplane, which landed a few hundred meters away from me. Mr. W. took my little suitcase and started running, together with me, in the direction of the airplane. The boy ran with us. I got to the spot one minute after the airplane had left, and I saw a large group of people there. Since I thought that airplane was only taxiing to find an appropriate take-off point, I shouted, "Where's Rudy?" Młot replied that Rudy had just flown off. In everyone's presence, I sharply rebuked Młot, who didn't even try to explain.

Młot didn't do anything at all to make my return trip to Warsaw any easier — in fact he didn't make any attempt at all to justify himself. Together with Mr. W., I returned to the horse-cart, where both Mr. W. and Mr. S., outraged by this ignominious misdeed, spontaneously stated that they were prepared to submit statements in this matter, which they considered scandalous and which they had observed in detail.

Luckily for me, Mr. S. invited me and the messenger girl, who had been left to fend for herself, over to his house for the night, and on the next day he took me to the train station, from which I returned to Warsaw — alone and without anyone's help. I had verbally asked the messenger girl, who had left before me, to submit a report on the whole matter at once, to be submitted to Chief Commanding Officer, and also asked her to relay to the Commander my wish that he send out a telegram immediately, ordering that all documents, papers and all my personal things be registered and stamped and given to you, Mr. Prime Minister, for safekeeping.

Sadly, however, I must state that even five days later that report has not made it to the ears of the Chief Commanding Officer.

As for my demand, seconded by the Chief Delegate, that an investigation be launched into this matter to find and punish the guilty parties, the Commander took a positive stance, of course, promising to carry through an investigation as soon as possible.

/-/ Salamander

Appendix 2.
Source Documents

I. Microfilm Frames 19–22 and 56

The author refers repeatedly to a large volume of "mail" being delivered from Poland to the Government-in-Exile and military command in London. This "mail" was primarily microfilm frames, rolled up tightly into special tins which had self-destroying charges inside them in case they were intercepted. There was a special procedure for opening them, and the frames were then printed out. Chciuk's orders on the inbound mission (Operation Salamander) make mention of over 1,200 such frames, containing political, military and intelligence messages to be delivered to the Polish authorities. On the outbound trip (Operation Wildhorn III), there was a significantly larger volume of these microfilm frames, to be delivered to London. They contained not only intelligence material, including detailed eyewitness reports from the concentration camps at Auschwitz and Majdanek (among others), but also cultural items including musical works by contemporary Polish composers — all using pseudonyms — and a few other creative pieces, such as the poem preserved on frame 56, written by an unknown female inmate at Auschwitz-Birkenau. She probably died. This heartbreaking poem is presented here for the first time, alongside a literal translation. Sadly, deterioration of the films has rendered one line illegible.

Following that, Frames 19–22 constitute one of several reports about conditions in the concentration camps, in this case Auschwitz, the most notorious of them all. This original source material has never been published before.

Frame 56

List z Rewiru / Birkenau /
Piszę do Ciebie, Mamo,
Co miesiąc list oficjalny,
Zawsze prawie to samo,
Tekst dobrze znany, banalny,
    Że żyję, że jestem zdrowa
    I że za paczki dziękuję ...
Co myślisz czytając te słowa?
Jak je rozumiesz, co czujesz?
Czy wiesz, jak straszną są blagą?
ą ....
    ....
    ....
    Minęły dni uniesienia,
    Romantyzm djabli wzieli.
    Czy wiesz jakie mam marzenia?
    Marzę o czystej pościeli.
I żeby się jeszcze udało
Mieć czasem gorącą wodę ...
Mamo, czy wiesz, moje ciało
Jest jednym, wielkim wrzodem ...
    To pchły i wszy mnie tak jedzą
    Że czasem wyję z rozpaczy ...
    A na wolności, czy wiedzą
    Co słowo "durchfell" znaczy?
Czy u was można iść lasem
I śpiewać gdy przyjdzie ochota?
Mamo, ty nie wiesz, jak czasem
Dzika ogarnia tęsknota ...
    A na stajennej pryczy
    Tuż obok człowiek umiera,
    Oczy ma błędne i mzyczy ...
    / śmierć zbliża się i wybiera ... /
Krzyczy, że żyć pragnie jeszcze,
Że chce do dzieci, do domu ...
Gorączka ją pali i dreszcze.
Śmierć zbliża się po kryjomu.
    O nie czekajcie już dzieci,
    Nie płaczcie w bólu, tęsknocie ...
    To lepiej, że nie wiecie,
    ze trup jej leżał w błocie,
Pod blokiem z innymi trupami ...
O nie leżała tam sama
Całymi godzinami,

Letter from the Infirmary / Birkenau
I'm writing you, Mom,
My monthly official letter,
It's always pretty much the same,
The text well known and banal,
    That I'm alive and well
    And thank you for the parcels ...
What do you think when you read
    /these words?
What do you make of them, what
    /do you feel?
Do you know what an awful load of crap
    /they are?
Umm ...
    Gone are the uplifting days,
    The devils have snatched romance.
    Do you know what I fantasize about?
    I dream of clean sheets.
And that I might still manage
To have some hot water sometime ...
Mom, do you know that my body
Is one big open sore ...
    It's the fleas and lice eating me so
    That sometimes I howl in despair ...
    And people who are free, do they know
    What the word "durchfell" means?[1]
Can people there take walks in the woods
And sing if they happen to feel like it?
Mom, you don't know how sometimes
This wild yearning grabs hold of me ...
    And on a plank bed in this stable
    Right next to me, somebody's dying,
    Her eyes look lost and they're seeping ...
    Death's getting closer and selecting ...
She yells that she wants to keep living,
That she wants to go home to her kids ...
She's burning with fever and shivering.
Death's getting closer, stealthily.
    Oh, don't wait any longer, children,
    Don't cry in your pain and yearning ...
    It's better that you not know
    That her dead body lay in the mud,
Under the block with the other corpses ...
Oh, she didn't lie there alone
For hours on end,

Appendix 2

```
              List z Rewiru / Birkenau /
Piszę do Ciebie, Mamo,                    Pod blokiem z innymi trupami...
Co miesiąc list oficjalny,                O nie leżała tam sama
Zawsze prawie to samo,                    Całymi godzinami,
Tekst dobrze znany,banalny,               Ukochana wasza mama.
Że żyję,że jestem zdrowa                  ..........................
I że za paczki dziękuję ...                   Tam druga dobiega kresu,
    Co myślisz czytając te słowa ?           Jęczy i żebrze pomocy.
    Jak je rozumiesz,co czujesz ?            Pomocy?ktożby się trudził?
Czy wiesz jak straszną są blagą?             Wszak i tak skończy tej nocy...
§..........................               Dwadzieścia lat ma dziewczynka
..........................                Każdy się nią zachwycał.-
    Minęły dni uniesienia,                Dziś chora,wyschła,sina...
    Romantyzm djabli wzięli.              Zeżarła ją pęcherzyca.
    Czy wiesz jakie mam marzenia?             A w domu matka wciąż czeka,
    Marzę o czystej pościeli.                 Czekają siostry i bracia,
I żeby się jeszcze udało                      Nie wątpią ani na chwilę,
Mieć czasem gorącą wodę...                    Że rychło wróci ich Wacia.
Mamo,czy wiesz,moje ciało                 I narzeczony się smuci
Jest jednym,wielkim wrzodem...            I modli się najgoręcej...
    To pchły i wszy mnie tak jedzą        Ona już nigdy nie wróci,
    Że czasem wyję z rozpaczy...          Nie wróci,jak tyle tysięcy...
    A na wolności,czy wiedzą              ..........................
    Co słowo "durchfell" znaczy?          ..........................
Czy u was można iść lasem                 ..........................
I śpiewać gdy przyjdzie ochota?           Dokoła siebie wciąż widzę
Mamo,ty nie wiesz,jak czasem              Tyle tych ciał świerzbowatych.
Dzika ogarnia tęsknota...                 Mamo,jak ja się brzydzę!
    A na stajennej pryczy                 To obóz trędowatych...
    Tuż obok człowiek umiera,             ..........................
    Oczy ma błędne i mżyczy...            Kiedy nareszcie zasypiam,
    /Śmierć zbliża się i wybiera.../      Myśląc o tobie,mamo,
Krzyczy,że żyć pragnie jeszcze,           Kocem się z głową nakrywam
Że chce do dzieci,do domu...              I śni mi się ciągle to samo...
Gorączka ją pali i dreszcze.              Że się pochylasz nade mną,
Śmierć zbliża się pokryjomu.              Jak niegdyś nad mą kołyską.
    O nie czekajcie już dzieci,           Rękę masz taką przyjemną...
    Nie płaczcie w bólu,tęsknocie...      Stoisz tak długo i ślisz..
    To lepiej,że nie wiecie,              Nie czuję durchfallu się
    że trup jej leżał w błocie,           Ni...
```

Microfilmed text of a poem written by a female inmate in the infirmary at Birkenau, addressed to her mother. The anonymous poet must have died. This page bears the frame number 56 and has deteriorated quite a bit. Never before published. Please see translation in this chapter (Chciuk-Celt Family Archives).

Ukochana wasza mama.	Your beloved mother.
....	....
Tam druga dobiega kresu,	Over there another one's end is nigh,
Jęczy i żebrze pomocy.	She's moaning and begging for help.
Pomocy? któżby się trudził?	Help? who on earth would bother?
Wszak i tak skończy tej nocy ...	She won't last through tonight anyway ...
Dwadzieścia lat ma dziewczynka	The girl is twenty years old
Każdy się nią zachwycał.—	All the guys were crazy about her.—
Dziś chora, wyschła, sina ...	Now she's sick, dried out, bruised up
Ze żarła ją pęcherzyca.	Eaten alive by blistering skin lesions.
A w domu matka wciąż czeka,	And at home her mother's waiting yet,
Czekają siostry i bracia,	Her sisters and brothers are waiting,
Nie wątpią ani na chwilę,	They don't doubt for even a minute
Że rychło wróci ich Wacia.	That their Wacia will soon be home.
I narzeczony się smuci,	And her fiancé is so sad
I modli się najgoręcej ...	And he prays most fervently of all ...
Ona już migdy nie wróci,	She's never coming back anymore,
Nie wróci, jak tyle tysięcy ...	Not coming back, like so many thousands
............................ą	...........................umm
....	....
....	....
Dookoła siebie wciąż widzę	All around me I keep seeing
Tyle tych ciał świerzbowatych.	So many of these scabies-ridden bodies.
Mamo, jak ja się brzydzę!	Mom, this is so disgusting!
To obóz trędowatych ...	This place is a lepers' colony ...
....	....
Kiedy nareszcie zasypiam,	When at last I start to fall asleep,
Myśląc o tobie, mamo,	Thinking of you, Mom,
Kocem się z głow nakrywam	I pull my blanket over my head
I śni mi się ciągle to samo ...	And dream the same dream every time ...
Że się pochylasz nade mną,	That you're leaning over me,
Jak niegdyś nad mą kołyską.	The way you used to lean over my crib.
Rękę masz taką przyjemną ...	Your hand is so pleasant ...
Stoisz tak długo i blisko ...	You stand there so long and so close ...
Nie czuję durchfallu wtedy	I don't feel the dysentery then
Nie--------------------	I don't--------------------
ą	umm ....

FRAME 19

OŚWIĘCIM.

"Konzentrationslager Auschwitz"

    The concentration camp at Oświęcim was created on June 14, 1940. At that time, 750 prisoners were transported to the camp from provincial prisons in Kraków, Tarnów and other places. These were mostly "tourists" captured

O Ś W I Ę C I M.
/"Konzentrationslager Auschwitz"/.

Obóz koncentracyjny w Oświęcimiu powstał w dn.14.VI.1940 roku. Przywieziono doń wówczas 750 więźniów z Krakowa, Tarnowa i innych więzień prowincjonalnych. Byli to przeważnie "turyści", schwytani na granicy węgierskiej czy słowackiej w drodze do wojska za granicą. W sierpniu i wrześniu przybyły do Oświęcimia pierwsze transporty z W-wy, złożone częściowo z więźniów z Pawiaka, w przeważającej części jednak z ofiar łapanek ulicznych i blokad domowych. W październiku 1940 roku numer bieżący więźnia dochodził już do 6.000. W pierwszych miesiącach istnienia obozu śmiertelność była nieznaczna, w związku z organizacją i przewidzianą rozbudową otwierała się dla więźniów dawniej przybyłych pewna ilość funkcyj, zapewniających znośne warunki życia. Stan ten uległ radykalnej zmianie w październiku i listopadzie, gdy zła pogoda wpływać zaczęła decydująco ujemnie na zdrowie więźniów, źle odżywianych, źle odzianych, pracujących przeważnie przy taczkach, bitych przy każdej okazji. Napływ nowych transportów równoważył ciągły ubytek wskutek chorób. Śmiertelność dzienna w listopadzie i grudniu r.40 dochodziła do 100 osób /t.j. do 2% ówczesnego stanu obozu/ dziennie. W końcu grudnia numer bieżący zbliżył się do 10.000, w międzyczasie przybył transport więźniów z Dachau. Od lutego 1941 roku rozpoczęły się w obozie pierwsze egzekucje. Wyroki nadchodziły z G-po z miejsca aresztowania. Komunikowano je skazanemu na chwilę przed egzekucją w miejscowym "Politische Abteilung". Skazańców wyprowadzano boso, w bieliźnie, ze związanymi rękami. W jednej z pierwszych egzekucyj zginął m.inn. prof. Uniw. Jagiellońskiego, Adam Heydel. Marzec i kwiecień 1941 roku przynoszą dalszy gwałtowny przypływ więźniów. Numer bieżący skacze do 17 tysięcy, rzeczywisty jednak stan liczebny obozu podwyższa się nieznacznie. Ciężka, długa zima i dżdżysta wiosna powodują niekończące się choroby i epidemie. Straszliwa biegunka, zwana "durchfallem"", dyfteryt, zapalenie płuc, serce, ropienie, wrzody, flegmony, wreszcie - ogólne wyczerpanie fizyczne /t.zw. Körperschwäche/ - kładą do 200-300 ludzi dziennie. W odgrodzonym od reszty obozu bloku "SK" - /Straf-Kompanie - karna kompania/' w jego podziemnych bunkrach, giną nieraz w kilka dni po przyjeździe, kierowani tam wówczas z reguły: Żydzi, księża, oficerowie zawodowi. Ilość chorych w szpitalu obozowym, pozbawionym możliwości radykalniejszej pomocy i właściwego leczenia, wzrasta w silnym tempie. Zapada decyzja dobijania chorych "nieuleczalnie". Od lata 1941 roku stosowane są wobec "wysortowanych" częstokroć jedynie na podstawie wyglądu zewnętrznego, przez niemieckiego lekarza obozowego - uśmiercające zastrzyki fenolu. Jednocześnie w odległości kilku kilometrów od właściwego obozu w Oświęcimiu powstaje, budowany przez więźniów, nowy kompleks baraków w miejscowości Rajsko, "przechrzczonej" przez Niemców na Birkenau - Brzezinka. Tam działać będą komory gazowe, uśmiercające tysiące chorych z "Auschwitzu", dziesiątki tysięcy jeńców sowieckich, przywożonych od listopada 1941 roku, setki tysięcy Żydów z całej Europy. W Birkenau wreszcie rozbudowany zostanie w r.1942 obóz kobiecy, zainaugurowany wczesną wiosną 1942 roku przywiezieniem kilkuset kobiet więźnych - Niemek z Ravensbrück początkowo do kilku bloków we właściwym Oświęcimiu.

Przytoczone poniżej relacje więźniów Oświęcimia i Birkenau odnoszą się przeważnie do okresu 1943-44. Mimo swej fragmentaryczności, stanowią materiał cenny dzięki bezwzględnemu autentyzmowi wypowiedzi.

podpis nieczytelny Kolski.
25.5.44

19

Microfilmed report about Auschwitz Concentration Camp, part 1: General description and synopsis. The page bears the frame number 19, and Major Kolski signed off on it on May 25, 1944. Never before published. Please see translation in this chapter (Chciuk-Celt Family Archives).

at the Hungarian or Slovakian borders, on their way to join the army abroad. In August and September, the first transport trains from Warsaw arrived, partially consisting of prisoners from Pawiak Prison, the majority however being victims of street dragnets or house blockades. In October 1940, the total number of prisoners was already approaching 6,000. In the first months of the camp's existence, the mortality rate was insignificant; because of organizational work and the anticipated expansion, a certain number of functions were available to the earliest arrivals, assuring them of tolerable living conditions. This state of affairs changed radically in October and November, when the bad weather began to have a decidedly negative impact on the inmates' health — poorly fed, poorly dressed, mostly working with wheelbarrows, beaten at every opportunity. The influx of new transports compensated for the continual loss of life resulting from disease. The daily mortality rate in November and December of 1940 was near 100 people, that is up to 2% of the total concentration camp population at the time. By the end of December, the current number of inmates was approaching 10,000, as a major transport of inmates from Dachau had arrived in the meantime. Beginning in February 1941, the first executions commenced in the camp. The death sentences were issued by the Gestapo at the place of arrest. The inmate would be informed of his death sentence at the local "Politische Abteilung" (Political Department) a moment before his execution. The sentenced person would be led out barefoot in his underwear, with his hands tied. Professor Adam Heydel of the Jagiellonian University was killed, along with several others, in one of the first such executions. March and April 1941 brought a further drastic influx of prisoners. The total number of inmates admitted jumped to 17,000, although the actual population at the camp increased only slightly. The long, hard winter and the drizzly spring caused an endless succession of diseases and epidemics. Horrible dysenteric diarrhea, called "durchfall," diphtheria, pneumonia, heart failure, abscesses, open sores, phlegmon, and finally a general physical exhaustion (known as "Körperschwäche") laid low an average of 200–300 people per day. In the underground bunkers of the separate block known as "SK" (Straf-Kompanie or penal company), they generally died within a few days of arrival. As a rule, those directed there at the time were: Jews, Catholic priests and professional officers. The number of sick people in the camp hospital, denied any possibility of more radical help or actual treatment, grew at a powerful rate. The decision was made to finish off those people deemed "incurably" ill. Beginning in the summer of 1941, certain inmates "selected" by the German camp doctor, often solely on the basis of their external appearance, were given deadly injections of phenol. At the same time, at a distance of a few kilometers from the actual camp at Oświęcim, a new complex of barracks buildings arose, constructed by inmates at a place called Rajsko, "rechristened" by the Germans as Birkenau — Brzezinka. That's where gas chambers were installed, killing thousands of sick inmates from "Auschwitz," tens of thousands of Soviet prisoners of war brought there beginning in November 1941, and hundreds of thousands of Jews from all over Europe. Finally, in 1942 an expanded women's concentration camp was built at Birkenau, inaugurated early in the spring of 1942 by the delivery of several hundred female prisoners — German women from Ravensbrück, initially housed in several blocks at Oświęcim proper.

The reports of inmates at Oświęcim and Birkenau, attached below, refer primarily to the period of 1943–44. Despite their fragmentary nature, they constitute a valuable source of material, owing to the impartial authenticity of the testimony.
(handwritten) subcommander Maj. Kolski
24 May 1944

Frame 20

Letters and notes from an inmate at Oświęcim April–June 1943.

The total number of living inmates, including the camp at Birkenau, is about 33,000. The number of persons admitted and numbered at the camp is in excess of 90,000. Subtracting about 3,000 inmates transferred to other camps or released (very few), this yields a figure of about 57,000 people murdered in one way or another, some of them dying of hunger, suffering, or disease, some of them executed by gunshot. The mortality rate exceeds 10,000 per month, an average of 130 people per day *(sic)*. Sick people (unclear), such as the physically weak or unable to work, and people who are completely emaciated, worn down to death by conditions at the camp, are assigned either to a "Spritze" (meaning an injection of phenol) or, on a more or less monthly basis, to "the gas."

Healthy people are executed by gunshot, carrying out sentences imposed either by Berlin or on the local level. Executions happen weekly. In one of the larger executions, in November, 260 people from the Lublin area were shot in the courtyard of Block 11, which was covered with stacks of dead bodies. More recently, around the 10th of January, 65 people were executed for violations of camp rules.

Entire transports of inmates are brought straight to the gas chambers, without any kind of admittance procedure (numbered registration). The number of such cases already exceeds 500,000 people, mostly Jews. Recently, trans-

Listy i notatki więźnia z Oświęcimia
/kwiecień - czerwiec 1943 rok/.   **20**

Liczba żyjących wynosi w sumie /razem z obozem w Birkenau/ około
33.000. Liczba numerów w obozie przekracza 90.000. Odjąwszy około 3.000
przeniesionych do innych obozów względnie zwolnionych /bardzo mało/ daje
to cyfrę 57.000 osób w ten czy w inny sposób wymordowanych. Część z głodu,
z biedy, z chorób - część rozstrzelanych. Śmiertelność przekracza
również 10.000 miesięcznie, przeciętnie 150 osób dziennie. Chorych /nieczytelnie/
t.j. ludzi słabych fizycznie, niezdolnych do pracy, wycieńczonych,
wymordowanych warunkami obozu, przeznacza się albo na "szprycę" czyli
zastrzyk fenolu, albo co miesiąc mniej więcej "na gaz".
Zdrowych rozstrzeliwuje się wyrokiem Berlina lub miejscowym. Rozstrzeliwuje
się co tydzień. Jedna z większych rozstrzałek, to rozstrzelanie
w jednym dniu 260 osób z rejonu lubelskiego - w listopadzie - podwórze
bloku 11, zaścielone stosami trupów - ostatnio około 10 stycznia 65 osób
z powodu przewinień obozowych.
Całe transporty przewozi się wprost na gaz, bez jakiejkolwiek numeracji.
Liczba takich przekracza już 500.000 osób. Przeważnie żydzi. Ostanio
transporty Polaków z Lubelskiego idą wprost na gaz./mężczyźni i kobiety/.
Dzieci rzuca się wprost na ogień. Za Birkenau pali się t.zw. "wieczny
ogień" - stos trupów na wolnym powietrzu - krematorium nie może nadążyć.
Ostatnio robi się próby z gazowaniem na wolnym powietrzu, zamiast w komorze.
- dla celów wojskowych. Zanosi się na transport z Oświęcimia do kamieniołomów
- inteligencja - oficerowie jako -/nieczytelnie/.
W obozie straszne wsypy, pali się grunt pod nogami, strasznie będzie
przetrzymać te ostatnie dni. Prawdopodobnie nikt stąd-by nie wyszedł, gdyby
zbliżało się do końca. Żądać natychmiastowego odwetu na Londyn w tamtejszych
warunkach. Będziemy usiłowali wiać. Przeprowadza się obecnie kastrację
kobiet na większą skalę - króliki doświadczalne! Nowe krematorium
pali dziennie około 5.000 osób, przeważnie żydów.

5 - IV.43.
Obóz cygański - zwozi się obecnie znowu cyganów z całej Europy. Przyjechali
z Polski, Czech, Słowacji i Niemiec. Już jest przeszło 12.000.
Mają osobny obóz. Zwożą całe rodziny - starców, kobiety, dzieci, niemowlęta
i kobiety w ciąży. Kilkanaście porodziło już w obozie. Kilkanaście
dzieci już zmarło. Zwożą nietylko cyganów wędrownych, ale cyganów
zasymilowanych i osiedlonych, cygańską inteligencję z Niemiec i artystów -
- i .... żołnierzy niemieckich. Ostatnio po przyjeździe pewnego transportu
cyganów z Niemiec, gdy jeden z SS-manów zbyt ordynarnie potraktował
jednego z cyganów, ten poskoczył do niego i wymyślał go: "Ty tchórzu,
ty tu walczysz z kobietami i dziećmi, zamiast na froncie - ja byłem ranny
pod Stalingradem, mam odznaczenia, jestem starszy rangą od Ciebie, ty
śmiesz mi ubliżać!" SS-man odszedł, jak zmyty. Ten zniemczony cygan od początku
wojny wcielony, jak wielu innych cyganów do armii niemieckiej, bawił
poprostu na urlopie u rodziny i wraz z całą rodziną został, bez względu
na mundur i służbę wojskową wywieziony do obozu cyganów. Żołnierzy niemieckich
jest kilkudziesięciu. Większość z nich ma odznaczenia niemieckie
z tej wojny. Obecnie jest najkonkretniejsze - jak Wielka Rzesza ocyganiła
cyganów.
Ostatnio transporty Polaków do obozu w głąb Niemiec objęły około 5.000
Polaków: Sachsenhausen, Gross Rosen, Wengamme, Buchenwald, Flosenburg.
Zanosi się na następne - oby jak najmniej Polaków zostało tutaj. Właściwie
wszyscy Polacy mają wyjechać. Gazowanie chorych i słabych normalnie,
t.j. stale. Ostatnio przywieziono około 5.000 żydów greckich. Część poszła
odrazu na gaz, część do pracy. Te części, które wprost z transportu śląna
gaz, są poza wszelką obozową numeracją. Oprócz tego zagazowano ostatnio
przeszło 100 osób z wyroków. Ludzie ci nie byli jeszcze ponumerowani,
tylko w śledztwie. Z Zagłębia. Cyganów ostatnio zaczęto traktować prawie
jak więźniów. Oddzielone rodziny - dzieci pozabierano. Ubranie własne
pomalowano czerwoną farbą. Chorzy idą na "szprycę" jak normalny häftling.
Wszyscy muszą pracować.
Następny transport żydów z Grecji przeszło 2.000. Około 500 do obozu,
reszta na gaz. Blok 2a: około 1.000 ludzi w śledztwie /kobiety i mężczyźni

Microfilmed report about Auschwitz Concentration Camp, part 2: Eyewitness accounts. The page bears the frame number 20. Never before published. Please see translation in this chapter (Chciuk-Celt Family Archives).

ports of Polish people from the Lublin area are also being taken directly to the gas chambers — men as well as women. Children are thrown straight onto a fire. Behind Birkenau, a so-called "eternal flame" is burning — piles of corpses in the open air — the crematorium can't handle the load.

Recently, there have been experiments with gassing people in the open, rather than in the chambers, for military purposes. People transported from Oświęcim to the rock quarries include university graduates and officers considered (unclear).

In the camp, there are terrible betrayals and informants, the ground is burning under our feet, it's going to be awful, trying to survive these last days. It's likely that no one would get out of here if the end were near. You are to give an immediate response to London on the conditions in here. We're going to try to get the hell out of here.[2] They're currently performing sterilizations of the women on a large scale — guinea pigs! The new crematorium burns about 5,000 people a day, mostly Jews.

5 May 1943.

The gypsy camp — they're currently bringing in gypsies from all over Europe. They have arrived here from Poland, the Czech area, Slovakia and Germany. There are already over 12,000 of them. They have a separate camp. Entire families are brought in — old people, women, children, infants and pregnant women. Over a dozen have already given birth inside the camp. Over a dozen children have already died. They're bringing in not only the wandering gypsies, but also assimilated and settled gypsies, the gypsy intelligentsia from Germany and artists — and .... German soldiers. Recently, when a transport of gypsies from Germany arrived and one of the SS men was particularly mean to one of them, the man got in his face and told him off: "You coward, you're over here doing battle with women and children, instead of being on the front lines! I was wounded at Stalingrad, I have medals and decorations, I'm senior to you in rank, and you dare to disrespect me!" The SS man slunk away, humiliated. This Germanized gypsy, drafted into the German Army right at the beginning of the war just like many other gypsies, was simply enjoying a few days' leave with his family, and he was hauled off to the gypsy camp, along with his entire clan, without regard to his uniform and military service. There are scores of German soldiers in here. The majority of them have military decorations from this war. Now it's clearer than ever how the Great Empire has gypped the gypsies.

Recently, transports of Poles to camps in the interior of Germany have taken about 5,000 Poles: Sachsenhausen, Gross Rosen, Wengamme, Buchenwald, Flossenburg. It looks as though as few Poles as possible are to remain here. Basically, all the Poles are supposed to be taken away. The sick and the weak are being gassed as usual, i.e., all the time. Recently about 5,000 Greek Jews were brought in. Some of them went straight to the gas chambers, some of them were put to work. Those groups who are sent straight to the gas chambers are outside of any admittance procedure or registration. Besides that, over 100 people were recently gassed because they had been sentenced to death. These people were also not yet registered, just under investigation. They were from the depths of the country. The gypsies have recently started being treated like regular prisoners. Families are being separated, the children taken away. Their personal clothing gets painted red. Sick people get the "Spritze" just like the normal Häftlinge (inmates). Everyone has to work.

The next transport of Jews from Greece was over 2,000 people. About 500 went to the camp, the rest straight to the gas chamber. Block 2a: about 1,000 people under investigation — men and women–

FRAME 21

Isolated from the rest of the camp. Of course they don't get to go to work, instead they have to lie face-down on the floor all day without moving. Lots of sick people — bedsores and ulcers. This has been going on for two months. They are guarded in the hall all day by a machine gun escort. Upon completion of the investigation, some of them are sent to the concentration camp like regular inmates, the rest go to the gas chambers.

Block 10: Experiments on women: artificial insemination, sterilization using X-rays.

All the Poles are to leave here in the course of the next few weeks. There have already been several transports. There's no camp discipline, and a great deal less tension. There's generally quite a bit of food. Typhus is raging in Rajsko in the women's camp. Among the gypsy inmates, there are active, decorated officers of the army, who fought on the eastern front. (unclear) This isn't a Schutzlager (protective camp) but rather a Sammellager (collection point). Slightly less rigorous here, but severely sick people (generally completely exhausted) are taken for a "Spritze," i.e., an injection of phenol into the heart, as stated by the Krankenhaus (hospital).

Block Rkl. Auschwitz — a group of Communists and Socialists, about 200 to 300 people, from the Dąbrowski Basin, they have to lie on their stomachs in two halls, men and women. The same system of detention and investigation as in Mysłowice. This is nothing more than an extension of that camp. Terrible conditions.

Izolacja od reszty obozu. Do pracy oczywiście nie chodzą, tylko cały dzień
muszą leżeć bez ruchu na podłodze na brzuchach. Dużo chorych - odleżyny.
Trwa to już dwa miesiące. Cały dzień pilnuje na sli eskorta z karabinem
maszynowym. Po śledztwie część do obozu, jako normalni więźniowie, część
na gaz.
Blok 10. Doświadczenia z kobietami: Sztuczne zapłodnienie, kastracja
promieniami Roentgena.

Wszyscy Polacy w ciągu najbliższych tygodni wyjadą s'ad. Już było kilka transportów. Rygoru co w lagrze nie ma. Jest duże odprężenie. Jedzenia
naogół dość dużo. Tyfus plamisty panuje w Rajsku w obozie kobiecym. Wśród
cyganów są oficerowie czynni armii z odznaczeniami - walczący na froncie
wschodnim. /nieczytelne/ Nie jest to Schutzlager tylko Sammelnlager. Trochę
mniejszy tu rygor, ale ciężko chorych /ogólne wyczerpanie/ biorą na "szprycę" t.j. zastrzyk fenolu w serce /jak podaje Krankenhaus/.
Bl. Rkl. Auschwitz - grupa komunistów i socjalistów /200 do 300/ osób
z Zagłębia Dąbrowskiego, leżą na brzuchach /w dwóch salach mężczyźni i ko-
biety/. System lagru i więzienia śledczego w Mysłowicach. Jest to poprostu oddział więzienia śledczego stamtąd. Warunki straszne.
3.IV. rozstrzelano w bloku 11. 27 Häftlingów z Bielska.
Za ostatnie 3 miesiące do 15 marca b.r. włącznie liczba zmarłych wynosi 20.000 osób. Nie liczy się tu transportów bezpośrednio wysyłanych na
gaz i nie rejestrowanych. Paczki są obecnie dozwolone w normalnej wielko-
ści 3 kg. W innych lagrach w Niemczech jest też odprężenie. K.L.Auschwitz
będzie wkrótce wyłącznie obozem żydowskim. Blok 10 będzie stacją doświad-
czalną dla kastracji, sterylizacji i sztucznego zapładniania. Dzieje się
to z ramienia instytutu higieny der Waffen SS z Berlina. Kobiety już w nim
są. Możliwe, że tak jak w innych lagrach powstanie i tutaj burdel dla
Häftlingów, co wywoła już kompletne zezwierzęcenie.

3.V.43.

Końcowy numer kolejny na dzień 1 marca 43: 113.272. Stan żyjących w obozie 29.415. Zmarłych w okresie od 14.VI.40 do 1.III.43 - 76.721. Zwolnionych: 1.117. Transporty do innych obozów - 6.469. Rubryka zmarłych
/76.721/ xxxxxxxxxxxxxxxxxxxxxxxxxxxxxxxxxxxxxxxxxxxxxxxxxxxxxxxxxxx
dzieli się na zmarłych naturalną śmiercią /brak lekarstw, bicie i t.d.
p. 31.524 rozstrzelanych 11.274, i pozbawionych życia w komorze gazowej
33.923/ oprócz tego oczywiście całe transporty żydów i innych z całej
Europy bez numeracji wprost na gaz. Między rozstrzelanymi: Minister Oświa-
ty Pieracki, były szef leg. Ewal, pułkownik Kaser, Ditinski, Komarnicki,
Hiltmer, Stawarz, kpt. Piasecki Edward, Suchowski, Jabłoński, Kawecki i wie
lu innych.
Wrzesień 1941. Stworzono obóz jeńców wojennych rosyjskich. Liczba wynosiła 11.572. Z tego rozstrzelano 6.314 w partiach po 150 dziennie. Reszta zmarła z głodu i bicia tak, że już 15.IV.42 liczba jeńców wynosiła 161.
Rozstrzeliwanych zakopywano w dwóch szychtach, polewanych wapnem. Obecnie
resztę grobów na gwałt się wykopuje, zwłoki się pali, celem całkowitego
zatarcia śladów.
Stan obozu z dnia 25.IV.1943. Birkenau - 11.671; Buna Werke - 3.301;
Goleszów - 289; Jankowice - 1.184; Kobier - 156; nieczytelny - 91; nieczytelny - 149; Auschwitz - 17.037. Razem 34.055. Polaków - 6.816, Czechów -
- 2.029, żydów - 3.138, jeńców wojennych 126 rosyjskich 600 ukraińców.
Lager cyganów około 12.000 /większe zwolnienia V.D. i R.D./. W Birkenau odkopują na gwałt masowe groby 11.000 jeńców rosyjskich, wykończonych
w ciągu dwu miesięcy zimowych 42 roku - palą zwłoki, by zatrzeć ślady.
Gazownia i szpryca od 14 dni wstrzymane.

10.VI.43.

Dookoła lagru od strony szosy budują schrony, kopią rowy w celach obron-
nych. W samym lagrze napięcie i zdenerwowanie. Odprawa oficerów S.S. na
temat niebezpieczeństwa ze strony ludności okolicznej. Wzmożona czujność
i uwaga na kontakt z jeńcami, dopatrywanie się kontaktu politycznego, któ-
ry istnieje. Żądanie jeńców o odwet, bombardowanie lagru bez względu na
ofiary jeńców. Zmiana nazwy Vernichtugslager na Arbeitslager ze względu
na wielkie zapotrzebowanie sił roboczych. Wyroki więcej uzasadnione i nie
tak częste. Wykańczanie na dłuższą metę. Arbeitslager: Dąbrowa, Jaworzno,

Microfilmed report about Auschwitz Concentration Camp, part 3: Further eyewitness reports detailing executions, experiments on inmates, and mass executions of Russian POWs. The page bears the frame number 21. Never before published. Please see translation in this chapter (Chciuk-Celt Family Archives).

Appendix 2 193

April 4th–27 Häftlinge from Bielsko were executed by gunshot.

For the last three months, up to the 15th of March, the number of deaths is 20,000 people. This is without taking into account those transports of people taken straight to the gas chambers and not registered. Parcels are currently allowed in the standard size of up to 3 kilograms. In other camps in Germany, there has also been a certain relaxation of tensions. Konzentrationslager Auschwitz is scheduled to shortly become an exclusively Jewish camp. Block 10 will be the experimental station for castration, sterilization and artificial insemination. This is happening under the auspices of the Hygiene Department of the Waffen-SS in Berlin. The women are already there. It's possible that, much as at the other camps, there will be a brothel for the Häftlinge here, too, which will bring about completely animal conditions.

3 May 1943.

The final intake number for the date of March 1st 1943: 113, 472. Number of inmates living in the camp: 29,415. Deceased in the time span of 14 June 1940 to 1 March 1943: 76,721. Inmates released: 1,117. Inmates transported to other camps: 6,469. The Deceased figure of 76,721 is subdivided as follows: died of natural causes, such as lack of medical care, beatings, etc.: 31,524; executed by gunshot: 11,274; deprived of life in the gas chamber: 33,923. In addition to these, of course, entire transports of Jews and others from all over Europe, sent straight to the gas chamber without being registered. Among the executed: Minister of Education Pieracki, the former chief of legal evaluation Colonel Kaser, Ditinski, Komarnicki, Hiltner, Stawasz, Captain Edward Piasecki, Suchowski, Jabłoński, Kawecki and many others.

Autumn 1941. A camp for Russian prisoners of war was created. The number of POWs was 11,572. Of these, 6,314 were executed by gunshot in groups of 150 per day. The rest died of starvation and severe beatings, such that by April 15, 1942 the number still alive was only 161. The ones who had been executed were buried in two layers, covered with lime. At present, the remaining graves are being dug up at a feverish pace and the bodies are being burned, with the aim of completely obliterating all traces.

State of the camp as of 25 April 1943: Birkenau — 11,671; Buna Werke — 3,301; Goleszów — 289; Jankowice — 1,184; Kobier — 156; (unclear) — 91; (unclear) — 149; Auschwitz — 17,037. Total: 34,055. Poles — 6,816; Czechs — 2,029; Jews — 3,138; Prisoners of War — 126 Russian and 600 Ukrainian.

Gypsy camp around 12,000. Major releases of Volksdeutsche and Reichsdeutsche. At Birkenau they're hurriedly digging up the mass graves of 11,000

Russian prisoners who were wiped out in the course of two months in the winter of 1942 — they're burning the bodies to erase all traces. The gas chamber and the injections have been suspended for the last 14 days.

10 June 1943

All around the camp, along the road, they're building shelters and digging ditches for defensive purposes. In the camp itself there's a high state of tension and irritability. The SS officers are being briefed on the subject of the threat of danger coming from the local population. Heightened sensitivity and attention to contacts with the prisoners, scrutiny of political contacts, which do exist. Inmates required to respond in case the camp is bombarded, without regard for their losses. Camp name being changed from Vernichtungslager (Extermination Camp) to Arbeitslager (Labor Camp) because of the pressing need for workers. Death sentences are more often for cause, and not as frequent. Finishing off in the long run. Arbeitslager: Dąbrowa, Jaworzno,

FRAME 22

Będzin and Chrzanów being prepared. Nationalities sticking together in the camp, the Häftlinge are cooperating with each other. Germans with green patches — bandits and criminals — being sent to the army. 17 have already left for Sachsenhausen for military retraining, they were sent off with a band playing. Gypsy camp around 13,000.

<u>Camp authorities.</u>

Hauptführer:	Hess (Chief Executive)
Lagerführer:	Hauptsturmführer Aufmeger (Camp Executive)
Lagerkommandant:	Schwartz (Camp Commander)
Standortsartzt:	Würtz (Chief Doctor)
Lagerartzt:	Kitt (Camp Doctor)
Politische Abteilung:	Jubner (Political Department)
Raportsführer:	Palitsch (the executioner, carries out sentences, **to be liquidated**) (Reporting Executive)
Transportführer:	Stienitz (Palitsch's deputy) (Transport Executive)

28 May 1941. The camp's political department ordered a roundup, as a result of which 180 prisoners were shot immediately. That same day, the Penal Company saw the arrival of 320 prisoners with red patches. Between May 28 and June 9, a further 28 of these 320 were shot. It was clear that all inmates

Będzin, Chrzanów w przygotowaniu. Węzły narodowościowe w lagrze, współpra-
ca Häftlingów. Niemcy zieloni /bandyci/ - do wojska 17 poszło już do Sachsenhausen na przeszkolenie wojskowe /żegnani muzyką/. Obóz cygański około
13.000.

Władze lagrowe.

Hauptführer: Hess
Lagerführer: Hauptsturmführer Aufmeger
Lagerkomendant: Schwartz
Standortsartzt: Würtz
Lagerarzt: Kitt
Politische Abteilung: Jubner
Raportsführer: Palitsch /kat, wykonawca wyroków, należy zlikwido-
                       wać/
Transportführer: Stienitz /zastępca Palitscha/.

28 maja 1941 r. Wydział polityczny obozu zarządził zbiórkę, w wyniku któ-
rej 180 więźniów rozstrzelano natychmiast. Tegoż dnia przybyło do kompanii
karnej 320 z czerwonymi punktami. W czasie od dnia 28 maja do 9 czerwca
z liczby 320 rozstrzelano jeszcze 28 więźniów. Jasnym było, że wszyscy posiadacze czerwonych punktów przeznaczeni byli na rozbicie. Dzień 10 czerwca od rana samego był dziwnie niezdrowy. Pracowaliśmy o 3 km. od obozu
w Königsgraben. Regulowaliśmy rzeczkę, położoną między dwoma wałami. Teren
pracy strzeżony przez kilkunastu wartowników, uzbrojonych w karabiny maszynowe. Praca szła opornie. Rozmiękła glina nie dała się wydobywać. Około
3 pp. Oberscharführer Moll, kierownik robót, dał sygnał końca pracy. Po
gwizdku Molla chwilę panowała cisza, poczym nagle grupa M. Lachowicza
z Warszawy rzuciła się w stronę zwału, kilka skoków - byli za wałem. Zagra-
ły karabiny maszynowe. Capowie niemieccy z siekierami wskoczyli na wał,
stwarzając zaporę. W minutę później sytuacja była opanowana. Zarządzono
zbiórkę - brakowało 20 więźniów. Grupkami wracaliśmy do obozu, pełni po-
sępnych myśli. Od x xxxxxx czasu do czasu ktoś padał, by nie wstać więcej.
To capowie odrabiali pałkami swe niezadowolenie z ucieczki. Po drodze za-
bito trzech więźniów, resztę dnia i noc spędziliśmy zbici w jedną gromadę
po jednej stronie bloku. Po gongu porannym zarządzono, by posiadacze czerwonych punktów ustawili się ma z lewej strony, czarne punkty zaś, to zna-
czy "starzy S.K.-owcy" z prawej strony. Wkrótce po tym przybył w asyście
podoficerów Obersturmführera Schwarza dowódca obozu Anmeier. Przemawiał
krótko: "psy! ja wam pokażę bunt! przeklęci bandyci polscy, popamiętacie
nas". Podszedł do pierwszego z szeregu czerwonych punktów i ....."obróć się"
..... blady z wrażenia wykonał rozkaz. W następnej chwili nie żył. Hauptsturmführer Anmeier celnie strzelał z odległości pół metra, nie chybił
pierwszego, ani żadnego z następnych 20. Sto trupów zaległo podwórze S.K.
Staliśmy spokojnie, czekając naszej kolejki ...... uspokoił się - spo-
kojnym głosem powiedział: "daję wam czas do 5 pp. Jeśli nie wydacie spraw-
ców buntu, czeka was wszystkich to samo......" wskazał na zwał trupów.
Wrażeń godzin następnych opisywać nie trzeba. O 5 pp. przyjechał Raportführer Tietze z kilkoma żołnierzami. Z listy wyczytano wszystkich czerwo-
no-punktowców. Powiązanych drutem poprowadzono do gazowni w Brzezince. Po
godzinie nie żyli już wszyscy. W bramie S.K. urządzili owację. Opuszczali
nas z uśmiechem na ustach i z okrzykami "Jeszcze nie zginęła, niech żyje"
i t.p. Na drugi dzień wzięto się do nas starych S.K.-łowców. W czasie pracy ze stanu 82 zaduszono i utopiono w rzece 7, w dzień później - 9, 3 dnia
- 12. Jakoś ocalałem. Wyszedłem z S.K. Dostałem się do pracy w młynie w Ba-
bicach. Przy pierwszej okazji, a nadarzyła się po półtora miesiąca, ucie-
kłem. Jestem wolny!

Microfilmed report about Auschwitz Concentration Camp, part 4: List of the Germans in authority, eyewitness account of a particularly harsh incident and the witness' eventual escape. The page bears the frame number 22, and is signed off by Major Kolski on May 24, 1944. Never before published. Please see translation in this chapter (Chciuk-Celt Family Archives).

wearing the red patch were being marked for destruction.[3] The day of June 10 was weirdly unhealthy, right from the very morning. We were working 3 km from the camp in the Königsgraben. We were regulating a little river which lay between two embankments. The work area was guarded by over a dozen sentries armed with machine guns. The work went slowly. The soft clay was hard to dig up. Around 3 P.M., Oberscharführer Moll, the director of works, gave the signal to cease working. After Moll's whistle there was a moment of silence, after which all of a sudden the group led by H. Lachowicz of Warsaw dashed toward the embankment, took a few jumps — and they were on the other side of it. The machine guns opened fire. The German capos, armed with axes, jumped up on the embankment, forming a wall. A minute later, the situation was under control. A roundup was ordered — there were 20 inmates missing. We returned to the camp in small groups, filled with gloomy thoughts. From time to time, someone would fall down, never to get up again. That was the capos, using their truncheons to work out their frustration over the escape. On the way back, they killed three inmates. We spent the rest of the day and night herded into one group on one end of the block. After the morning assembly gong, all inmates with red patches were ordered to line up on the left side, whereas those with black patches, which signify "Senior SK inmate," were to line up on the right. Shortly thereafter, camp leader Anmeier arrived, accompanied by Obersturmführer Schwartz's officers. His speech was brief: "You dogs! I'll show you a plot! You God-damned Polish bandits, you'll remember us!" He went up to the first guy in the red-patch row and ... "turn around!" Pale with fear, the inmate did as he was ordered. The next moment, he was dead. Hauptsturmführer Anmeier fired accurately from a distance of half a meter, he didn't miss the first guy nor any of the following twenty. 100 dead bodies littered the courtyard of the S.K. We stood there calmly, awaiting our turn ... he calmed down. In a calm voice, he said: "I'm giving you until 5 P.M. If you don't reveal who organized this plot, the same thing awaits each of you..." He pointed at the mound of corpses.

I don't need to describe what the next few hours felt like. At 5 P.M., Raportführer Tietze arrived with several soldiers. The names of all red-patch inmates were read from a list. Tied together with wire, they were all led to the gas chamber in Brzezinka. An hour later, they were all dead. At the gate of the S.K. the soldiers were given an ovation. They left us with smiles on their faces, shouting "Long Live Poland!" and "Poland isn't dead yet as long as we're alive" (our national anthem) and the like. The next day, the senior S.K. inmates were let loose on us. During the work day, out of 82 of us, 7 were strangled and drowned in the river, the next day it was 9 more, and the following day, 12 more. I managed to survive somehow. I got out of the S.K., and got work at the mill in Babice. At the very first opportunity, which presented itself a month and a half later, I escaped. I'm free!

(handwritten note) Please note the narrow scope of this information. It is precise and without any fantasizing. Kolski. 24 May 1944

II. Tadeusz Chciuk's Orders

(English translation)

<u>First and last name:</u> Tadeusz Tomasz CHCIUK, born 17 October 1916 in Drohobycz

<u>Father's name:</u> Michał

<u>Mother's name:</u> Maria, née Śpiewak

<u>First and last name on passport:</u> Marek JURKIEWICZ, born 6 June 1915 in Lwów

<u>In case of death please notify:</u> Stanisława Sklenarz, 51 Belsize Park Gardens, London NW 3

<u>Pseudonym: CELT.</u>

Assignment

Celt will take with him two belts labeled as follows:
1/ DR 105/20 containing   54,000 U.S. Dollars
2/ DR 106/20 containing   90,000 U.S. Dollars
    Total   144,000 U.S. Dollars

The money will be bundled and packaged; furthermore in belt DR 105/20 he will have his own money, separately packaged, in a pocket labeled X. He will also be taking mail in the form of microfilm, in a can specially prepared by the Commander-in-Chief's staff. The can is to be opened in Celt's presence by a specialist from the S Team. The microfilmed mail contains 1,223 frames.

Celt is a special political envoy, sent by the Prime Minister and his government to the Chief Delegate and the National Unity Council to familiarize them in detail with the current political situation, the course of Polish-British and Polish-American talks on the subject of Polish-Soviet relations — in order to get a clear picture of the situation in Poland and of public opinion, particularly in relation to these questions. He will relay to the political parties in all clarity the positions of the Government, the President and the party leaders.

He is ordered to return to Headquarters as soon as possible, via Budapest if possible, where his assignment is to get relations back on track.

Celt is also an official envoy of the Supreme Council of the Association of Polish Boy Scouts in Great Britain, to all Scouting organizations in the nation.

On technical matters: he is to give a detailed presentation on Anusia's work, and is to check and confirm her network of correspondents. He absolutely must see to a change of code, installing the new code which he is taking with him. He will report on the work of the Rapid Telegraph and will familiarize himself with its difficulties regarding communications between the nation and Headquarters. He will report on the possibility of a northerly route.

Celt is coming to you for the second time. He accomplished his first mission superbly, overcoming numerous difficulties. He was awarded the Virtuti Militari medal. He deserves your full confidence, and the Government attaches great weight to his mission as well as his return. I request that you, Mr. Vice Premier, give instructions that he is to be given help in the execution of his assignments.

Celt is supplied for six months.

M.p., 18 February 1944

ORKAN. ("Hurricane")

PS. Disk's assignment is in Celt's mail.

(handwritten)

In addition, not on the list
5 unnumbered files
2 from Dr. Schwarbart

III. Parachutist's Pamphlet

2nd Lieut. Tadeusz Chciuk carried this passage, taken from a training pamphlet published by the 4th Polish Brigade, in his diary.

It would be wrong to consider the parachutist only as a soldier who has learned an extremely important kind of modern warfare. Parachutist-training is a school of character and a test of leaders' capacities. It teaches us to know better ourselves and to dominate the self-preserving instinct. It enables us to govern ourselves and gives a criterion of our self-control without which it would be impossible to command other people. It teaches us to be strong and only such men are wanted by our motherland.

The difficult tasks of the parachutist compel him to be universally trained and educated. He must acquire special qualities united with one idea: to go by "the shortest way" to Poland and to fight for her.

A parachutist is always ready for efforts and sacrifices. He does not pay any regard to danger. He wants to be strong, courageous and highly disciplined and well-trained. He does not hesitate to lose his life if it is necessary for fulfilling his task. In this he is supported by his comrades.

Never abandon a comrade in a grave moment; keep smiling even in front of death.

If you are looking for death — come in for a while.

Chapter Notes

The notes are annotated to identify the source. Notes from the original Polish edition are identified by the initials *MC* (Marek Celt, also referred to as "the author" in original notes) and *WF* (the editor, Wojciech Frazik). *WF/JC* (Wojciech Frazik/Jan Chciuk-Celt) indicates notes that I expanded on and *JC* (Jan Chciuk-Celt) indicates notes that I wrote for this translation.

Introduction

1. Dariusz Baliszewski, "Misja Salamandra" in *Wprost* #28/2004(1128), 66–68. *JC*
2. Władysław Bułhak, "Wokół Misji Józefa Retingera do Kraju, Kwiecień-Lipiec 1944r.," *Zeszyty Historyczne* No. 168, Paris, 2009, ISSN 0406-0393, 9–14. *JC*
3. This is an edited and paraphrased version of the brief online biography of J.H. Retinger that I wrote and posted at http://home.teleport.com/~flyheart/retinger.htm.
4. Joseph Retinger, *Memoirs of an Eminence Grise* (Brighton, UK: Sussex University Press, 1972), 2. *JC*
5. Zdzisław Najder, *Joseph Conrad: A Life* (Rochester, NY: Camden House, 2007), 471. *JC*
6. Joseph Retinger, *Conrad and His Contemporaries* (London: Minerva, 1941; New York: Roy, 1942). *JC*
7. Herbert Henry Asquith (1852–1928) British politician, leader of the Liberal Party 1908–26, Prime Minister, 1908–16. *JC*
8. Georges Clémenceau (1841–1929) French journalist, physician, and statesman, member of the Radical Party. He was twice the prime minister of France, and was one of the principal architects of the Treaty of Versailles. *JC*
9. Alfred Charles William Harmsworth, 1st Viscount Northcliffe (1865–1922) Hugely influential British newspaper magnate. He founded the *Daily Mail* in 1896 and the *Daily Mirror* in 1903, and also owned the *Times* from 1908 to 1922. *JC*
10. Philippe Berthelot (1866–1934) influential French diplomat. *JC*
11. Bailey bridges, invented by a British civil servant named Donald Bailey, were lightweight, portable pre-fabricated bridges that could be carried in a truck and set up by hand, yet were strong enough to carry tanks. The design is still used today. *JC*
12. Marek Celt, *Biali Kurierzy* (Łomianki: LTW, 2005) (and other earlier editions). Deals in detail with the author's exploits as a "white courier" during the early part of World War II. Not yet translated into English. *JC*
13. Stasia's surviving daughter, Krystyna M. Sklenarz, M.D., described this harrowing ordeal through a child's eyes in her memoir, *Two Trains From Poland*, Xlibris, 2011. *JC*
14. Marek Celt, *Koncert: Opowiadanie Cichociemnego* (Łomianki: LTW, 2002) (and other earlier editions). Tells the full story of the shootout and Operation Jacket. Not yet translated into English. *JC*
15. Marek Celt, *Raport z Podziemia: 1942* (Wrocław : Zakład Narodowy im. Ossolińskich, 1992) (and other earlier editions). Describes in detail what the author saw and experienced while in Poland's underground in 1942, and his long journey back to base in London. Not yet translated into English. *JC*
16. Sikorski's fatal plane crash is the subject of historian David Irving's controversial book, *Accident: The Death of General Sikorski* (London: Wm. Kimber & Co., 1967). *JC*
17. Another copy (incomplete) is in the archives of the Polish Institute and Sikorski Museum in London: Collection 25, Case 9. *WF*

18. "Dzidek" dobry "reizer," chodzi jak "młody bóg." (Dzidek's a good traveler, he walks like a young god.) This is the quotation from Jan Freisler's report, archived at the Sikorski Museum in London. *WF*
19. Baliszewski. *JC*

Chapter 1

1. Paweł Siudak (1905–1972), high-ranking official of the Polish Interior Ministry, whose responsibilities included communications between the Government-in-Exile and the country from 1941 to 1944. *WF*
2. Władysław Banaczyk (1902–1980), Interior Minister, 1943–1944. *WF*

Chapter 2

1. Marian Hemar (1901–1972) was a Polish poet and cabarettist. During the war he was a lieutenant, living in London. This quotation is from *Kawał i Morał*. *WF/JC*
2. Paweł Siudak. *WF*
3. Winston Churchill's speech to the House of Commons, February 22, 1944. *WF*
4. The BBC's Polish Service was broadcast in Polish for the Polish listening audience, and was the principal source of news reporting independent of Hitler's propaganda. *WF*
5. The Union of Polish Patriots (ZPP — Związek Patriotów Polskich) was a political organization founded by Polish Communists in the Soviet Union and controlled by Soviet authorities. Led by Wanda Wasilewska, one of their primary goals was to lay the groundwork for the Communist Party to take control of postwar Poland. *JC*
6. This refers to a public exchange of diplomatic notes which commenced after Soviet troops crossed the pre-war border into Polish territory in Wołyń on January 4, 1944. The Polish declarations of January 5 and 15 were answered by the Soviets on January 11 and 17. *WF*
7. In view of the subsequent controversy regarding just who sent Retinger to Poland, it would be worthwhile — reaching into the future a little bit here — to recall an event which spoke volumes about JHR's way of doing political business. In the summer of 1944, several weeks after Mikołajczyk's return from Moscow, there was a significant cooling of relations between the two men. According to Retinger, the matter at hand was his urgent desire to travel to Moscow in order to prepare the ground for a new visit by Mikołajczyk, so that it would produce fruitful results in the form of establishing Polish-Russian relations and coming to some kind of agreement. Retinger says that when he discussed this plan with Mikołajczyk, the latter agreed to it. Armed with this news, Retinger went to Eden, notifying him of his departure and requesting an airplane. Eden contacted Mikołajczyk to confirm that this was true, and the latter stated that he hadn't agreed to it at all. Retinger got angry with Mikołajczyk about this. In Mikołajczyk's circles, on the other hand, it was said that when Retinger first came to talk to him about it, he said he was going on Eden's advice and that Eden had agreed to give him an airplane — but then it turned out that Eden hadn't known anything about it before then. In the end, as is now known, Mikołajczyk went to Moscow in October 1944 without Retinger. *WF*
8. Stanisław "Cat" Mackiewicz (1896–1966) was an ultraconservative figure. In his self-published 1945 book *Lata Nadziei — 17 września 1939 r.— 5 lipca 1945 r.* (reprinted in 1990 by Głos [ISBN 83-85088-01-6]) he makes disparaging comments and insinuations about Józef Retinger even as he praises him. *WF*
9. Professor Stanisław Kot (1885–1975) — historian, PSL political party activist, member of Sikorski's innermost circle, minister responsible for contact with the country, ambassador to the Soviet Union 1941–1942. *WF*
10. "Cable" was actually Lieut. Wiktor Karamać. *MC*
11. Stasia and her husband, Leopold Sklenarz, were living in London at the time. *JC*
12. "Dakota" was a popular nickname for the Douglas DC-3, the American transport airplane in widespread use by the Allies in World War II. *WF*
13. This could have been a simple mistake, or it could just as well have been an act of minor sabotage. *JC*
14. Again, this could have been a mistake, but it also appears as though someone might be sabotaging the mission in bigger and smaller ways. One spark at this point would have ended the mission. *JC*
15. Radio Kościuszko broadcast the pro-Soviet programs of the Union of Polish Patriots (ZPP). *WF*

Chapter 3

1. Jerzy Zubrzycki, Otolia's brother. He later went on to become a university professor in Australia. *MC*
2. Section VI of the commander-in-chief's staff, responsible amongst other things for communications with the country. *MC*
3. Paul Henri Spaak (1899–1972), Belgian foreign minister during the war. *WF*
4. Retinger did give Celt a copy of *Conrad and his Contemporaries* after the war, with the inscription: "To Dzidek — the best companion, most patient victim, most energetic commander! Gratefully, J.H. Retinger, November 1944." The other book is *Polacy w Cywilizacjach Świata — do końca XIX-go Wieku*, originally published in Warsaw in 1937 and republished in 1991. *JC*
5. Robert Baden-Powell (1857–1941), the founder of the Boy Scouts. *WF*
6. "Tempi passati" is Italian for "times gone by." *MC*
7. *Stars and Stripes* is the regular newspaper of the U.S. armed forces. *JC*
8. He is referring to the original form of the combat paratrooper insignia worn by Polish forces. It was replaced on November 20, 1944, by an eagle with a golden wreath in its talons. *WF*
9. A *franc tireur*, literally a "free shooter," is a civilian, especially guerilla, fighter or sniper who operates outside of the regular military structure. *JC*
10. I admit that at the time, I didn't fully understand the meaning of this term, "European Agent." It wasn't until much later, after the war and after our return to Poland, that the words "European Agent" took on their proper meaning. For it is JHR who must be seen as the *spiritus movens* (driving force) behind the creation of the European Community, by all means one of those who had a vision of a United Europe when hardly anybody was thinking of it. Western publications bear witness to the fact that this was no ordinary person, and that he had a share in the attainment of a unified Europe. I'm a crown witness to testify that he was held in high esteem by European politicians. *MC*
11. "Going to see Tito" (i.e., going to Yugoslavia) refers to Josip Broz Tito (1892–1980), the head of the Communist partisans in Yugoslavia during World War II and leader of Yugoslavia for decades afterward (premier, 1945–53; president, 1953–80). Great Britain was already supporting the partisans by this time. *WF/JC*
12. "Station W" (or *Placówka W*) was the code name for the Hungarian outpost of the Polish couriers — "W" for *Węgry* (Hungary). *JC*
13. "Lech" was Wacław Felczak (1916–1993), the author's good friend at "Station W," who was later held in prison by the Communists from 1948 to 1956 and subsequently went on to be a distinguished professor of history at the Jagiellonian University in Kraków. *JC*
14. "Béla" was the magnificent Hungarian priest Béla Varga (1903–1995), member of the Hungarian Parliament; guardian of the Polish High School in Balatonboglár, at which the author's fiancée Ewa Lovell was enrolled; he gave the author invaluable help in his previous mission in 1942, getting him safely from Hungary to Switzerland at great personal risk to himself. *WF/JC*
15. Peter A. Wilkinson, who, while still a captain, was in charge of the Polish section of the early SOE, later to become General Colin Gubbins's closest cohort. Wilkinson was deployed by sea on a mission to Yugoslavia on December 3, 1943, and had just returned. *WF*

Chapter 4

1. Lieut. Alfred Chłapowski, adjutant commander of the Polish 1586 Squadron, which carried out these flights to Poland. *WF*
2. The Handley Page Halifax was a four-engine English heavy bomber, also used for air drops of men and equipment. *WF/JC*
3. Flight Officer Kazimerz Szrajer, a cheerful airman who radiates an air of calm. There's nothing official about him, nothing ceremonious, "easy does it" and that's that. His calm calms my unease. *MC*
4. The Focke-Wulf Fw-190 was one of the principal German fighter planes. *WF*
5. Sergeant Józef Petryszak. *WF*
6. Messerschmitts were German fighter planes: the single-engine Me-109 or the twin-engine Me-110. *WF*
7. The Armstrong Whitworth A.W.38 Whitley was an English twin-engine medium bomber, also used for parachute training. *WF/JC*
8. Second Lieutenant Jerzy Mara-Meyer, code named "Filip," *Cichociemny* courier dropped into Poland on March 31st, 1942 in

Operation Belt. Killed in action in Warsaw on May 27, 1943. *WF/JC*

9. "Buka" was Wiktor Strzelecki, *Cichociemny* emissary dropped into Poland with the author on December 28, 1941, in Operation Jacket. Arrested by the Germans in 1942 and murdered in Berlin. *WF/JC*

10. In various works written about the *Cichociemni* and the fighting Polish underground, it's been written that Salamander "broke his leg during the parachute jump" or "seriously sprained his foot." Not true! It was I who suffered a slight contusion of the shins. Nothing happened to him. *MC*

11. Lieutenant Florian Kortus, code name "Krzysztof," a pilot. He died in 1988. *MC*

Chapter 5

1. This house, our first house on Polish soil, was an estate in Olesin Duży, commune of Dębe Wielkie, district of Mińsk Mazowiecki. Its owners were a young married couple, Jerzy and Jolanta Gruhnów. Almost half a century after the date of 4.4.44, I received a beautiful letter from Jerzy, living in Wrocław. He had tracked me down thanks to reading my book *Biali Kurierzy*, and figured out that the author was his guest paratrooper of years ago. From that time on, I kept in friendly contact with this brave person. Jolanta, unfortunately, died years ago. Jerzy remarried with a magnificent Polish woman who raised his children from the previous marriage and generally held the whole family together. The Communists had split Olesin Duży up into smaller lots—"The estate's falling apart," as Jerzy put it in a letter. Jerzy's great-grandfather, who took part in the Rebellion of 1863, was the uncle of two-time Nobel laureate Marie Skłodowska-Curie. My reunion with Jerzy after so many years was a huge experience for me. I was a guest at the Gruhnóws' house in 1991 during my first visit in 43 years, and many memories came alive. Sadly, Jerzy didn't live to see this book published; he died in 1994. *MC*

2. I met her again eight years later. At first we couldn't believe our eyes. She was a secretary in the editorial department at Radio Free Europe, the voice of free Poland, and I was an editor. Her name: Marysia Natanson; mine (on-air) was Michał Lasota. *MC*

3. Aurelia Śpiewakowa, my aunt, lived there. She was married to Col. Władysław Śpiewak, who was in German captivity at the time. Their daughter Hanka Mittelstaedt also lived there. She died in 1993. *MC*

4. The famous, magnificent Michalina Wieszeniewska, director of Personnel Evacuation Referral at the "Import" Company, formerly called the "Syrena" Company (i.e., the cell handling air drops in the Department V of AK Headquarters) which included *Cichociemni* parachute missions. *MC*

5. After the war, her last name was Lipińska. *WF*

6. "Sobol" was the code name for Jan Stanisław Jankowski (1882–1953), who was the Chief Delegate at that time—the fourth man to hold that position since the war started. He was sentenced to eight years' prison by the Soviet Union in 1945 in egregious violation of international law, and was murdered in a Soviet prison in 1953, a fortnight before completion of his sentence. *JC*

7. "Wartski" was the code name for Cyryl Ratajski (1875–1942), the second chief delegate. He resigned his position in August 1942 because of ill health, and died in October 1942. *JC*

8. "Non possumus" means "we can't" in Latin. The reference is to the Christian martyrs of Abitina in 304 A.D., who were ordered by Emperor Diocletian on pain of death to stop meeting on Sundays to celebrate the Eucharist. They famously said, "We can't do that," and were executed. *JC*

9. "Sine ira et studio" means "without anger or fondness" in Latin. It refers to Tacitus's quote about writing about history "without either bitterness or partiality." *JC*

10. "Marta" was the code name for Wanda Modlibowska, the secretary at the presidial office of the Delegature. *MC*

11. "Roman" was really named Jan Domański. *MC*

12. "Wernic" was the code name for Prof. Jan Piekałkiewicz, third chief delegate. He was arrested by the Gestapo on February 19, 1943, and was tortured and murdered at the Gestapo prison on Szuch Alley. He died on June 19, 1943. *JC*

13. "Grabowiecki" was the code name for Stefan Pawłowski, the new chief of the presidial office of the Delegature. *JC*

14. These were the three principal Scouting organizations active in the resistance during the war. The boys and girls of the *Szare Szeregi* (the Grey Ranks) took active part, carrying out sabotage missions and taking up

arms against the Germans with unbelievable bravery; the regular scouts of the ZHP were organized into regiments; and the Wigry Battalion was a unit of armed Boy Scouts. The author's two missions into occupied Poland both expressly included making contact with scouting groups, and he devoted a broad chapter of his 1942 report to matters pertaining to the Scouts. *WF/JC*

15. "Drogowski" was the code name for Konstanty Regamey (1907–1982), composer, orientalist, Swiss citizen. *MC*

16. "Nowak" was the code name for Stefan Korboński (1901–1989), director of Civil Resistance for the underground government at that time. *MC*

17. Anthony J. Drexel Biddle, Jr. (1897–1961), U.S. ambassador to the Polish Government-in-Exile. Rudolf Emil Schönfeld (1895–1981), U.S. chargé d'affaires assigned to the Polish government. *WF/JC*

18. Edvard Beneš (1884–1948), president of Czechoslovakia, 1935–38; president of the Czechoslovak Government-in-Exile, 1940–45; president of Czechoslovakia, 1945–48. *MC*

19. "Black Wanda" was the code name for Wanda Kamienicka-Gryckowa, an outstandingly fearless and solid commander of the Warsaw Girl Scouts' Council, married to Stanisław Grycko, director of radio communications between the Interior Ministry in London and the underground. "Nika" was the code name for Weronika Dzierżek of the Peasant Women's Union, messenger for the Peasant Battalions headquarters, press distributor for the Peasants' Party. *MC*

20. Alojzy Horak, chief of the Training and Operational Department of the Peasant Brigade "Chłostry," attached to the Peasant Battalions headquarters. *MC*

21. "Andrzej" was the code name for Second Lieut. Benedykt Moszyński, *Cichociemny* courier for the Interior Ministry, dropped into Poland on January 7, 1942, in Operation Shirt. *WF/JC*

22. "Wera" was the code name for Napoleon Segieda, *Cichociemny* dropped into Poland on November 8, 1941, in Operation Ruction, one of the very earliest such missions. The author incorrectly went along with rumors of the day, stating that Segieda died in the autumn of 1942 while trying to make his way back to London. In fact, Segieda made his way across Austria, Switzerland, France, Spain and Portugal and got to London in February 1943. (*Cf.* Wojciech Frazik, "Wojenne losy Napoleona Segiedy, kuriera Rządu RP do Kraju" in *Studia Historyczne* 1998, Vol. 3). *WF/JC*

23. This was where the author thought things stood in 1944, of course. "Włodek" was the code name for Bombardier Czesław Raczkowski, *Cichociemny* courier dropped into Poland on February 16, 1941, as part of Team Zero in Operation Adolphus, the very first such mission. He survived interrogation by the Gestapo and reported to base in London in 1945. He was a Peasant Party (Emigré) activist after the war and stayed in contact with the author. *WF/JC*

24. *Congressus vivorum* is Latin for "meeting of the men" or "gathering of heroes." *MC*

25. "Marcin" was the code name for Zygmunt Zaremba, Socialist Party activist, member of the Socialist Party leadership before the war, one of the leaders of the Socialist "Freedom, Equality, Independence" movement. "Michniewski" was the code name for Franciszek Białas, another Socialist Party activist. Head of the Public Anticommunist Committee from October 1943 onward. *WF*

26. The Sejm is the name of the Polish parliament. *JC*

27. *Non plus ultra* means: the uttermost point, perfection, the best there is. *JC*

28. Section II — Military Intelligence and Counter-espionage. *JC*

29. The Dorchester Hotel, whose owner, Victor Cazalet, was a great friend of Poland. Many Poles resided there during the war years. *WF*

Chapter 6

1. One of the key men he spoke with was Szmul Zygielbojm (1895–1943), the leader of a Jewish organization called the Bund, who committed suicide in 1943 to protest the fact that the Allies hadn't done anything about the Holocaust for eleven months, even though they knew it was happening from reports delivered by Jan Karski and my father, among others. His suicide telegram is a scathing, heartbreaking indictment. *JC*

2. The author related to me personally that he and other Poles had repeatedly asked the British authorities in London why nothing was being done while the Holocaust was raging. Jan Karski and Tadeusz Chciuk, among others, had provided detailed, graphic,

first-hand reports, after all, and for eleven months the British and Americans sat by, doing nothing. My father told me that those queries were always met with the same one-line response: "We have other strategic priorities." *JC*

3. This was a patrol of regular German soldiers. The author related to me personally that they were preceded by a swaggering group of about half a dozen Hitler Youths — armed teenagers — who delighted in taking wild pot shots on the street and scaring the daylights out of the people there. *JC*

4. The author related to me personally that the soldier was laughing as he made target practice out of a small child falling to its death. He was having fun! *JC*

Chapter 7

1. "Rudy" was the code name for Colonel Roman Rudkowski, group captain of the air wing attached to Section III of AK Headquarters. One of the highest-ranking *Cichociemni*, he was first dropped into Poland on January 26, 1943, in Operation Brace; picked up and flown back to London on May 30, 1944, in Operation Wildhorn II; dropped into Poland again on October 17, 1944, in Operation Poldek 1 as an emissary of the chief of staff of the AK's commander-in-chief. *WF/JC*

2. The author's depiction of events at this point is contradicted by the statements of Izabella Horodecka, the nurse/assassin from Unit 993/W who had been sent with orders from the top to poison Retinger. She says she was assigned to watch over him during the days he spent waiting for the airplane. His own relation of events, written on June 5th, tclearly states that he was in the company of a female messenger. This is supported by the statements of Kazimierz Strzelecki (quoted in Terlecki, Olgierd, *Kuzynek Diabla*, Kraków 1988) and Stefan Musiałek-Łowicki (in his article about Wildhorn II, "Akcja Drugi Most — lądowanie alianckiego samolotu pod Tarnowem 29. maja 1944 r. [relacja dowódcy akcji]" in *Studia Historyczne 1978, Vol.3)*, who state unequivocally that Retinger was accompanied by a woman. The author may have been relying here on a description of events provided by Retinger, who was known to tell various people differing versions of what happened on his adventure. *WF*

3. As far as the British were concerned, Retinger's return aboard Wildhorn II was of vital importance. General Colin Gubbins, the head of the Special Operations Executive, was reportedly waiting for him at the airfield in Bari. *JC*

4. According to other accounts, the cart didn't exactly turn over; it was more like it went down a steep ditch and into the water of Uszwica Creek, and Retinger was thrown from his seat by the sudden stop. *WF*

5. He didn't mean a medical doctor — he was referring to Jan Stanisław Jankowski, the chief delegate, who was also known as "The Doctor." *WF*

6. The Omega Clinic was located at Aleje Jerozolimskie 51. *WF*

7. That was Professor Marian Grzybowski, enormously valuable to the underground. After the war he was murdered by the UB (Security Police). *WF*

8. The reference here is to two nuns' orders in Poland. The Barefoot Carmelites (Bose Karmelitanki) are known to be pious to the point of asceticism, whereas at Bielany, the Feast of the Pentecost is celebrated with jubilation. *JC*

9. This is a play on the names of two famous Swiss watchmakers, Omega and Schaffhausen. The author wore a Schaffhausen on his wrist until his dying day. *JC*

10. The Battle of Monte Cassino was one in which Polish forces led by General Władysław Anders, suffering tremendous losses, played a decisive role in achieving victory for the Allies on May 18, 1944. It is considered by many to be the Poles' "finest hour." *JC*

11. *Casus belli* is Latin for "reason for war." *MC*

12. Allan Graham, conservative member of Parliament, president of the Anglo-Polish Friendship Society. *WF*

13. Fryderyk Voigt was a British publicist sympathetic to Polish matters. *WF*

14. Combat Organization "East" (*Bojowa Organizacja "Wschód"*) was founded by members of the Boy Scouts led by Bronisław Jastrzębski. *WF*

15. Oskar Lange (1904–1965), a leftist economist, led a diversionary campaign in the US, agitating against the Polish Government-in-Exile. In April 1944, he went to Moscow at Stalin's invitation for a propaganda visit; in June 1944 he met with Mikołajczyk during his visit to the U.S., forwarding certain sup-

posedly amiable Soviet proposals. It is now known that he was a Soviet agent. *WF*

Chapter 8

1. The German administration of occupied Poland, and the land itself, was called the "Generalgouvernement," as distinct from Germany proper, "Deutsches Reich." They issued postage stamps which are now a philatelic curiosity. *JC*
2. The Fieseler Fi-156 Storch was a single-engine German liaison and reconnaissance plane. *WF/JC*
3. He did — 47 years later. *WF*
4. Hopping out of the plane were: Lieut. Zdzisław Jeziorański, aka Jan Nowak (later to become the head of the Polish Section of Radio Free Europe and therefore the author's boss), Major Bogusław Wolniak, Capt. Kazimierz Bilski and Second Lieut. Leszek Starzyński. *WF/JC*
5. He was eager to get to 100 combat flight missions because that was the generally accepted point at which a pilot was deemed to have fulfilled his mission — if he should be lucky enough to survive a hundred flights. *JC*
6. Flight Lt. F.G. Culliford of New Zealand was the pilot. *JC*
7. *Author's Note:* It wasn't until a few days later, when the Warsaw Uprising began and I was sitting in London, biting my fingernails to the quick out of sheer frustration, that I realized how much meaning, how much truth was contained in his stubbornly shouted exhortation. *MC*

Chapter 9

1. As it turned out, I never saw him in person again. Later, when I was working at Radio Free Europe, I heard his voice in a recorded interview he gave in Brazil on the subject of the V-1 and V-2 rockets. I relied heavily on the things he'd told me in Rabat, in my later radioplays about the Third Bridge. *MC*
2. Toward the end of the author's stay in Poland, the underground resistance was severely shaken up by the murders on June 13th of Jerzy Makowiecki, his wife Zofia, and Ludwik Widerszal, who all worked for the Information and Propaganda Bureau of AK Headquarters. The ONR mentioned above was a group called the National-Radical Organization, and they were widely accused of instigating these murders. However, an investigation by former AK officers right after the war revealed this accusation to have been false. *WF*
3. Sir Richard Stafford Cripps (1889–1952) was a Labour politician, British Ambassador to the Soviet Union 1940–42 and a key figure in forging the alliance between the Soviet Union and the Western powers, later Minister of Aircraft Production; Ben Smith (1879–1964) was another Labour politician and MP. He drove one of London's very first taxicabs; Major General Sir Colin Gubbins (1896–1976) was the head of the Special Operations Executive, created by Winston Churchill in June, 1940; Brendan Bracken, 1st Viscount Bracken (1901–1958) was a Conservative politican, Minister of Information in the British government 1941–45; Archibald Sinclair, 1st Viscount Thurso (1890–1970) was the head of the Liberal Party, and Secretary of State for Air 1940–45; Mariel-Henri Jaspar (1901–1982) was a Belgian politician, and served as Belgian envoyé to the Czechoslovakian government; Jan Masaryk (1886–1948) was the Czechoslovakian Foreign Minister 1940–48. *WF/JC*
4. John Ward (1921–1995) was an RAF flight lieutenant, ex–POW and active member of the AK in Poland. *WF/JC*
5. Beginning on August 21, 1944, the British cabinet deliberated on the matter of recognition of AK soldiers as combatants, but they first wanted to secure the approval of the American and Soviet authorities. The British and American governments issued virtually identical statements on this subject on August 29 and 30, and a policy recognizing AK soldiers as combatants was announced in the press on the 30. The Agricola medals were awarded on August 28. *WF*

Appendices

1. "Durchfell" is a cruel play on words in German. "Durchfall" is the German word for severe diarrhea; in the context of the concentration camps, it means dysentery. "Durchfell" refers to a person's skin being so completely riddled through and through ("durch") with holes from thousands of fleabites and lice, that it hangs loose, like some kind of perforated hide ("Fell"). *JC*

2. Reports were filed by escapees which indicated that they were hoping — and preparing — for some kind of help to arrive from outside. This is corroborated by *Raport W*, filed in 1945 by the unbelievably heroic Captain Witold Pilecki (1901–1948), who deliberately got himself sent to the "Konzentrationslager Auschwitz" in 1940 in order to gather first-hand information. He escaped in 1943. He was put to death by his own countrymen in 1948 after a Communist show trial, in which he stood accused of spying for the West. His story, translated by Jarek Garliński, is now available in English as *The Auschwitz Volunteer: Beyond Bravery* (Los Angeles, CA: Aquila Polonica, 2012). *JC*

3. There was a system of colored triangular patches, stitched onto the outer garment, used to identify types of inmates. The red patch signified political prisoners — most of the Poles were classified as such. Two yellow patches, one on top of the other to form a Star of David, marked Jewish prisoners. A green patch was used to indicate criminals; the black patch was for "asocial" prisoners, which eventually came to include gypsies; the pink patch was for homosexuals, many of them shipped over from Germany; a purple patch was for Jehovah's Witnesses, whom the Germans considered a threat; a blue patch was for emigrants. *JC*

Index

Numbers in **bold italics** indicate pages with photographs.

Agricola Officers' Training Academy 174–176
"Air Bridge" operations 40, 45, 65–68; *see also* Operation Wildhorn I; Operation Wildhorn II; Operation Wildhorn III
Algiers 46
Anders, Gen. Władysław 172
Anticommunist Committee 136–137, 205
Antosia 92–95, 105
Arciszewski, Tomasz ("Stanisław") 145, 154–155, ***163***, 166, 170
Armia Krajowa *see* Home Army
Atlantic Charter 38
Auschwitz (Oświęcim) concentration camp 114, 182–197
Austro-Hungarian Empire 11

Baden-Powell, Gen. Robert 54
Balatonboglár 13
Banaczyk, Min. Władysław 28, 135, ***176***
Bari, Italy air base 43, 44
BBC Polish Service 35
Beneš, Pres. Edvard 103
Bernhard, Prince 10
Bień, Deputy Chief Delegate 111
Bilderberg Conferences 10
Birkenau (Brzezinka) concentration camp 186
Bonnard, Pierre 5
Bór, General 12
Bracken, Brendan 172
Brzoza, Józef 23

Bund (Jewish Socialist Organization) 114
By Parachute to Warsaw 114–116

"Cable" (agent) 43, 44, 51
Cadogan, Sir Anthony 3
Calles, Elias Plutarco 8
Castellane, "Boni" 5, 7
Celt, Marek (Tadeusz Chciuk-Celt) 11–18
Chciuk, Maria 12
Chciuk, Michał 12
Chciuk, Władysław 12, 86
Chief Delegate 14, 35, 37, 42, 92–93, 95; Marek Celt meetings with 100–102, 109, 112, 135–136, 139
Chmielewski, Capt. Jerzy ("Rafał") 145, 162
Churchill, Winston 8, 20, 24, 26, 35, 37, 41, 58, 101, 102, 134, 166
Cichociemni 1–2
Claubert, SOE Officer 161
Combat Organization "East" 135
concentration camps 114
Concerto for Four Colts 14, 51, 58, 90
Conrad, Joseph 7, 54
Cripps, Richard Stafford 172
Curstins 172
Curzon Line 21–22, 35, 37, 39, 65, 167; *see also* Teheran Conference

Davies, Norman: *Rising '44: The Battle for Warsaw* 4
Dęblin Air Force Academy 86

delegature 44
Demel, Col. Franciszek 25
Dermatological Clinic 130
Dorchester Hotel 26, 113, 172–173
Drogowski 96, 139
Drohobycz 11

Eden, Anthony 9, 20, 24, 26, 37, 40, 65, 101, 102, 172
European League for Economic Cooperation 9

Frankfurter, Felix 8
Frazik, Dr. Wojciech 1

Galicia 4, 11
Geneva Convention 175
Ghetto (Warsaw) 116
Gibraltar 46
Gide, André 5–6
Government Delegature 36
Grabowiecki, Chief of Staff to Chief Delegate 95–96, 99
Grabski, Stanisław (National Unity council chairman) ***163***
Graham, Allen 134
Gubbins, Gen. Colin 172

Haller, Gen. Józef 7
Hazell, Major 48
Hemar, Marian 31
Hewitt, Maj. Richard 53
Holsworth, SOE Officer 161
Home Army (Armia Krajowa) 4, 23, 105, 111–112, 123
Horak, Col. Alojzy (Nestorowicz) 104

209

Index

Horodecka, Izabela 25
Hungary, Polish Underground outpost in 44
Illuminati 11
Interior Ministry *see* Polish Ministry of the Interior
Iranek-Osmecki, Col. Kazimierz 25

Jankowski, Jan Stanisław ("Sobol") 23, 139; *see also* Chief Delegate
Jasiukowicz, Deputy Chief Delegate 111
Jaspar, Mariel-Henri 172
Jewish Socialist Organization (Bund) 114
Jews, liquidation of 114–116
Jurkiewicz, Marek 23, 97, 128

Karamać, Wiktor (agent "Cable") 43, 44, 51
Karczewski, Marceli *163*
Karski, Jan 115
Katyń massacre 21, 36
Koncert see *Concerto for Four Colts*
Konopacki, Scoutmaster Eugeniusz 174
Kot, Professor 42, 56–58, 91

Lange, Prof. Oskar 135
Lasota, Michał 20
Lieberman, Mrs. 36
Łódź concentration camp 114
Lovell, Ewa 12, 16, *17*, *19*, 23, 58–59, 64
Lublin Committee (PKWN) 164
Lwów 37, 39, 138, 165, 167

Mackiewicz, "Cat" 41
Majdanek concentration camp 114, 182
Małkowska, Olga 44, 174
Małkowski, Andrzej 6, 54
Mara-Meyer, Jerzy 81
Markowski, Colonel *163*
Marta 95–96, 100
Marysia, Miss 91
Masaryk, Jan 172
Mauersberger, Father Jan (Krzemień) 104
Memoirs of an Eminence Grise 8

Michniewski (leader, Anticommunist Committee) 136–137
Miciński, Colonel Czesław 145
Miesięcznik Literacki i Artystyczny 6
Mikołajczyk, Stanisław 2, 9, 16, 20, 24, 28, 65, 102, *163*–167, 174, *176*
Mittelstaedt, Hanka (cousin) 23, *99*, 110, 117–118, 124–125
Mniszek, Aleksander *163*
Molotov, Vyacheslav 17
Monte Cassino 172
Morel, Stella 8
Morones, Luis Negrete 8
Moscow Conference 102
Moskal, Franciszek *15*

Najder, Zdzisław 7
National Unity Council 35–36, 137
Nestorowicz (Colonel Alojzy Horak) 104
Nika 103
NKVD 21, 35, 137
"Northern Route" 113, 124, 126, 132, 139
Nowak (chief, Directorate of Civil Resistance) 97–98

Omega Clinic 126–129
Operation Jacket 14–16, 45
Operation Salamander 1, 2, 24
Operation Wildhorn I 112
Operation Wildhorn II 25, 113, 179–182
Operation Wildhorn III 1, 145
Ossowski, Władysław 12, 19, 21
Oświęcim (Auschwitz) concentration camp 114, 182–197

Paisley, Capt. Edward 4, *22*, 44, 70
Pajdak, Deputy Chief Delegate 111
Pascal, Blaise 61
Pawiak Prison 162
Peasant Battalions 103
Perkins, Col. Harold *163*, 165–167

Polish Constitution of 1935 38
Polish Government-in-Exile 2, 25, 35, 38
Polish Home Army (Armia Krajowa) 4, 23, 105, 111–112, 123
Polish Ministry of the Interior 31–32
Polish Peasants' Party ("Triangle") 100
Polish People in the World's Civilizations 54
Polish Socialist Party 145
Polish Underground 28, 65, 94, 130
Polish Workers' Party (PPR) 103, 136–137
Powązki Polish National Cemetery 18

Rabat, Morocco 162
Raczyńksi, Ambassador 102
Radio Free Europe 17–18
Radio Kościuszko 48
Radio Świt 16, 31, 34, 35–36, 98
Ravel, Maurice 5, 54–55
Report from the Polish Underground 1942 27
Retinger, Józef Stanisław 5
Rising '44: The Battle for Warsaw 4
Romer, Foreign Minister Tadeusz 102, *163*, *176*
Roosevelt, Franklin D. 20–21, 102, 165
Rowecki, Gen. Stefan (Grot) 104
Rudkowski, Colonel ("Rudy") 118, 122–123, 144, 172–174, 179–180

Sabbat, Scoutmaster Kazimierz 44, 174
Scouting, Supreme Council in London 44
Section II (Home Army Intelligence Department) 111, 123
Seyda, Minister 37
Sikorski, Gen. Władysław 4, 8, 16, 24, 27, 38, 41–42, 55, 58–59
Silent Shadows 1, 13
Sinclair, Archibald 172
Sinclair, Lady 172
Siudak, Counselor 28, 32

Index

Sklenarz, Leopold 13
Smith, Ben 172
Sobol (chief delegate) 23, 92, 100–102
Sosnkowski, Gen. Kazimierz **15**, 24, 174
Soviet secret police *see* NKVD
Soviet Sphere of Influence 20, 103
Spaak, Paul Henri 172
Special Operations Executive (SOE) 2, 48
Śpiewakówna, Hanka (cousin) *see* Mittelstaedt, Hanka
Stalin, Joseph 2, 20, 25, 27, 166
Starzyński, Lt. Tadeusz 45–46
Stem 22, 31
Strasburger, Henryk (mideast affairs delegate) 167, 171
Sulima, Marek 11, 23, 44, 47, 70, 71
Sweden, northern access route to 44

Szare Szeregi (Scout fighting units) 96, 104, 174, 177
Szrajer, Lt. Kazimierz 73–75, 156

Targowica Group 93
Teheran Conference 2, 20, 27, 33, 35, 37, 39, 44, 93, 101
Tobruk 9, 55
Treblinka concentration camp 114
Truszkowski, SOE Officer 161, 167

Underground *see* Polish Underground
Union of Polish Patriots 38, 65, 171

V-1, V-2 rockets 145–146, 163
Vilnius 37, 39, 138
Virtuti Militari medal 13, 15, 16

Ward, John (*Times* correspondent) 172
Warsaw, Fund for 172

Warsaw Ghetto 116
Warsaw Uprising 4, 26, 172, 175–176
Wartski 95, 104
Weber, Hans von 6
White Couriers 12, 21, 58, 70
Wigry units 96, 177
Wildhorn *see* Operation Wildhorn I; Operation Wildhorn II; Operation Wildhorn III
Wilkinson, SOE Major 64
William of Orange 61
Wiśniewski sisters 92–93

Zamoyski, Count Władysław 5
Żarański, Józef **163**
Zażuliński, Tadeusz (Polish envoy to Cairo) 167
Zubrzycka, Otolia "Tola" 6–8
Zubrzycki, Jerzy "Jurek" 51–52, 69

www.ingramcontent.com/pod-product-compliance
Ingram Content Group UK Ltd.
Pitfield, Milton Keynes, MK11 3LW, UK
UKHW042000140426
5217IPUK00015B/892